DHCP for Windows 2000

DHCP for Windows 2000

Neall Alcott

O'REILLY®

Beijing · Cambridge · Farnham · Köln · Paris · Sebastopol · Taipei · Tokyo

DHCP for Windows 2000

by Neall Alcott

Copyright © 2001 O'Reilly & Associates, Inc. All rights reserved.
Printed in the United States of America.

Published by O'Reilly & Associates, Inc., 101 Morris Street, Sebastopol, CA 95472.

Editor: Sue Miller

Production Editor: Leanne Clarke Soylemez

Cover Designer: Ellie Volckhausen

Printing History:

> January 2001:   First Edition.

Library of Congress Cataloging-in-Publication Data can be found at:

http://www.oreilly.com/catalog/dhcpwin2000

ISBN: 1-56592-838-5

[M]

Table of Contents

Preface

Dynamic Host Configuration Protocol (DHCP) provides a means of allocating and managing IP addresses dynamically over a network. Before the advent of DHCP, administrators configured each host on a network with an IP address, subnet mask, and default gateway. Maintaining the changes and the logs of the changes took a tremendous amount of time and was prone to error. DHCP uses a client/ server model in which the network information is maintained and updated dynamically by the system.

This book discusses DHCP in a Windows 2000 environment. It provides an introduction to the DHCP protocol and shows how to implement a DHCP server into the network. It also covers the more advanced features of DHCP.

The book begins with an overview of the TCP/IP protocol suite and shows how DHCP coexists with the rest of the TCP/IP suite. It identifies DHCP's predecessors, RARP and BOOTP, and explores the reasons that DHCP was developed. DHCP design considerations are discussed, as well as the different methods of deployment. The book shows how to install and configure DHCP servers in routed and non-routed environments and how to configure a client to use DHCP. It also discusses how to administer a DHCP server in Windows 2000 using DHCP scopes, options, and leases. Finally, the book covers DHCP's close relationship with Dynamic DNS, as well as some of the future directions for DHCP.

Conventions Used in This Book

The following conventions are used throughout this book:

Italic
> Used for URLs, filenames, email addresses, and new terms when first defined.

Constant width
> Used in examples to show the contents of files or the output from commands.

Constant bold
> Used in examples to show commands or other text to be typed by the user.

Constant italic
> Used in examples and command syntax definitions to show variables for which a context-specific substitution should be made.

 Indicates a tip, suggestion, or general note.

 Indicates a warning.

How to Contact Us

We have tested and verified the information in this book to the best of our ability, but you may find that features have changed (or even that we have made mistakes!). Please let us know about any errors you find, as well as your suggestions for future editions, by writing to:

O'Reilly & Associates, Inc.
101 Morris Street
Sebastopol, CA 95472
(800) 998-9938 (in the U.S. or Canada)
(707) 829-0515 (international/local)
(707) 829-0104 (fax)

We have a web site for the book, where we list errata, examples, or any additional information. You can access this page at:

http://www.oreilly.com/catalog/dhcpwin2000

To ask technical questions or comment on the book, send email to:

bookquestions@oreilly.com

For more information about our books, conferences, software, Resource Centers, and the O'Reilly Network, see our web site at:

http://www.oreilly.com

Acknowledgments

Acknowledgments, acknowledgments, acknowledgments! They are oh so difficult. What if I forget someone?! Well, let me try my best. If I left anyone out, please take me to lunch so I can personally thank you . . . your treat of course . . .

This book began to take shape during a phone call with Robert Denn at O'Reilly. We discussed the curious situation where there were many books for many subjects, but very few for the oft-used, but little discussed, DHCP. Thus, this book was born. I would also like to thank Neil Salkind, my agent, and everyone at Studio B for all of their help.

At O'Reilly, I would like to thank Sue Miller, my editor. Sue was instrumental in keeping this project moving forward and sharpening my work. I especially need to thank Leanne Soylemez for her thoroughness as the production editor and Rob Romano for redrawing my crappy . . . err . . . displeasing figures.

And of course, the tech reviewers honed the details and, in the end, created a better book. I must thank André Paree-Huff, Rory Winston, and Jim Boyce.

I must say I was very fortunate to work with the finest IT team around: System Support at AstraZeneca Chesterbrook. Many thanks and memories go to Bill "The Fridge" Friedgen, Chuck "Chooch" Boohar, Frank "No, not Kathy Lee's hubby, the decent one" Gifford, Mark "When I was a . . . " Clayton, Richard "This is Richard!" Muir, Mike "Polly" Kliwinski, Matt "Good eats" McWilliams, Tina Hughes, Tina Mohler, Adara Santillo (J), Paul "Hoagie Man" Kern, Sandy "Could you please come to the data center" Garlinski, Ed "Salt Shaker" Cartright, Steve Urick, The Honorable Marvin Mayes, George "The Agent" Oschenreither, Chris Pignone, Ed Murawski, David Short, Rich Donato, and finally, the Men in Black: Brian "Morphius" Seltzer and Jeff "The Angry Man" Sisson. Tell the Culinary Engineer at the Deltaga I said hello and the coffee is weak.

Nor shall I ever forget the Ghosts of System Support's Past (kill the lights and queue the sad music):

> Jeff Tincher and Mark Marshall, both currently haunting Brandycare.
> Jim Lange, rattling chains at Merck.
> Bill Juliana, the only spirit wearing boat shoes and changing CDs at Comverse.
> Lise Leonard, casually floating through the halls of Yoh.

And most of all I must thank my wife, Ginny, and my daughters, Lauren and Lindsey. Thank you for always making me laugh and letting me know that play must always be more important than work. The breaks that I took with you made it possible to recharge my batteries and forge ahead with this project. I am forever grateful for your love and support.

—Neall Alcott

1

TCP/IP Overview

Dynamic Host Configuration Protocol (DHCP) is an Internet standard protocol designed to dynamically allocate and distribute IP addresses as well as additional TCP/IP configuration information. DHCP is defined by RFCs 2131 and 2132. Working with the Internet Engineering Task Force (IETF) and a number of other vendors, Microsoft was instrumental in the development and standardization of DHCP.

Before the advent of DHCP, most TCP/IP configurations were maintained statically. An administrator configured each individual host with a valid IP address, subnet mask, and default gateway, as well as other TCP/IP configuration parameters. As you can guess, configuring and administrating static TCP/IP configurations for multiple workstations and network devices can be a burdensome task, especially if the network is large and/or changes frequently. The exception to the rule was the use of two predecessors to DHCP, the RARP and BOOTP protocols. These protocols are covered in more detail in Chapter 2, *In The Beginning: RARP and BOOTP*.

DHCP uses a client/server model of operation (see Figure 1-1), where a DHCP client makes a request to a DHCP server for an IP address and other configuration parameters. When the DHCP client makes the request, the DHCP server assigns it an IP address and updates its database, noting which client has the address and the amount of time that the address can be used. This amount of time is known as a *lease*. When the time expires, the DHCP client needs to renew the lease or negotiate a new lease for a different IP address. Through the use of leases, the DHCP server can reclaim unused IP addresses.

Using DHCP allows an administrator to make changes to a client's IP configuration without the need to visit each and every client. The user at the workstation only needs to release and renew their DHCP lease. That is the power and benefit of DHCP.

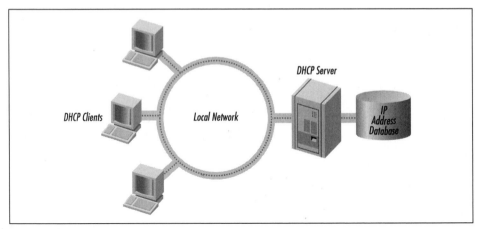

Figure 1-1. The DHCP client/server model

The purpose of this chapter is to provide an overview of the data that DHCP is expected to deliver: TCP/IP configuration information. The TCP/IP protocol suite is the common language of the Internet and by far the dominant networking protocol suite in use today. One must understand the many different facets of the TCP/IP protocol suite in order to configure, maintain, and troubleshoot a Windows 2000 DHCP server.

This chapter begins with an overview of the TCP/IP protocol suite, describing the different functions at the different layers of the Open Systems Interconnection (OSI) Model. It then covers Media Access Control (MAC) addresses—what they are and how they operate, followed by a very important area that one must understand: IP addressing and subnetting. The next two sections finish up the chapter by giving an overview of the two types of name resolution used in Microsoft Networking: DNS and WINS.

The TCP/IP Protocol Suite

In the 1960s, the Department of Defense's Defense Advanced Research Projects Agency (DARPA) was in charge of developing a means of communication that would still function in the event of a nuclear war. Development focused on the new theory of the *packet-switched network*. All forms of networking up to this time (i.e., the phone system) had used a *circuit-switched network*.

A circuit-switched network connects the sending and receiving stations by a single, direct physical path. Circuit-switched connections are not shared with other traffic; they are meant to be one-to-one. The telephone system is an example of a circuit-switched network. When a person dials a phone number, the phone company equipment establishes a direct connection between the caller's phone and the receiving phone. This connection lasts for the duration of the call.

A packet-switched network operates by breaking the data to be transmitted into smaller datagrams or packets. Each of these packets is numbered and sent out across the network. Because the packets are individually numbered, they can take multiple paths to their destination. There they will be put back in order and reassembled into the original data.

Figure 1-2 illustrates the concepts of these two types of networks.

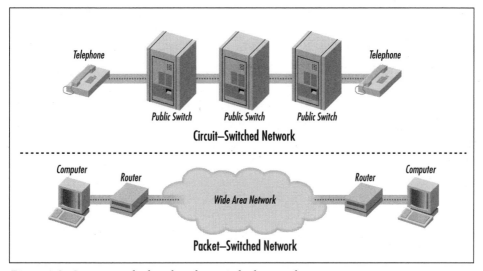

Figure 1-2. Circuit-switched and packet-switched networks

The weakness with a circuit-switched network is that communication links have to be set up ahead of time. If a circuit goes down, communication stops. The beauty of a packet-switched network is that if a point of communication goes down, the data is automatically rerouted through another location dynamically. In the end, it had great battlefield potential—which is what DARPA was looking for. If a command center was taken out, communications could continue by rerouting the data across any available medium: packet radio, satellite links, land links, etc.

The TCP/IP protocol suite was developed and refined as part of the packet-switched network project.

The OSI and DOD Reference Models

The TCP/IP protocol suite can be used to communicate over any type of networking medium. This includes Local Area Network (LAN) and Wide Area Network (WAN) environments. TCP/IP accomplishes this by using a modular design. The blueprint of this modular design comes from the Department of Defense (DOD) Reference Model. The International Standard Organization (ISO) also developed a seven-layer reference model called the Open Systems Interconnection (OSI)

Model. These models provide networking hardware and software vendors with guidelines to create products that will be compatible in form and function across multiple hardware and operating system platforms.

The DOD Reference Model consists of only four layers that are closely aligned with the OSI Reference Model (see Figure 1-3):

Application Layer

> This layer provides application interfaces, session establishment, data formatting, and data conversion for applications running on a host system. This layer coincides with the upper three layers of the OSI Model: Application Layer, Presentation Layer, and Session Layer.

Transport Layer

> This layer defines the method of communication between two systems: connection-oriented or connectionless. This layer maps directly to the Transport Layer in the OSI Model.

Internet Layer

> The Internet Layer defines internetworking communications (i.e., routing). This layer maps directly to the Network Layer of the OSI Model.

Network Interface Layer

> This layer defines data-link and media access methods (i.e., Ethernet, Token Ring, FDDI). This layer includes the remaining two layers of the OSI Model: Data Link and Physical Layers.

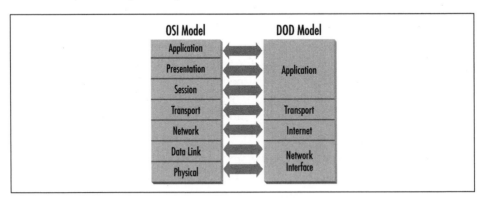

Figure 1-3. Comparing the OSI and DOD Models

The Application Layer

The Application Layer defines protocols that provide email, file transfer, remote logins, and drive-mapping capabilities to user applications. Some examples of protocols from the TCP/IP Protocol Suite that reside at this layer are Telnet, FTP (File Transfer Protocol), SNMP (Simple Network Management Protocol), SMTP (Simple Mail Transport Protocol), and DNS (Domain Naming System).

The Transport Layer

The Transport Layer defines two protocols: Transmission Control Protocol (TCP) and User Datagram Protocol (UDP). These protocols provide two separate functions:

Transmission Control Protocol (TCP)

TCP is a connection-oriented protocol. This means that TCP will provide a reliable connection between two systems. TCP accomplishes this by sending acknowledgments periodically to determine that datagrams are being received. If the datagrams were not received, TCP resends them, thus insuring reliable delivery. TCP is also responsible for breaking the data down into individual segments, numbering them, and reassembling them at the destination.

User Datagram Protocol (UDP)

UDP is a connectionless protocol. Unlike TCP, UDP does not use any acknowledgments, sending data blindly out onto the network to the destination. UDP assumes that another layer, usually provided by timers and timeout periods, will handle error correction. Implementations such as these are integrated into applications by the developer. Since UDP does not have the overhead of TCP, it is considered quick and efficient.

The Internet Layer

The Internet Layer is responsible for the delivery of packets across an internetwork. There are two protocols that operate at this layer, Internet Protocol (IP) and Internet Control Message Protocol (ICMP).

IP is the engine of TCP/IP, in charge of routing packets to and from logical addresses (i.e., IP addresses). These logical addresses correspond to particular systems located on the network.

IP addresses are organized in a hierarchical manner, allowing networks to be subdivided into subnets.

When a system wants to transmit data to a destination on a local network, IP takes the data segment provided by TCP. It then adds a header to the segment that includes the destination IP address and determines the destination's local subnet. IP sends the resulting packet to the source's network interface, and thus to the local network. At the destination, IP receives the packet, strips off the header information, and sends the resulting segment up to TCP. TCP reassembles the data and sends it to the appropriate application (see Figure 1-4).

If the destination is not located on the same local network as the source, IP performs additional steps to transmit the data.

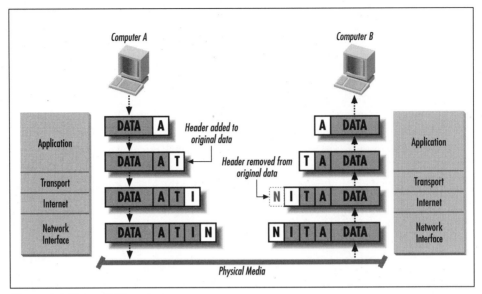

Figure 1-4. IP in a LAN environment

IP first takes the data segment provided by TCP. It creates and attaches the header to the data segment and determines whether the destination is on a local or remote subnet. In this case, since the source and destination are not on the same local network, IP sends the packet to the default gateway (i.e., the router on the local subnet).

At the router, IP receives the packet and, after analyzing the destination IP address, determines that the packet is destined for another host on a remote subnet. IP determines the subnet address for the destination and routes the packet to the network interface attached or closer to the destination's local subnet.

Finally, the destination receives the packet, strips off the header, and sends the data segment to TCP for reassembly (see Figure 1-5).

I will discuss IP addresses and subnetting in more detail later in this chapter.

ICMP provides message packets that report errors and other information, such as network congestion, that may be affecting IP packets. There are some situations when this may occur:

1. The destination may be unreachable because there is no route.

2. The host may be unreachable because of a configuration issue or because a gateway does not have the buffering capacity to forward the packet.

3. ICMP can also notify the source host that a more efficient route exists.

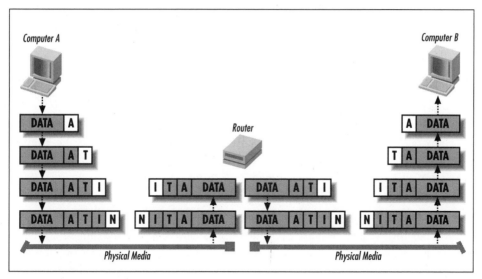

Figure 1-5. IP in a WAN environment

ICMP also provides an echo-request message. These messages are created by the `ping` command and are used to test connectivity between hosts on an internetwork. The `tracert` command also uses this mechanism to determine the router list and report the time between routers (known as hop time).

Finally, if an IP packet's Time to Live (TTL) field has reached zero, a router discards the packet. The router then generates an ICMP time-exceeded message to notify the source host that the packet was discarded.

Network Interface Layer

The Network Interface Layer provides data link and media access capabilities to the upper-level layers via hardware addresses. This layer allows TCP/IP to function across multiple media-access protocols, such as Ethernet, Token Ring, FDDI, Frame Relay, ISDN, and xDSL.

Ethernet

Invented by Xerox, Ethernet is a baseband LAN specification that uses Carrier Sense Media Access/Collision Detection (CSMA/CD). Ethernet can operate at 10 Mbps over various cable types. There are also newer and faster implementations of Ethernet available.

Token Ring

Invented by IBM, Token Ring is a token-passing LAN specification. Computers in a Token Ring environment are connected to the network media in a closed ring. Whichever computer possesses the Token is permitted to transmit data on the ring. When the computer is finished transmitting, it passes the token on to the next computer in the ring. If the next computer does not need to transmit, it, too, passes the token on. By employing a token-passing scheme, collisions are avoided, since only one computer is permitted to transmit. Token Ring can operate at 4 or 16 Mbps.

Fiber Distributed Data Interface (FDDI)

FDDI is a 100 Mbps, token-passing LAN standard using fiber-optic cables. FDDI uses a token-passing scheme similar to Token Ring. FDDI consists of two fiber-optic rings, a primary ring and a backup ring in case the primary fails. FDDI using multimode fiber can operate up to a distance of 2 km. FDDI using single mode fiber can operate to a distance of 40 km.

Frame Relay

Frame Relay is a telecommunications service meant to be used as a WAN technology. It is the medium by which multiple LANs can be linked together. Frame Relay operates by placing data into a frame for transmission. A virtual circuit connection is created between two end devices, over which the frame is sent. Frame Relay provides no error correction, so the devices on either end of the connection must supply error correction. A switched data link layer protocol, Frame Relay can handle multiple virtual circuits.

Integrated Services Digital Network (ISDN)

A digital communication protocol, ISDN can carry voice and data through conventional copper telephone networks. An ISDN line is comprised of two different channels, B and D. B (or bearer) channels are the main conduits for data and voice communications. D (or data) channels are used to transmit setup and control signals for the entire ISDN connection. ISDN comes in two levels of service: Basic Rate Interface (BRI) and Primary Rate Interface (PRI). BRI consists of two B channels (64 Kbps) and one D channel (16 Kbps). As a result, BRI ISDN operates at speeds up to 128 Kbps. PRI consists of 23 B channels and one 64 Kbps D channel. PRI ISDN operates at up to 1.544 Mbps. An ISDN adapter must be installed on both ends of the connection to handle the digital signal.

xDSL

A digital technology that uses the existing copper telephone infrastructure to transmit voice and data. Typical telephone wire in the United States contains four wires. Only two of the wires are used for telephone service; the other two remain unused. xDSL utilizes all of the wires to carry a digital signal at a frequency higher than that of voice communications. As a result, a telephone line utilizing xDSL can carry voice and data communications simultaneously. xDSL is a faster alternative to ISDN and operates at a number of speeds such as 640 Kbps, 1.6 Mbps and up. Currently xDSL suffers from major distance limitations, usually less than 20,000 feet from the central telephone office.

I briefly describe Ethernet here because it is by far the most popular LAN technology. It is cheap, easy to use and understand, and flexible.

Ethernet uses a media access process known as CSMA/CD (Carrier Sense Media Access/Collision Detect). This works by allowing any host on the network to transmit at any time, but before transmitting, the host must listen for traffic on the network. If no traffic is detected, the host can proceed. If two hosts on the network transmit at the same time, a collision occurs. When a collision occurs, the offending stations are each set to wait a random length of time before retrying the transmission.

Ethernet comes in primarily three flavors: IEEE 802.3 (10 Mbps), Fast Ethernet (100 Mbps), and Gigabit Ethernet (1000 Mbps).

IEEE 802.3
The standardized version of Ethernet. It operates at a data rate of 10 Mbps.

Fast Ethernet
A form of Ethernet that provides a data rate of 100 Mbps. Workstations that are equipped with IEEE 802.3 network adapters can connect to a Fast Ethernet-based network, however they are still limited to 10Mbps data transmission.

Gigabit Ethernet
Another form of Ethernet that provides a data rate of 1 Gbps, or 1 gigabit. Gigabit achieves its tremendous speed by using fiber-optic cable as the network medium. Copper cabling can also be used, but it severely limits the distance Gigabit Ethernet can operate at. Workstations equipped with IEEE 802.3 and Fast Ethernet network adapters can attach to Gigabit Ethernet, but they are still limited to their respective data transmission rates.

This essentially concludes the discussion of the DOD Reference Model. The remaining sections of this chapter deal with more specific TCP/IP concepts. This provides an understanding of some of the configuration parameters that a DHCP server provides to DHCP clients.

MAC Addresses

Media Access Control (MAC) addresses are hardware addresses that uniquely identify a network interface card (NIC) in a host.

MAC addresses are 48 bits in length and are written as 12 hexadecimal digits. The first 6 hexadecimal digits identify the manufacturer of the NIC. This is known as the Organizational Unique Identifier (OUI), which is administered by the IEEE. Each manufacturer of Ethernet devices must register with the IEEE. The remaining 6 hexadecimal digits are used as a serial number, which is administered by the individual manufacturer (see Figure 1-6).

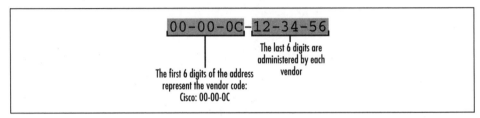

Figure 1-6. Example of MAC addresses

Table 1-1 lists the OUI numbers for several well-known NIC manufacturers.

Table 1-1. List of Common OUI Numbers

Manufacturer	OUI Number
Novell	00-00-1B
Cisco	00-00-0C
3Com	00-20-AF
HP	08-00-09
Apple	08-00-07
IBM	08-00-5A
Intel	00-90-27
Microsoft	00-50-F2

ARP

In order for communication to take place across an internetwork, a MAC address must be resolved to a logical network address (an IP address, which I will cover in more detail in the next section). This is accomplished by using the Address Resolution Protocol (ARP). ARP works slightly differently depending on whether it is used in a LAN or WAN environment.

In a LAN environment, ARP is used when a host needs to transmit data to another host (see Figure 1-7). To find out the destination host's MAC address, the source broadcasts an ARP request on the LAN. The ARP request includes the IP address to be resolved. Because it is a broadcast, all hosts connected to the LAN receive and process this request. When the destination host receives the broadcast, it responds directly with an ARP reply that contains its MAC address. Also, any other host that receives the ARP request can respond if the requested address is in their ARP cache. The source host will then add the destination's MAC address to its ARP cache and begin transmitting data.

 The ARP cache is dynamic and entries are removed after two minutes. If an ARP entry was reused, the entry remains in the ARP cache for ten minutes.

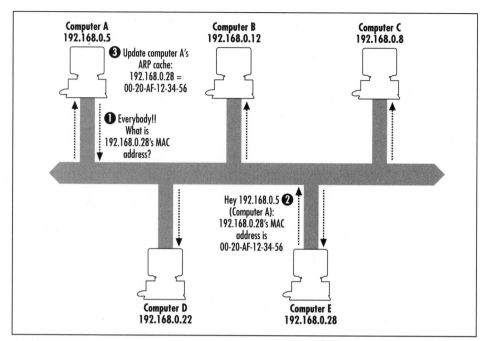

Figure 1-7. Example of ARP in a LAN environment

In a WAN environment, ARP operates mostly in the same manner, except that the source and destination are not on the same LAN (see Figure 1-8). In this case, the source host compares its IP address with the destination's IP address and determines that it is located on a different subnet (through a process called ANDing, which I'll discuss later in this chapter). At this point the source host broadcasts an ARP request to determine the MAC address of its default gateway. The router replies with its MAC address, which is then added to the source's ARP cache. Now, when the source wants to communicate with the destination host, it addresses its data packets to the router's MAC address. The packet's destination IP address still contains the destination's IP address. The router then forwards the information to the destination host on the other subnet.

IP Addressing

IP addressing is the heart of the TCP/IP-based internetwork. The process of routing IP packets is possible because of this logical addressing scheme.

An IP address is a logical 32-bit binary number that identifies a system on an internetwork. An IP address comprises two parts—the network portion and the host portion. The network portion of an IP address tells the host what logical network it is located on. The host portion identifies that particular host.

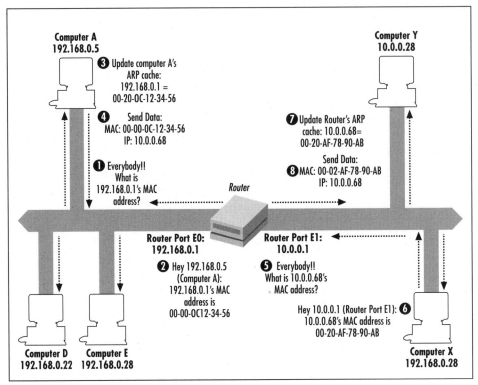

Figure 1-8. Example of ARP in a WAN environment

IP Address Format

Because humans tend to have trouble remembering and evaluating binary numbers, IP addresses are expressed in dotted decimal notation. A 32-bit binary IP address is written out in four octets, each of which contains eight bits. Each bit position in an octet represents a value (one of 128, 64, 32, 16, 8, 4, 2, 1); the sum of these values, when totaled, represents the octet's decimal value (see Figure 1-9).

IP Address Classes

Initially, when IP was developed, the IP address space was divided into distinct IP address classes to determine where the network portion stops and the host portion begins. The value of the first octet and its highest order (leftmost) bits determine the class. There are five IP address classes, three of which (A, B, and C) are available for commercial use (see Figure 1-10). Class D is reserved for IP multicasting. Multicasting allows multiple computers in the same multicast group to receive the same data transmission, sort of like a directed broadcast. Class E is strictly reserved for research use by the Internet Engineering Task Force (IETF).

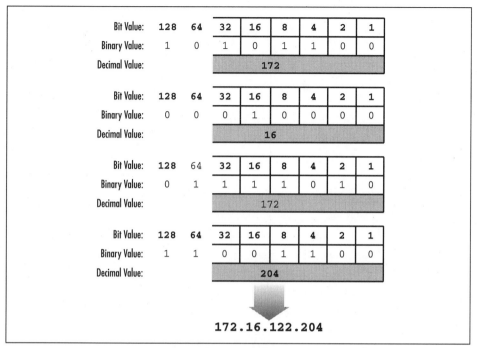

Figure 1-9. Dotted decimal example

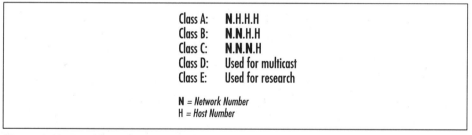

Figure 1-10. IP address classes

Class A

In a Class A IP address, the network portion is represented by the first octet; it has 0 in its leftmost bit. In other words, if you were to set all the remaining bits in the first octet to 0s, the resulting value for the octet would be 0. If you set all the remaining bits in the first octet to 1s, the resulting value would be 127. Therefore all Class A IP addresses fall into the 0-127 range for the first octet. This also results in 127 possible networks and a maximum of 16,777,214 hosts on each network. (Please note that the network 127.0.0.0 is reserved for loopback addresses.) Figure 1-11 summarizes the characteristics of the Class A address class.

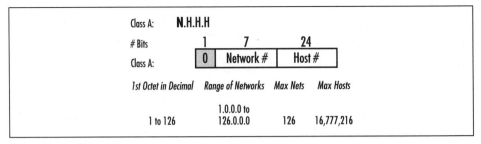

Figure 1-11. Class A

Class B

In a Class B IP address, the first and second octets represent the network portion; it has 10 in its two leftmost bits. A Class B IP address falls into the 128 to 191 range for the first octet. This results in 16,384 possible networks and a maximum of 65,534 hosts on each network. Figure 1-12 summarizes the characteristics of the Class B address class.

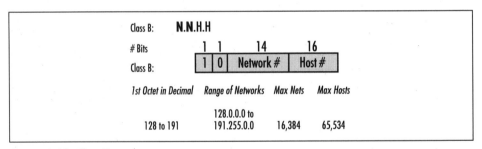

Figure 1-12. Class B

Class C

In a Class C IP address, the network portion is represented by the first, second, and third octets; it has 110 in its three leftmost bits. A Class C IP address falls into the 192 to 223 range for the first octet. This results in 2,097,152 possible networks and a maximum of 255 hosts on each network. Figure 1-13 summarizes the characteristics of the Class C address class.

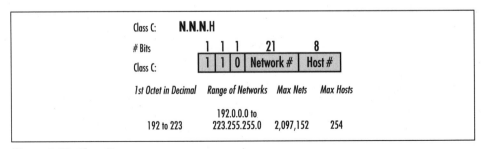

Figure 1-13. Class C

Please note that some host and network addresses cannot be used. These are discussed later in this chapter.

IP Subnetting

IP address classes are not always the most efficient way to design an IP addressing scheme. There aren't many companies that need a Class A address with 16 million hosts, and there may be smaller companies that need more addresses than a Class C network can provide. As you can see, this method could lead to a tremendous number of wasted IP addresses. The Internet Engineering Task Force (IETF) saw this and submitted RFC 950 to facilitate the addition of a third level to the existing two-level hierarchy created with IP address classes.

This third level is known as subnetting. Subnets are created by taking leftmost bits from the host portion of an IP address and applying them to the network portion (see Figure 1-14).

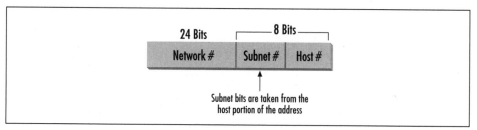

Figure 1-14. Subnetting a Class C address

Subnetting gives network designers and administrators the ability to divide larger networks into smaller, more efficient networks. Since subnets are under local administration, the outside world (via routing tables) does not need to know of their existence.

Subnetting is made possible by the use of a subnet mask. A subnet mask, along with the IP address classes, determines where the network and subnet portions of an IP address end and the host portion begins. A subnet mask is a 32-bit binary number. Starting at the leftmost bit, 1s are placed in every bit that is part of the network and subnet portions. The remaining bits contain 0s (see Figure 1-15).

So how does IP determine the subnet where a host is located? There is a set process that a router or host performs to determine the subnet address. This process is commonly known as Logical ANDing. Logical ANDing is simply a Boolean operation that follows three basic rules: 1 "ANDed" with 1 is 1; 1 "ANDed" with 0 is 0; 0 "ANDed" with 0 is 0. In other words, if 1 = True and 0 = False:

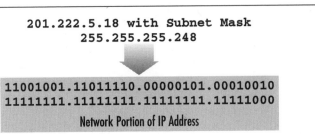

Figure 1-15. Subnet mask example

1 "ANDed" with 1 is 1	True AND True = True
1 "ANDed" with 0 is 0	True AND False = False
0 "ANDed" with 0 is 0	False AND False = False

The process begins with the IP destination address and the internal subnet mask. A Logical AND operation is performed which causes the host portion of the destination IP address to be removed—resulting in the subnet address. Here's an example where the ANDing operation is performed on a Class C subnet. Take a moment and observe the last octet in the IP address:

Destination IP Address:	192.168.0.214	11010110
Subnet Mask:	255.255.255.224	11100000
Resulting Subnet Address:	192.168.0.192	11000000

Given the preceding example, we have determined that the IP address 192.168.0. 214 with a subnet mask of 255.255.255.224 is located on the subnet 192.168.0.192.

Taking the example further, what is the maximum number of hosts on this segment and what are the starting and ending IP addresses?

Before we answer these questions, I want to introduce you to a little formula that makes life in the IP world easier. This formula is 2^n-2. Using this formula, one can determine the number of hosts in a subnet. 2^n represents the number of hosts that can be created, where 2 is the number of possible values for each bit (0 or 1— remember we're dealing in binary here!) and n is the number of bits taken from the host portion of the network address. I subtract two from 2^n because addresses of all 1s and all 0s cannot be used.

Now let's take a moment to answer the first question: what is the maximum number of hosts on this subnet, 192.168.0.192? This can be determined by examining the portion of the subnet mask that is not masked, or contains 0's. For the subnet mask of 255.255.255.224, the host portion contains 5 zeros. This means that the n exponent in our trusty little formula would have a value of 5. The number of hosts is then 2^5-2. Which results in...get out those calculators...30. So, on subnet 192.168.0.192, the maximum number of hosts is 30. That wasn't so bad, was it?

OK, we answered the first question. Now let's figure out the second question: what are the starting and ending IP addresses on subnet 192.168.0.192? Or another way to ask this question is, what is the range of IP addresses on subnet 192.168.0.192?

To answer this we need to again examine the subnet mask 255.255.255.224.

First, note that we are only concerned with the last octet, 224, since this octet contains the host addresses. Take 224 and convert it into binary. This results in 11100000. To figure out the address ranges possible with this subnet mask, we need to determine the value of the furthest bit to the right that is set to 1. For this subnet mask, there are three 1s, and the last set bit is 32.

This value, 32, is known as the *subnet offset value*. The subnet offset value tells you that every 32 addresses results in another subnet. We can now determine the subnet's address range by taking the subnet address, 192.168.0.192, and adding 32, which results in 192.168.0.224. 192.168.0.224 is the start of the next subnet after 192.168.0.192.

Since 192.168.0.224 is the start of the next subnet, let's subtract 1 from this address, which results in 192.168.0.223. This is the last host address in the 192.168.0.192 subnet. Determining the first host address is simple: add 1 to the subnet address, 192.168.0.192, which results in 192.168.0.193.

So, to answer the second question, 192.168.0.193 is the first host address, and 192.168.0.223 is the last host address in the 192.168.0.192 subnet.

Note that if we set another bit to 1 in the subnet mask, or, in other words, move the masked bits further to the right, the subnet offset value gets smaller. This results in a smaller address range, or fewer hosts per subnet. If we move the masked bits to the left, the subnet offset value grows larger, resulting in larger address ranges.

Now let's expand our discussion to the enterprise level. Here we will walk through a situation where subnetting would be used in a large internetwork environment. An organization has been assigned the Class C network address 201.222.5.0. This company has 20 remote offices, each containing 5 workstations and a server.

First, determine the subnet field size that will yield enough subnets in this situation. Remember the 2^n-2 formula? Using that formula again, one can determine the number of subnets created.

In our example, the network address is 201.222.5.0. We know that it is a Class C address because the first octet falls into the Class C range: 192 to 223. Given that it is a Class C address, the network portion is made up of the first three octets. This represents 24 bits from the 32 bits in the address. This leaves the remaining octet, or 8 bits, for the host portion. Now let's determine the number of bits required. Using the formula 2^n-2, simply plug in the number of bits. 2^5-2 = 30 possible subnets, which provides the required 20 subnets, with 10 left over for future growth.

Why use 5 bits? Why not use 4? 2^4-2 = 14 subnets, which is not enough. Using 6 bits, 2^6-2 = 62 subnets, which works for the subnets but does not leave enough host addresses.

Recall that the bit furthest to the right is the subnet offset value. This value determines the subnet addresses.

We used 5 bits for the subnet portion. The fifth bit value from the right is 8. Therefore the subnet addresses are all multiples of 8: the first subnet is 201.222.5.8, the next is 201.222.5.16, etc.

The host address range begins with the subnet address plus 1. The range ends with the next subnet address minus 2.

Our first subnet is 201.222.5.8. The host range for this subnet would be 201.222.5.17 through 201.222.5.22.

To conclude, IP subnetting happens to be one of those subjects that many people do not immediately comprehend. It needs to be studied and put to practical use. Once this happens, people understand it, and they never forget it. Give subnetting time and work with it. It will "click."

Classless Interdomain Routing (CIDR)

As the Internet unexpectedly grew in popularity, it became apparent that something must be done about the depletion of registered Internet networks and the growth of Internet routing tables. In particular, Class B networks were nearly completely allocated by the late 1980s. The reason for the depletion of this particular class was the lack of a class whose size was appropriate for a mid-size organization. A mid-size organization would require more than the maximum 254 hosts a Class C network provides, while the 65,534 hosts a Class B network provides were too many. If an organization needed more than 254 hosts, it would be assigned a Class B network, essentially wasting many IP addresses.

Classless Interdomain Routing (CIDR), defined in RFC1519, was implemented to slow the growth of the Internet routing tables and the need to allocate more network numbers.

CIDR slows routing table growth by aggregating multiple networks to form a single network. This is known as supernetting. Supernetting also alleviates the Class B address depletion problem by allowing multiple Class C networks to be aggregated. These aggregated Class C networks provide a number of hosts some-where between a Class C and a Class B network.

For example, a company requires 6500 host addresses. To achieve this without allo-cating a Class B address, the company is issued the network address 192.168.0.0/19. The /19 represents the number of bits in the network number, much like a subnet mask. This network actually represents 32 Class C addresses, 192.168.0.0 to 192.168. 31.0. The IP address utilization level of the 192.168.0.0/19 network is almost 80%, whereas the utilization level of a Class B network would have been about 10%. Also, only one route is added to the routing table. When a router outside the com-pany needs to send data to a host on subnet 192.168.16.0, it uses the 192.168.0.0/19 routing table entry. The company's router then forwards the data to the correct sub-net.

CIDR solves the two problems of growing router tables and the need for more net-work addresses quite nicely; however, there is an issue that needs to be consid-ered. If you are working entirely with modern routing technology, such as the routing protocol Open Shortest Path First (OSPF), using CIDR is possible and not entirely difficult. However, if you are using older technology such as Routing Information Protocol v.1 (RIP1), CIDR cannot be used. RIP1 uses IP address classes to determine routes to a network. It does not use subnet masks to determine the network address. It simply observes the address' first octet to determine which class the IP address belongs to. So keep this in mind if you want to use CIDR.

IP Address Restrictions

Certain IP addresses have special meanings and therefore cannot be used. Table 1-2 lists these addresses and describes why they cannot be used. Please note that some newer networking equipment allows some use of these restricted addresses. Refer to your equipment's operating manual for more information.

Table 1-2. Special IP Addresses and Their Uses

Special Address	Description
0.0.0.0	This host on this network. Can be used by the BootP process for a host that does not know its IP address but does have a hardware address.
255.255.255.255	This is used for a broadcast to all hosts on the same physical medium.
Host Address of All 1s	This is used for a broadcast to all hosts on the specified net-work or subnet.
Network Address of 127	This is used as an internal loopback address. Packets addressed like this are used only for testing the local TCP/IP stack.

DNS and Hostnames

Trying to remember many IP addresses is nearly impossible for anyone, especially with the growth of the Internet during the past 10 years. Hostnames make everyone's life easier by giving an IP address a memorable name. After all, remembering *microsoft.com* is much easier than remembering 207.46.130.149.

Originally, in the dark days of the Internet and TCP/IP, hostname resolution was left to a single text file, called the *HOSTS* file. Hostnames were manually added to this file, and then the file was downloaded and distributed to each TCP/IP host. *HOSTS* files work fine and are manageable if your network is small. *HOSTS* files in Windows NT and Windows 2000 are stored in the *%systemroot%\SYSTEM32\ DRIVERS\ETC* directory. Example 1-1 shows a sample *HOSTS* file.

Example 1-1. Sample HOSTS File

```
# Copyright (c) 1994 Microsoft Corp.
#
# This is a sample HOSTS file used by Microsoft TCP/IP for Chicago
#
# This file contains the mappings of IP addresses to host names. Each
# entry should be kept on an individual line. The IP address should
# be placed in the first column followed by the corresponding host name.
# The IP address and the host name should be separated by at least one
# space.
#
# Additionally, comments (such as these) may be inserted on individual
# lines or following the machine name denoted by a '#' symbol.
#
# For example:
#
#      102.54.94.97    rhino.acme.com        # source server
#       38.25.63.10    x.acme.com            # x client host

127.0.0.1          localhost
192.168.0.1        cg141484-a
192.168.0.254      proxy
192.168.0.2        nalcott
```

The *HOSTS* file method of hostname resolution became more cumbersome and inefficient as the Internet grew. In 1984, two new RFCs (882 and 883) were released detailing DNS. These RFCs have since been superceded by RFCs 1034 and 1035.

DNS is a distributed database that allows local administrators to maintain their portion of the DNS database while allowing access to it for hostname resolution across the entire Internet. DNS is implemented in a client/server arrangement. The server portion is driven by name servers. Name servers hold the segment of the DNS database (called a zone) that they have authority over. The client portion is known as a resolver. This can be any TCP/IP client that supports DNS. Whenever you are using the Internet, whether it is the World Wide Web or simply email, you are using DNS.

The structure of the DNS database can be described as an inverted tree (see Figure 1-16). The top of the tree (or the trunk) is known as the root domain. It is shown as a single dot (".").

Below the root domain are the top-level subdomains. Currently these include *com, edu, net, org, mil* and country domains, such as *jp* for Japan and *nz* for New Zealand. In 1998, the United States government turned Internet addressing and naming duties over to a private organization called the Internet Corporation for Assigned Names and Numbers (ICANN). ICANN is currently developing a new standard for top-level subdomain naming. This will expand the top-level domains into more recognizable domain names. These new top-level domains are *biz* (for corporations), *info* (for informational use), *name* (for people's names), *pro* (for professionals, such as doctors and lawyers), *museum* (for museums and nonprofit organizations), *aero* (for airlines), and *coop* (for cooperatives). This new domain naming standard will blur the line between the original top-level subdomains *com, net*, and *org*.

Subdomains are DNS management structures. The local administrators for those domains are responsible for maintaining that portion of the DNS database. These subdomains can also be broken into further subdomains, which can be delegated authority as well.

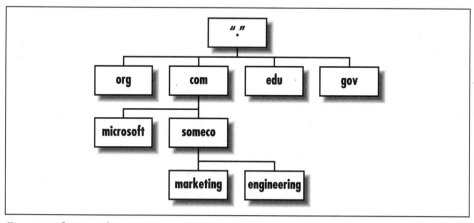

Figure 1-16. Example DNS structure

An absolute hostname in DNS is called the *Fully Qualified Domain Name* or FQDN. An FQDN begins with the hostname and proceeds to the root. For example, *www.microsoft.com* describes a host with the name *www* in the subdomain *microsoft* under the *com* top-level domain. Although you can also include the final "." for the root domain, it is typically left out and is not necessary.

As mentioned earlier, name servers have authority over one or more zones (see Figure 1-17). Zones are simply a subset of the DNS database. Please note that zones do not have to have any normal boundaries. A zone may contain a single domain, two subdomains, or multiple levels of the name space.

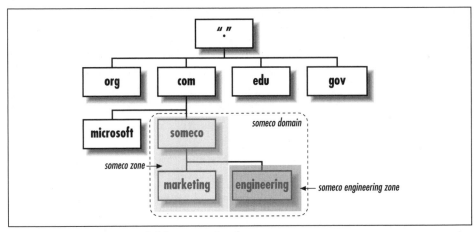

Figure 1-17. DNS zones and delegation of authority

Each zone must be serviced by a primary name server. The data for the zone is housed on the primary name server in files. To provide some redundancy for name servers, there is also a secondary name server. Secondary name servers update their files by periodically doing a *zone transfer*, a mechanism for replicating changes on the primary name server to secondary name servers.

DNS Name Resolution

When an application such as a web browser needs to resolve a hostname, it uses the client portion of DNS, known as a *resolver*. The resolver creates a DNS query specifying the hostname to be resolved and sends the query to a name server it was configured to use. The name server then queries the root domain's name server, which responds with the address of the appropriate top-level domain's name server. This continues until the request reaches the name server that can satisfy the query (see Figure 1-18).

Although it looks like it would take a long time for resolution to take place, in reality it's mostly a matter of seconds for the request to be resolved. Some of this speed can be attributed to the fact that name servers will cache results of queries. So the next time you type a web site's address into the address bar of your browser, count how long it takes to resolve.

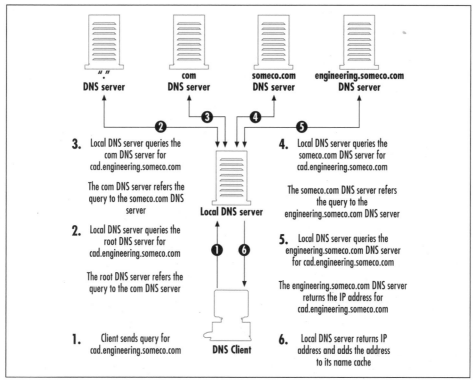

Figure 1-18. DNS name query process

WINS and NetBIOS Names

Windows 2000 is the first Microsoft operating system with the capability to rely completely on DNS for name resolution. The primary naming system for Microsoft networks before Windows 2000 was based on NetBIOS names. A computer's NetBIOS name, sometimes called its "computer name," is assigned by the administrator who first installs the operating system. Modifying the network properties on the operating system can also change the NetBIOS name. Although Windows 2000 relies heavily on DNS for name resolution, the installer must still assign the computer a computer name. This name is then used for the computer's hostname as well as its NetBIOS name. Each computer has its own NetBIOS name that it broadcasts to all other computers on the network.

As you can imagine, maintaining NetBIOS names on a local area network is extremely easy, because whenever it is booted up, a computer always either broadcasts its NetBIOS name or adds itself to the NetBIOS name database on a WINS server.

However, using NetBIOS names in a subnetted environment suffers the major limitation that routers do not forward broadcasts. Therefore computers in different subnets are never aware of each other.

One method of eliminating this problem is using an *LMHOSTS* file (see Example 1-1). Much like a *HOSTS* file, an *LMHOSTS* file is a text file listing NetBIOS names and their corresponding IP addresses. To facilitate NetBIOS name resolution on an internetwork, an administrator has to manually edit and distribute *LMHOSTS* files to all computers on the internetwork.

Example 1-2. Sample LMHOSTS File

```
192.168.0.2    nalcott     #PRE   #DOM:ALCOTT  #DC for network
192.168.0.254  proxy       #PRE   #Proxy Server for Network
192.168.0.1    cg141484-a  #PRE
```

To alleviate some of these problems, Microsoft introduced the Windows Internet Naming Service (WINS) with Windows NT. WINS maintains a NetBIOS name database much like *LMHOSTS*. However, unlike *LMHOSTS*, WINS is dynamic. When a computer is first booted up, it will register its NetBIOS name with the WINS server it is configured to use. Each entry in the database has a TTL that removes the entry after it expires. Figure 1-19 displays some example WINS NetBIOS registrations.

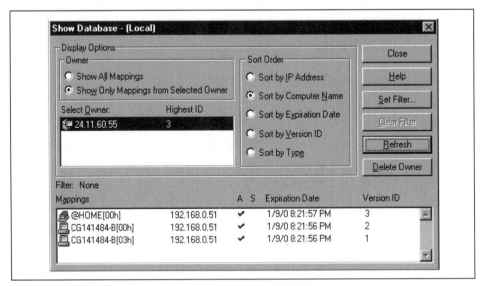

Figure 1-19. Snapshot of WINS Manager in Windows NT 4.0

NetBIOS Name Resolution

So how does a Microsoft-based client (DOS, Windows for Workgroups, Windows 9x, and Windows NT) know which type of NetBIOS name resolution to use? There are four NetBIOS name resolution modes that tell a client which method to use: B-Node, P-Node, M-Node, and H-Mode.

 The command `ipconfig /all` displays the current NetBIOS Name Resolution configuration on Windows NT 4.0 and Windows 2000. On Windows 95 and Windows 98, use the WINIPCFG utility.

B-Node

The B-Node (or broadcast) mode uses broadcast messages to resolve NetBIOS names on the network. This is the oldest and most basic form of NetBIOS name resolution used in Microsoft networks. It is also the default NetBIOS name resolution mode for clients not configured with the IP address of a WINS server. Figure 1-20 illustrates B-Node name resolution. When Computer A needs to send data to Computer E, Computer A sends a broadcast message to the network, looking for Computer E. If and when Computer E receives the broadcast, it responds directly to Computer A with its IP address. Computer A then updates its NetBIOS cache with Computer E's IP address.

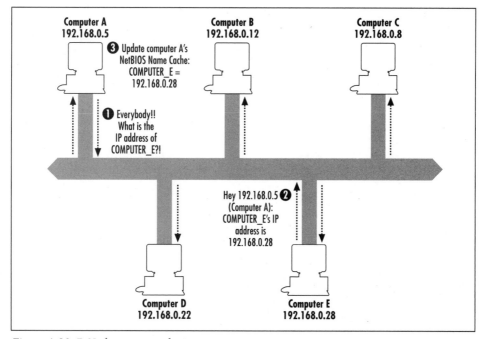

Figure 1-20. B-Node name resolution

B-Node resolution works great in small networks. However, as the network grows, the amount of bandwidth consumed by broadcasts grows, thus slowing down the network. Also, as noted earlier, routers do not forward broadcasts. Therefore B-Node name resolution mode will not work in a routed environment.

P-Node

Clients configured to use the P-Node (or point-to-point) mode will use WINS for NetBIOS name resolution. Figure 1-21 illustrates P-Node name resolution. To use P-Node mode, a client must be configured with the IP address of a WINS server. When Computer A needs the IP address for Computer E, it will contact the WINS server it is configured to use. The WINS server will then respond with the IP address. Computer A then updates its NetBIOS cache with Computer E's IP address.

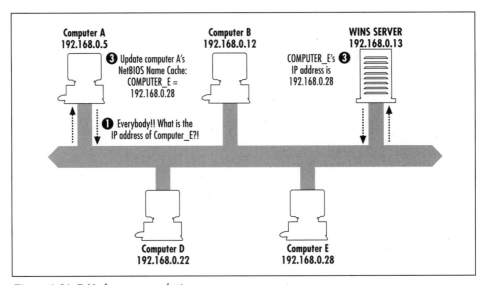

Figure 1-21. P-Node name resolution

P-Node resolution works great because it alleviates the two problems associated with B-Node mode: too many broadcasts and not working in a routed environment. Since all queries and responses used in P-Node name resolution are directly between the client and the WINS server, no broadcasts take place, which means P-Node mode works in a routed environment.

Some limitations of P-Node mode are that every client must be configured with the IP addresses of WINS servers, and NetBIOS name resolution will fail if no WINS server is available. Another issue to consider is that there must be a WINS server or WINS proxy on each subnet. A WINS proxy listens for broadcasts from clients configured to use B-Node. It takes the request and sends it directly to the WINS server it is configured to use.

M-Node

M-Node (or multiple) mode–configured clients try to resolve NetBIOS names with a broadcast first (B-Node). If the broadcast is not successful, the client tries to resolve the NetBIOS names via a WINS server (P-Node). Figure 1-22 illustrates M-Node name resolution.

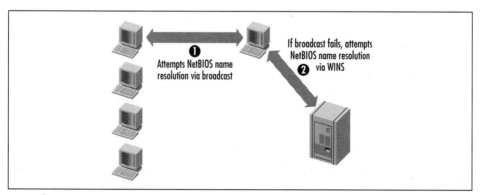

Figure 1-22. M-Node name resolution

M-Node mode allows name resolution to continue if a WINS server is down. Please note that since it uses broadcasts first, broadcast traffic may become a problem in a large network.

H-Node

An H-Node (or hybrid) mode client tries to resolve NetBIOS names using WINS first. If WINS fails, the client uses a broadcast. Figure 1-23 illustrates H-Node name resolution.

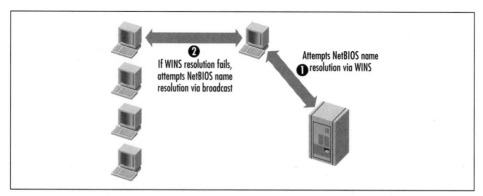

Figure 1-23. H-Node name resolution

H-Node mode is the default NetBIOS name resolution mode for clients configured with the IP address of a WINS server.

Summary

This chapter gave an overview of some of the configuration information that DHCP is expected to deliver to its clients.

TCP/IP is the dominant network protocol in use in today's network environments. It is also the network protocol for the Internet, and I strongly urge that you learn as much about it as you can. Understanding TCP/IP will help you configure, maintain, and troubleshoot many systems that a network engineer will encounter.

The chapter began with a discussion of the TCP/IP protocol suite. This included a comparison of the two common reference models: the Open Systems Interconnect (OSI) Model and the Department of Defense (DOD) Reference Model. During the discussion I delved into the various layers in the models and provided examples of how the various components in TCP/IP are implemented.

Next I moved into a discussion on hardware addresses. These addresses, also known as MAC addresses, are used to uniquely identify the network interface card (NIC) in a computer.

The next section described IP addressing. IP addressing is the heart of a TCP/IP-based network. An IP address is a 32-bit binary number that identifies a computer on a network. It contains two parts: the network portion and the host portion of the address. This section also included a discussion of IP address classes and how they are employed. The section concluded with a discussion of IP subnetting and Classless Interdomain Routing (CIDR). The entire concept of packet routing is made possible through the use of IP addressing.

The chapter concluded with a discussion of the various name resolution processes found on Microsoft TCP/IP-based networks. This included Domain Name System (DNS), which is the standard name resolution process for many corporate networks and the Internet. Windows Internet Naming Service (WINS) is used on Microsoft networks to provide NetBIOS to IP address name resolution.

2

In The Beginning: RARP and BOOTP

This chapter describes the predecessors to DHCP, the Reverse Address Resolution Protocol (RARP) and the Bootstrap Protocol (BOOTP). These two protocols are illustrated here to highlight the need for a more robust and dynamic configuration protocol as well as to provide a basic foundation to understanding DHCP.

RARP

RARP is a protocol that exists at the Data Link Layer. Think of it as the exact opposite of ARP (described in Chapter 1, *TCP/IP Overview*). It provides a mechanism for a host to determine its IP address when it is only aware of its MAC address.

RARP typically is utilized when a diskless workstation is booted. Since it does not have any IP configuration data stored locally, it must use RARP to find out its IP address. RARP accomplishes this by using a client/server process. The RARP server contains a database that simply maps IP addresses to their corresponding MAC addresses.

When a RARP client wants to find out its IP address, it sends a broadcast Ethernet frame (target MAC address = FF:FF:FF:FF:FF:FF) containing its MAC address. The RARP server, upon receiving the message, looks up the requester's MAC address in its RARP table. If a match is found, the RARP server creates a reply packet that contains the requester's IP address (see Figure 2-1). If no match is found, the packet is discarded.

Although very basic in functionality, RARP can determine and configure a diskless workstation with an IP address. However, it does not contain a method for determining and delivering other configuration data (e.g., subnet mask, default gateway, etc.). Another downside of RARP is that an RARP server can service only a

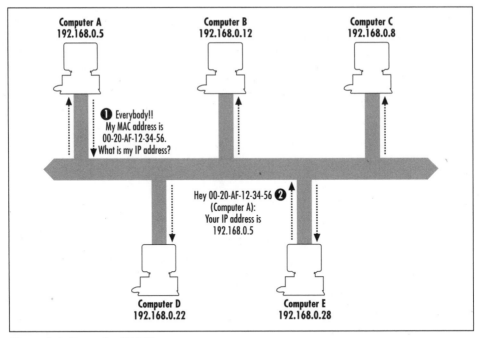

Figure 2-1. Example of RARP

single subnet because of its complete reliance on Ethernet broadcasts. To overcome these shortfalls, another protocol was developed, called BOOTP.

What Is BOOTP?

BOOTP, much like RARP, is a protocol that allows a diskless host to request an IP
address. It also provides other configuration parameters, as well as supplying a
boot file. BOOTP is an IP-based protocol that uses UDP to provide the communication between a BOOTP client and a BOOTP server. More importantly, BOOTP
allows hosts (e.g., desktop PCs, servers, X terminals, etc.) to be dynamically configured to use the TCP/IP protocol suite. So instead of manually configuring each
TCP/IP-based host on a network, BOOTP delivers the information automatically
without user intervention.

BOOTP is a client/server process where the BOOTP client, during the boot phase,
requests configuration information from a BOOTP server. The BOOTP server,
upon receiving the request from the BOOTP client, looks up the client's MAC
address in its BOOTP configuration database and sends a reply containing IP configuration information. The client receives the reply and configures its TCP/IP
stack. The BOOTP client will also load a boot file if the BOOTP server supplies a
path using the fully qualified filename. A major improvement is the *magic cookie,*

which is a mechanism for a BOOTP server to supply vendor-specific operating system (OS) options to a BOOTP client. These options could include DNS servers, WINS or NetBIOS name servers (NBNS), time servers, etc.

There are many configuration options (known as vendor options) available. Refer to RFC-1533 (*http://www.ietf.org/rfc/rfc1533.txt*) for a complete listing.

Some of the more important information supplied includes:

- IP address
- IP subnet mask
- IP address of the default gateway for the client's subnet
- IP addresses of primary and secondary DNS servers
- IP addresses of primary and secondary WINS or NBNS

Additional information supplied by a BOOTP server may include:

- IP address of a boot server
- The fully-qualified name of a boot file to be used
- The domain name of the client (i.e., *microsoft.com*)
- IP address of a time server
- Time offset (in seconds) from Coordinated Universal Time (CMT)

Microsoft-based operating systems (as well as other OSs) support only a limited subset of vendor options. The Microsoft-supported options are discussed in a later chapter.

BOOTP Packet Structure

Before delving into the conversation between a BOOTP client and a BOOTP server, I will examine the packet structure of the BOOTP protocol (see Figure 2-2).

A BOOTP packet's transmission order is from left to right, top to bottom—just as you are reading this page. The number shown in parentheses is the number of octets (or bytes) each field occupies.

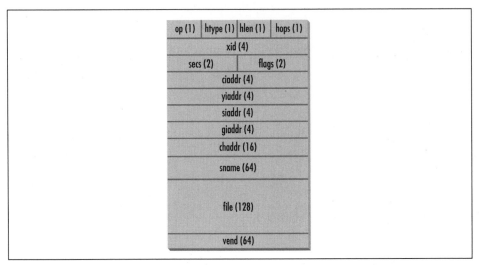

Figure 2-2. BOOTP packet structure

Field Definitions

Table 2-1 lists the available fields in a BOOTP packet and describes the type of information each field is to supply.

Table 2-1. BOOTP Field Definitions

Field	Definition
op	Specifies the message type: if 1, the message is a BOOTPREQUEST; if 2, the message is a BOOTPREPLY.
htype	Specifies the hardware address type (i.e., Ethernet or Token Ring). 10 Mbps Ethernet = 1.
hlen	Specifies the hardware address length. Ethernet = 6.
hops	Specifies the number of hops or routers between the client and the server.
xid	Specifies the transaction ID number. This is a random number that is used to match up the request with the reply that is returned.
secs	Specifies how long it has been since the client was booted up.
flags	Specifies whether the BOOTPREPLY message should be sent as a unicast message or a broadcast message.
ciaddr	Specifies the client's IP address if known. This is only used in a bootprequest message.
yiaddr	Specifies the IP address assigned to the client by the server. This is only used in a BOOTPREPLY message.
siaddr	Specifies the IP address of the server. This is only used in a BOOTPREPLY message.
giaddr	Specifies the gateway address if the message crossed a router.
chaddr	Specifies the client's MAC address.

Table 2-1. BOOTP Field Definitions (continued)

Field	Definition
sname	Specifies the server name that the client wishes to boot from.
file	Specifies a filename the client should use to boot from. The filename must contain a fully qualified path.
vend	Specifies optional vendor-specific information. This field is also referred to as the magic cookie.

The BOOTP Conversation

Let's explore the BOOTP conversation in more detail. There are two types of BOOTP messages, the BOOTPREQUEST and the BOOTPREPLY. The packet structure of these messages is identical; the only difference is in the type of information they contain.

Sending the BOOTPREQUEST

When the BOOTP client firsts boots up, it constructs a BOOTPREQUEST message and broadcasts this message across the network. This message includes information that allows the BOOTP server to determine what configuration data it must supply to the requesting host.

The BOOTPREQUEST message contains the following information:

Source's MAC address
    From the client's LAN adapter

Destination's MAC address
    FF:FF:FF:FF:FF:FF (Ethernet broadcast)

Destination's IP address
    255.255.255.255 (IP broadcast)

Source's IP address
    0.0.0.0 (unless the requester knows its IP address)

Destination server hostname
    If requester prefers a specific server

Boot filename
    If requester prefers a specific boot file

Vendor-specific data
    Configuration data relating to operating system-specific functions.

Let's take a moment to examine the contents of a BOOTPREQUEST message. In this example, I will work my way up the OSI Model starting with the Data Link Layer.

At the Data Link Layer, you find the Ethernet header, which contains hardware addressing, such as MAC addresses. The Ethernet header is also referred to as a frame. The Ethernet header's destination address is an Ethernet broadcast, designated by the hexidecimal address FF:FF:FF:FF:FF:FF. The source address (00:60:97: 93:CF:BF) is derived from the sender's MAC address (see Figure 2-3, callout 1). The Ethernet header also contains information about the upper-level protocol it is housing, in this case IP.

Moving up the OSI Model, we arrive at the Internet Layer. Here you will find the IP header, which contains logical networking address information. Some of this information is used by IP to maintain the data, such as the IP version, time to live, and packet length.

With a BOOTPREQUEST message, the client has two choices when attempting communication with the BOOTP server. The client set the destination address for the IP header to broadcast (255.255.255.255) (see Figure 2-3, callout 2). However, if the client knows the IP address of a BOOTP server, it can address the message directly to the server's IP address via a unicast packet, thus avoiding broadcasting to the entire network.

Finally, the client needs to enter source address information. Since the client most likely does not have an IP address, the source address for the packet is 0.0.0.0 (i.e., this host on this network) (see Figure 2-3, callout 2). If the client does know its IP address, it will place the address in the `ciaddr` field.

Next stop on the OSI Model: the Transport Layer. BOOTP utilizes the UDP protocol at this layer, since the data transmission is noncritical. UDP does not provide any error control, so if a packet is lost, it will not be automatically retransmitted. When utilizing UDP, the protocols found in upper layers, in this case BOOTP, are responsible for retransmitting their requests if a packet is lost or discarded.

At this layer it is important to note the UDP source and destination ports. All communications from a BOOTP client are sent via UDP port 68. The destination UDP port is 67, which is the port the BOOTP server is listening on (see Figure 2-3, callout 3).

Let's step up to the upper layers of the OSI Model and enter the heart of this discussion: BOOTP.

While constructing the BOOTPREQUEST, the BOOTP client sets the `op` field to 1 (BOOTPREQUEST). The `op` field simplifies the BOOTP protocol because the protocol needs only a single packet structure for both bootprequests and bootpreplys. Simply changing the `op` field from 1 to 2 turns a BOOTPREQUEST into a BOOTPREPLY message (see Figure 2-4, callout 1).

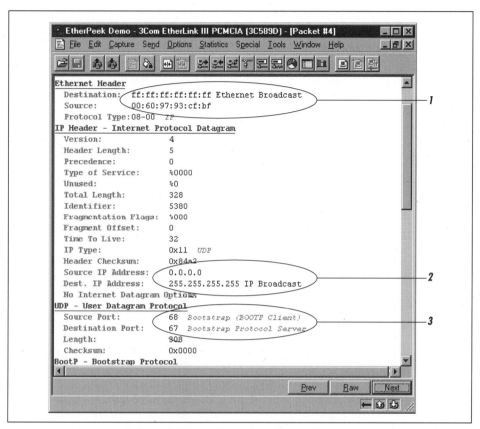

Figure 2-3. Packet trace of a BOOTPREQUEST message: BOOTP information

Other information included in the BOOTPREQUEST is addressing information regarding the client. Remember that the structure of all BOOTP messages remains the same. Since a BOOTPREQUEST message is sent from a BOOTP client requesting an IP address, most of the information will be set to 0.0.0.0.

The most important piece of information included in the packet is the MAC address of the source, placed in the **chaddr** field. This has a dual role: it provides the BOOTP server with a hardware address to use for lookups, and it provides the client's hardware or MAC address for the BOOTPREPLY message from the server (see Figure 2-4, callout 2).

Receiving the BOOTPREQUEST

So the BOOTP client broadcasts the BOOTPREQUEST message to the network. Now what? A BOOTP server listens for bootprequests being broadcast on UDP port 67. When the BOOTP server receives a BOOTPREQUEST, it performs a few checks on the message before processing it.

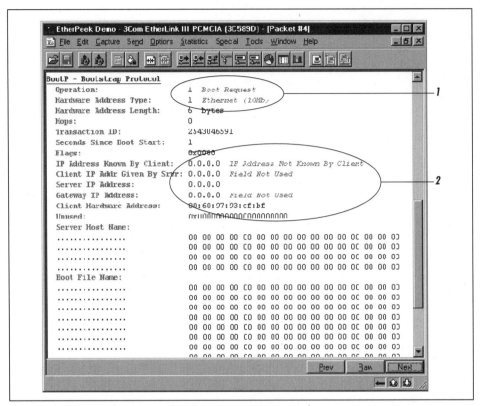

Figure 2-4. Packet trace of a BOOTPREQUEST message: Ethernet, IP, and UDP information

The first check is to determine whether the client specified a server name. If no
server name was specified or if the server name matches the BOOTP server's hostname, it continues to process the packet. If a server name was specified and does
not match the BOOTP server's hostname, it discards the packet.

The BOOTP database located on the BOOTP server is simply a static text file containing MAC addresses and their corresponding IP configuration information.
Example 2-1 gives a sample BOOTP database file.

Example 2-1. Example BOOTP Database File

```
# bootptab: database for bootp server
# Blank lines and lines beginning with '#' are ignored.
#
# Legend:
#
# first field -- hostname
#
# hd -- home directory
# bf -- bootfile
# ds -- domain name servers
```

Example 2-1. Example BOOTP Database File (continued)

```
# gw -- gateways
# ha -- hardware address
# ht -- hardware type
# ip -- host IP address
# sm -- subnet mask
# to -- time offset  of local time from GMT (seconds)
# ts -- time servers
#
#
# <devicename>:ht=ethernet:ha=<MACaddress>:ip=<ipaddress>:sm=<subnetmask>
:gw=<gatewayaddress>:ds=<DNSserver>
#
BOOTPCLIENT1:ht=ethernet:ha=00105A897960:ip=192.168.0.20:sm=255.255.255.0
:gw=192.168.0.1:ds=192.168.0.10
BOOTPCLIENT2:ht=ethernet:ha=00C0A8358A12:ip=192.168.0.21:sm=255.255.255.0
:gw=192.168.0.1:ds=192.168.0.10
BOOTPCLIENT1:ht=ethernet:ha=00E0293642FE:ip=192.168.0.22:sm=255.255.255.0
:gw=192.168.0.1:ds=192.168.0.10
```

After checking the server name, the BOOTP server attempts to look up the client's MAC address in the server's BOOTP database. If the BOOTP server finds the address, the server places the corresponding IP address in the `yiaddr` field of the BOOTPREPLY message (see Figure 2-5, callout 2). If no match is found, the server discards the packet.

Next, the server checks the BOOTPREQUEST message to see if the client specified a boot file. If it was specified, the server uses the requested filename along with the IP address (from the previous lookup) to perform a database lookup. If there is a match, or if there is a generic file specified in the BOOTP database, the server places the fully qualified filename in the `file` field of the BOOTPREPLY.

Finally, the server checks for any requested vendor-specific options. If there are any, it places the data in the `vend` field of the BOOTPREPLY.

Now that the BOOTP server has looked up the requested information and placed it in the appropriate fields of the BOOTPREPLY message, the server finishes the message. It sets the `op` field to BOOTPREPLY (see Figure 2-5, callout 1) and places its IP address in the `siaddr` field (see Figure 2-5, callout 2).

Sending the BOOTPREPLY

Sending the BOOTPREPLY back to the client causes a dilemma: how does the server send a reply to a client that does not know its IP address? The server performs a few operations before trying to transmit the BOOTPREPLY.

First, if the original BOOTPREQUEST's `ciaddr` field was nonzero, the server sends the packet just like any other packet: directly to the corresponding IP address.

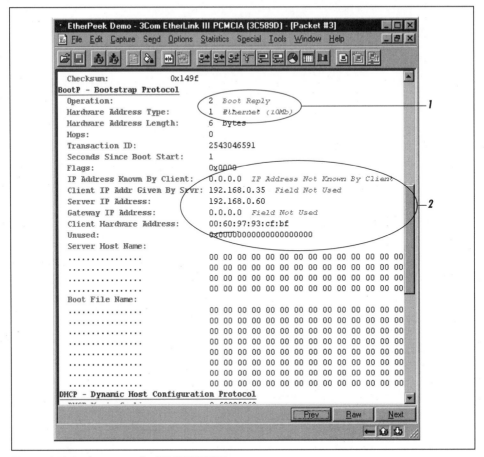

Figure 2-5. Packet trace of a BOOTPREPLY message

Once the client receives it, it reconfigures its IP stack using the newly supplied IP address and configuration data.

If the client does not know its IP address, it will not be able to respond to ARP requests from the BOOTP server. In the case, there are two possibilities:

1. The server can create an ARP cache entry using the client's MAC address and the IP address the server just assigned.

2. The server can simply address the packet as a broadcast (255.255.255.255) (see Figure 2-6, callout 2).

In later implementations of BOOTP, the `flags` field is used to specify whether the reply should be sent as a unicast or broadcast message. The `flag` field is 2 octets long (16 bits), out of which only the first bit is used. If the bit is 1, the message should be sent as a broadcast. If the bit is 0, the message should be sent as a uni-cast. Since only the client knows whether or not it can receive unicast messages at this point, the client is responsible for setting this bit in the original BOOTPRE-QUEST packet.

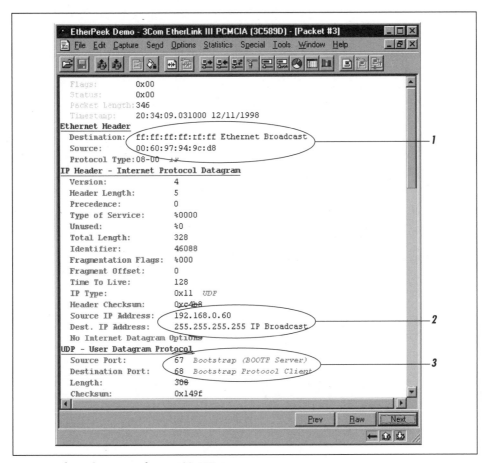

Figure 2-6. Packet trace of a BOOTPREPLY message

After the server determines how and where it will transmit the packet, the BOOTP-REPLY message is sent on UDP port 68 with the source port set to 67 (see Figure 2-6, callout 3).

Receiving the BOOTPREPLY

The BOOTP client continues to listen for the BOOTPREPLY on UDP port 68. When the BOOTP client receives a BOOTPREPLY, it configures its IP stack with the information provided in the BOOTPREPLY. It finds its IP address in the ciaddr field and default gateway address in the giaddr field (see Figure 2-5, callout 2).

Summary

RARP and BOOTP were simply the first steps in figuring out a method to deliver IP configuration information. After RARP was developed, it became apparent that it had a couple of major shortfalls. First, a RARP server could only operate on a single subnet. Second, it lacked the critical ability to provide any IP configuration information other than the IP address.

Although BOOTP provided a vast improvement over RARP, it also suffered some serious shortfalls. First, the BOOTP database was a static text file. This meant that administrators needed to maintain the file by hand as changes were made to the network. A simple change like replacing a host's network interface card required the administrator to update the BOOTP database file. Another shortfall was the inability to dynamically allocate and distribute IP addresses. In the age of depleted IP address space, dynamic IP addressing was a critical feature.

Seeing this, the IETF started work to create a new protocol that would overcome these shortfalls: Dynamic Host Configuration Protocol (DHCP).

3

Making Life Easier: DHCP

This chapter provides an introduction to the Dynamic Host Configuration Protocol (DHCP). As you will see, DHCP shares many traits with BOOTP. However, they are two separate protocols and as such operate in different ways. I will also detail the DHCP conversation that takes place between a DHCP client and DHCP server. Finally I will cover DHCP relay agents, which allow DHCP to operate in a subnetted environment by relaying requests between the client and server, and how relay agents operate.

Why DHCP?

As shown in the previous chapters, RARP and BOOTP made inroads towards creating a way to dynamically configure a host on a TCP/IP-based network. RARP provided a means of obtaining an IP address; however, it could only function on a single subnet and did not provide any other configuration information, such as the subnet mask and default gateway. BOOTP alleviated some of the problems of RARP, but an administrator still had to maintain static configuration files on the BOOTP server. Also, BOOTP clients could not renew their configurations until the system was restarted, thus triggering the BOOTP process.

DHCP, defined in RFC2131 and RFC2132, was developed to alleviate many of these shortcomings and to accomplish the following:

- DHCP allows administrators to control configuration parameters on their network.

- Clients using DHCP can be dynamically configured. This allows additions and changes to networks without the need to visit each individual host or workstation.

- For fault tolerance, multiple DHCP servers can service one or more subnets.

- DHCP servers, via BOOTP relay agents, can service more than one subnet.

- DHCP provides a dynamic database for IP address allocation. These IP addresses, when no longer in use, can also be reclaimed via lease durations.

- Clients can continue to use a DHCP-allocated IP address even after the client is rebooted. BOOTP clients must always obtain an IP address from a BOOTP server when they are booted.

It is important to remember that DHCP is based on the earlier BOOTP protocol. They share many of the same characteristics:

Client/server operating model

IP configuration information is allocated when a client requests an IP address from the server. The server holds and maintains the configuration information via either static files (on the BOOTP server) or a dynamic database (on the DHCP server).

Packet structure

BOOTP and DHCP have nearly identical packet structures. Each packet is a 576-byte UDP datagram. The only difference between the two structures is the field dedicated to providing optional configuration information. In a BOOTP packet this field is called the **vend** field; it can hold a maximum of 64 octets of information. In a DHCP message, the field is known as the **options** field. This field can be of variable length, but a client must be prepared to receive an **options** field of at least 312 octets.

UDP port numbers

Both BOOTP and DHCP use the same well-known UDP port numbers, 67 (for client request messages) and 68 (for server replies).

The *Services* file located in *%systemroot%\system32\drivers\etc* provides a list of well-known port numbers. Some applications use this file to determine the number of a well-known port. For example, Exchange Server uses the *Services* file to determine which port is used for initiating Network News Transfer Protocol (NNTP) connections. In Windows 95 and Windows 98, the *Services* file is located in the *Windows* directory.

Because DHCP and BOOTP share these characteristics, DHCP servers can service existing BOOTP clients.

Using Static IP Configurations

Installing the TCP/IP protocol suite on a host requires careful configuration of an IP address, subnet mask, and default gateway. The host will not be able to communicate with other hosts on the network if any of these parameters are incorrect. It is also important to correctly configure the host with IP addresses of DNS servers and WINS servers. If these items are incorrectly configured, the host may not be able to perform name resolution correctly.

There are many scenarios where a statically configured host may not be able to communicate:

- The user changed the IP address. If the user enters an IP address that is not valid, the host will not be able to communicate. Or worse, the user may enter an IP address that is already in use, creating multiple problems on the network.

- The user or network administrator mistyped the IP address, subnet mask, or default gateway. As people are not perfect and make mistakes, this problem can be very common in a statically configured environment.

- A computer is physically moved from one subnet to another. Statically entered information needs to be updated whenever a computer is moved. This increases administrative overhead because it requires the network administrator to physically visit and change each moved system.

Of course, a static IP address can be utilized when a device needs to be stable and dependable. Here are some situations where static IP addressing is useful and necessary:

- Most, if not all, servers on a TCP/IP-based network should be configured with a static IP address. A server is a central point of network activity. Their configurations must be static and stable, providing consistent network connectivity. Servers will be configured and maintained by experienced network engineers. Although there is always a chance of user error, misconfiguration of an IP address on a server is rather unlikely.

- Network printers should be configured with a static IP address. A network printer is a critical point in the printing process. Configuration with a static IP address ensures that print queues located on print servers always find the correct network printer to handle a user's job.

- Other devices that benefit from static IP addresses include network infrastructure equipment, such as routers, switches, and hubs. Much like servers and network printers, these devices are important and necessary in the health of the network. They are configured and maintained by experienced network engineers, reducing the likelihood of misconfiguration.

Using DHCP for IP Configurations

Using DHCP to distribute and manage IP configurations alleviates most of the problems associated with a statically maintained environment. Simple problems such as a wrong IP address, subnet mask, or default gateway are completely eliminated. Also, configuration information central to the operation of the network can be updated automatically. If the IP addresses of DNS or WINS servers change, the administrator simply updates the DHCP database, and the changes are sent to the DHCP clients upon next boot or when their lease expires.

In essence, DHCP allows the network configuration to become transparent to the user. For the user, it becomes a "Plug and Play" operation. When the user starts a new desktop, he simply plugs in the network cable and boots it up. The desktop, or DHCP client, receives the configuration information from the network's DHCP servers and updates its configuration settings. At this point the user can start accessing the resources on the network.

 Of course·the new computer must also be configured as a DHCP client. DHCP client settings differ among hardware vendors. Check with your hardware vendor to determine its default DHCP client settings.

DHCP also simplifies life for users with laptops. Users with laptops can roam from one area in the company to another or even to multiple sites across the country. When the user plugs her laptop into the network, the laptop contacts a DHCP server that tells it the correct configuration to use for that site. Once the laptop receives this information, the user can begin using network resources.

DHCP accomplishes many of these tasks through the use of scopes and leases.

A *scope* is a collection of IP configuration parameters that will be used by all DHCP clients on a given subnet. For instance, a scope would encompass a single contiguous range of IP addresses. Because these IP addresses make up a subnet, other parameters such as subnet mask and default gateway would also be defined in the scope.

A *lease* is the period of time that the DHCP server permits the DHCP client to use an IP address. By using a lease, the DHCP server can dynamically allocate IP addresses and reclaim them once the lease has expired.

As you can see, the entire DHCP process occurs without the knowledge of the user. It also does not require a network administrator to configure the user's machine when it is initially added to the network. Nor does it require the administrator to visit and reconfigure laptops as users move throughout the organization. All of this translates into savings for the organization and the LAN administrator.

DHCP Packet Structure

Let's examine the packet structure of the DHCP protocol. As you will see, the DHCP packet structure is fundamentally the same as the BOOTP packet structure. There are only two differences: the **vend** field was changed to the **options** field, and this field was expanded from 64 octets in length to a minimum of 312 octets.

As shown in Figure 3-1, a DHCP packet's transmission order is from left to right, top to bottom. The number shown in parentheses is the number of octets (or bytes) each field occupies.

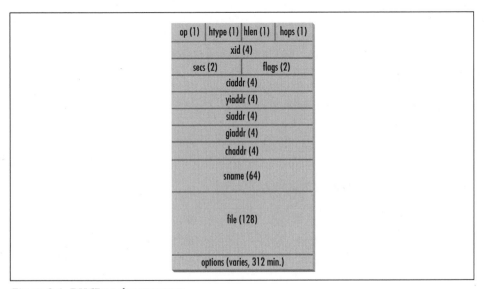

Figure 3-1. DHCP packet structure

Field Definitions

Table 3-1 lists the available fields in a DHCP packet and describes the type of information each field supplies.

Table 3-1. DHCP Field Definitions

Field	Definition
op	Specifies the message type: if 1, the message is a BOOTPREQUEST; if 2, the message is a BOOTPREPLY.
htype	Specifies the hardware address type (i.e., ethernet or token ring). 10 Mbps Ethernet = 1.
hlen	Specifies the hardware address length. Ethernet = 6.
hops	Specifies the number of hops between the client and the server.
xid	Specifies the transaction ID number. This is a random number that is used to match up the request with the reply that is returned.

Table 3-1. DHCP Field Definitions (continued)

Field	Definition
secs	Specifies how long it has been since the client was booted.
flags	Specifies whether the BOOTPREPLY message should be sent as a unicast message or a broadcast message.
ciaddr	Specifies the client's IP address, if known. This is only used in a BOOTP-REQUEST message.
yiaddr	Specifies the IP address assigned to the client by the server. This is only used in a BOOTPREPLY message.
siaddr	Specifies the IP address of the server. This is only used in a BOOTPREPLY message.
giaddr	Specifies the gateway address if the message crossed a router.
chaddr	Specifies the client's MAC address or some other type of identifier unique to that client.
sname	Specifies the server name that the client wishes to boot from.
file	Specifies a filename the client should use to boot from. The filename must contain a fully qualified path.
options	Specifies optional vendor-specific information. This field was formerly referred to as the **vend** field.

The DHCP Conversation

There are three main components in a DHCP conversation, as shown in Figure 3-2.

The first component, the DHCP client, is the software portion of an operating system that is designed to request IP addresses and other related configuration information. Once it receives the requested information, the software reconfigures the operating system.

The second component, the DHCP server, is a program that listens for requests from DHCP clients on the network and supplies them with the information that is requested. The DHCP server is maintained by a network administrator. It is configured with a database that houses the configuration information, including IP addresses, subnet masks, default gateways, and DNS and WINS server addresses. The database also tracks which IP addresses are currently in use and which MAC addresses are using them.

The third component is the DHCP relay agent. Identical to the BOOTP relay agent, the DHCP relay agent listens for DHCP broadcasts on its local subnets. The DHCP relay agent is configured with IP addresses of DHCP servers. If it receives a DHCP broadcast from a DHCP client, the DHCP relay agent will send the request as a unicast message directly to a DHCP server. I will examine BOOTP and DHCP relay agents later in this chapter.

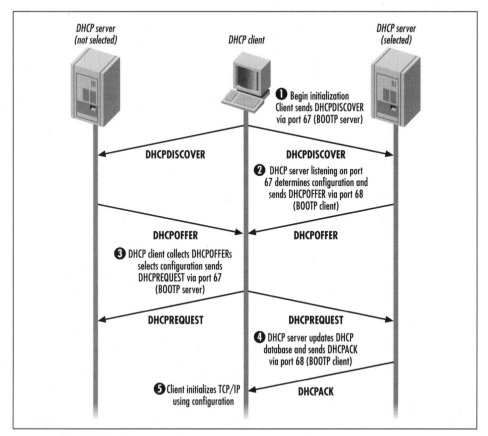

Figure 3-2. The DHCP conversation

DHCP greatly differs from BOOTP in how it handles the conversation between DHCP clients and DHCP servers. The DHCP conversation is more robust, so DHCP is more dynamic and flexible. Whereas BOOTP provides a simple conversation between a BOOTP client and a single BOOTP server, DHCP provides a full conversation, allowing multiple DHCP servers to respond to a DHCP client's single request.

Let's take a moment and walk through a typical DHCP conversation between a DHCP client and DHCP server on a local subnet. Later in this chapter, I will discuss how DHCP relay agents allow DHCP to operate in a multiple-subnet environment.

The DHCPDISCOVER Message

The DHCP conversation begins when a DHCP client sends a DHCPDISCOVER broadcast message across its local subnet (see Figure 3-3). This message is used to discover any DHCP servers that are on the network and available to fulfill the client's request.

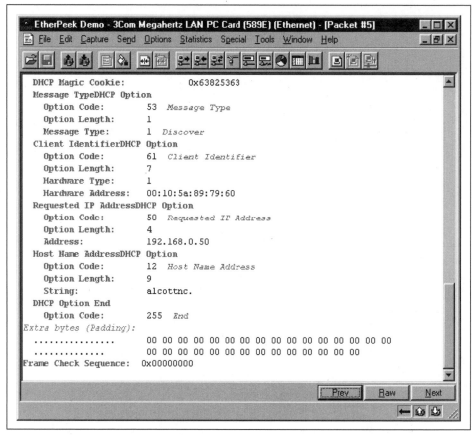

Figure 3-3. DHCPDISCOVER message

The destination Ethernet address is set to FF:FF:FF:FF:FF:FF, or an Ethernet broadcast. The source Ethernet address is set to the client's MAC address.

The source IP address is set to 0.0.0.0 because the client does not yet have an IP address. The destination IP address is set to 255.255.255.255, i.e., an IP broadcast. Because it is sent as an IP broadcast, all IP hosts on the subnet will receive this message. Any DHCP servers receiving this broadcast may respond if configured to do so.

DHCP, like BOOTP, uses UDP ports 67 (BOOTP server) and 68 (BOOTP client). For the DHCPDISCOVER message, the source UDP port is set to 68. The destination UDP port is set to 67.

The remainder of the message follows the packet structure described earlier in the chapter. The DHCPDISCOVER message is simply a BOOTPREQUEST (op field = 1). The fields `ciaddr`, `siaddr`, and `giaddr` are all zeroed out (i.e., set to 0.0.0.0) since the client does not have any IP configuration. The `chaddr` field is set to the client's MAC address.

The `options` field begins with the DHCP magic cookie and then specifies the DHCP Message Type Option (53) as 1, Discover. Once the DHCPDISCOVER message is complete, the client broadcasts it on its local subnet (see Figure 3-3).

The DHCPOFFER Message

The DHCPOFFER message is a broadcast message sent by the DHCP server offering a DHCP lease. The destination Ethernet address is set to FF:FF:FF:FF:FF:FF. The source Ethernet address is set to the DHCP server's MAC address.

The source IP address is set to the DHCP server's IP address, and the destination IP address is set to be an IP broadcast, 255.255.255.255.

For the DHCPOFFER message, the source UDP port is set to 67 (BOOTP server). The destination UDP port is set to 68 (DHCP client).

The DHCPOFFER message is completed by setting the `op` field to 2 (BOOTP-REPLY). The `yiaddr` field is set to the IP address the server has determined should be used by this client. The `chaddr` field is set to the client's MAC address.

The `options` field specifies the DHCP Message Type Option (53) as 2, i.e., Offer. The number in parentheses is the DHCP option number, which is defined in RFC2132, *DHCP Options and BOOTP Vendor Extensions*. The `options` field is completed with the following IP configuration information (see Figure 3-4):

Subnet Mask Option (1)
This option specifies the subnet mask to be used by the client.

Renewal Time Option (58)
Also known as T1, this option specifies the amount of time, measured in seconds, that should elapse before the client attempts to renew its IP address lease. This is set to 50% of the time allocated for the lease.

Rebinding Time Option (59)
Also known as T2, this option specifies the amount of time, measured in seconds, that should elapse before the client attempts to renew its IP address lease via a broadcast message. This is set to 87.5% of the time allocated for the lease.

IP Address Lease Time Option (51)
This option specifies the total amount of time that the client has a valid lease on this IP address.

Server Identifier Option (54)
This option specifies the IP address of the DHCP server that is sending this DHCPOFFER message, and thus is offering this lease.

DHCP Option End (255)
This option designates the end of the `options` field.

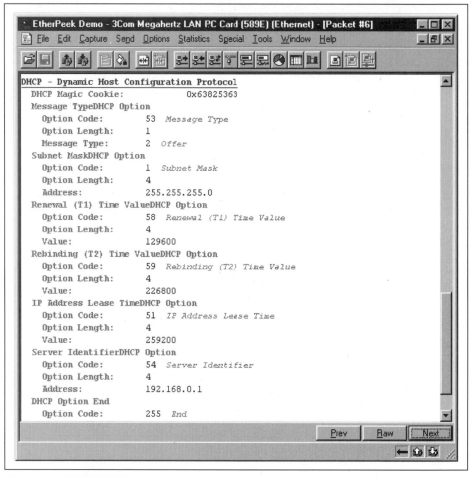

Figure 3-4. DHCPOFFER message

Once the DHCPOFFER message is complete, the server broadcasts it on its local subnet. Because the DHCPDISCOVER message is sent as a broadcast, more than one DHCP server may respond. In this case, each DHCP server will determine the IP configuration that should be sent to the client. Once the determination is made, each DHCP server sends a DHCPOFFER.

The DHCPREQUEST Message

Because more than one DHCP server may respond with a DHCPOFFER message, the DHCP client will respond with a DHCPREQUEST message to the first DHCPOFFER it receives.

The DHCPREQUEST is a broadcast message sent by the client making the DHCP request. Why are we still using broadcast messages instead of unicast messages?

Using a broadcast message for the DHCPREQUEST kills two birds with one stone. First, it lets the DHCP server from which the client is accepting the offer know that the client is accepting the offered IP address. It also notifies all of the DHCP servers that sent DHCPOFFERs that the original request has been fulfilled.

Much like the other messages, the destination Ethernet address is set to FF:FF:FF:FF:FF:FF. The source Ethernet address is set to the DHCP client's MAC address.

The source IP address is set to 0.0.0.0, and the destination IP address is set to be an IP broadcast, 255.255.255.255.

In a DHCPREQUEST message, the source UDP port is set to 68 (DHCP client). The destination UDP port is set to 67 (BOOTP server).

The DHCPREQUEST message is completed by setting the `op` field to 1 (BOOTP-REQUEST). The fields `ciaddr`, `siaddr`, `giaddr` are all zeroed out (i.e., set to 0.0.0.0) as the client still does not have any IP configuration. The `chaddr` field is set to the client's MAC address.

The `options` field specifies the DHCP Message Type Option (53) set as 3, Request. The `options` field is completed with the following IP configuration information (see Figure 3-5):

Client Identifier Option (61)
> This option specifies the MAC address of the DHCP client making the request.

Requested IP Address Option (50)
> This option specifies the IP address that the DHCP client is requesting to lease.

Server Identifier Option (54)
> This option specifies the IP address of the DHCP server that the DHCP client is requesting the lease from.

IP Address Lease Time Option (51)
> This option specifies the total amount of time that the client has a valid lease on this IP address.

Server Identifier Option (54)
> This option specifies the IP address of the DHCP server that is sending this DHCPOFFER, and thus is offering this lease.

Parameter Request List Option (55)
> This option lists the DHCP configuration information the client would like to receive, in addition to the IP address and subnet mask. For Microsoft products, the requested parameters are Subnet Mask (1), Routers (3), Domain Name (15), Domain Name Servers (6), NetBIOS Name Servers (44), NetBIOS Node Type (46), and NetBIOS Scope (47).

DHCP Option End (255)
> This option designates the end of the `options` field.

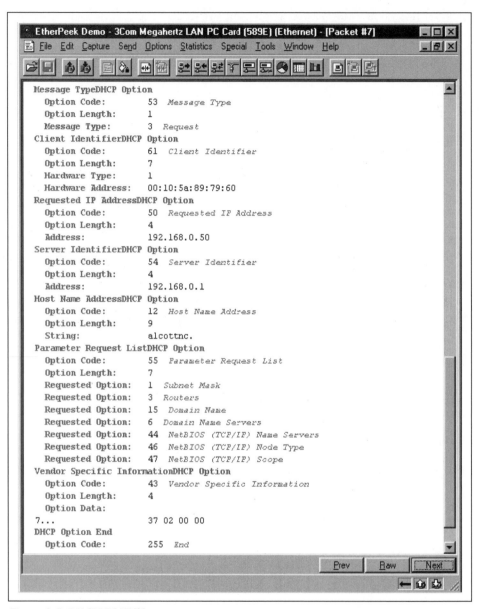

Figure 3-5. DHCPREQUEST message

With the DHCPREQUEST message complete, the DHCP client broadcasts it on its local subnet. All DHCP servers that sent a DHCPOFFER see that the client accepted another offer. The DHCP server that made the accepted DHCPOFFER sends a DHCPACK with the remaining configuration parameters.

The DHCPACK Message

Once the DHCP server receives the DHCPREQUEST, it creates a DHCPACK message, or *DHCP Acknowledgment*. The DHCPACK is used to acknowledge the client's request and to notify the client that the IP address it requested has now been reserved. It also returns the configuration parameters that the DHCP client asked for in the DHCPREQUEST.

DHCPACK is a broadcast message sent by the DHCP server acknowledging the DHCP request. The destination Ethernet address is set to FF:FF:FF:FF:FF:FF. The source Ethernet address is set to the DHCP server's MAC address.

The source IP address is set to the DHCP server's IP address, and the destination IP address is set to be an IP broadcast, 255.255.255.255.

Again, the UDP ports are switched. The source UDP port is set to 67 (BOOTP server). The destination UDP port is set to 68 (DHCP client).

The DHCPACK message sets the op field to 2 (BOOTPREPLY). The yiaddr field is set to the IP address the server has determined should be used by this client. The chaddr field is set to the client's MAC address.

The options field specifies the DHCP Message Type Option (53) set as 5, i.e., ACK. The options field is completed with the following IP configuration information (see Figure 3-6):

Renewal Time Option (58)
> Also known as T1, this option specifies the amount of time, measured in seconds, that should elapse before the client attempts to renew its IP address lease. This is set to 50% of the time allocated for the lease.

Rebinding Time Option (59)
> Also known as T2, this option specifies the amount of time, measured in seconds, that should elapse before the client attempts to renew its IP address lease via a broadcast message. This is set to 87.5% of the time allocated for the lease.

IP Address Lease Time Option (51)
> This option specifies the total amount of time that the client has a valid lease on this IP address.

Server Identifier Option (54)
> This option specifies the IP address of the DHCP server that is sending this DHCPOFFER, and thus is offering this lease.

Routers Option (3)
> This option specifies the default gateway.

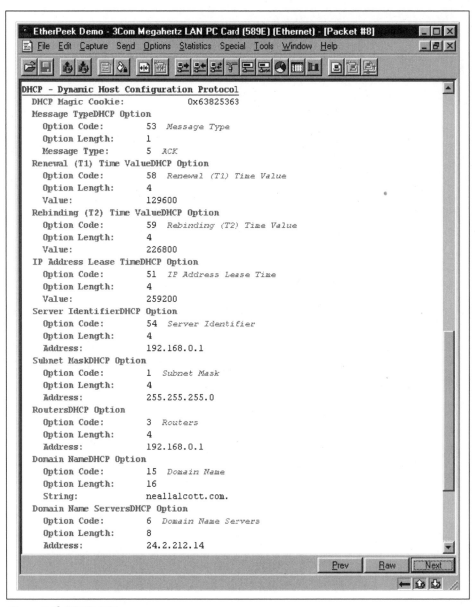

Figure 3-6. DHCPACK message

Domain Name Option (15)

This option specifies the domain name to be used by the client.

Domain Name Servers Option (6)

This option lists the DNS servers to be used for hostname resolution by the client.

NetBIOS Name Servers Option (44)
This option lists the WINS servers to be used for NetBIOS name resolution by the client.

NetBIOS Node Type Option (46)
This option determines the NetBIOS node type to be used by the client.

DHCP Option End (255)
This option designates the end of the `options` field.

The server broadcasts the DHCPACK on its local subnet once the message is complete. Once the DHCP client receives the DHCPACK, it initializes its TCP/IP stack and begins participating on the network.

The DHCPNACK Message

What if another DHCP client is now using the IP address offered by the DHCP server? In this case, when the DHCP client responds with the DHCPREQUEST message, the DHCP server responds with a DHCPNACK message or *DHCP Negative Acknowledgment*. When the DHCP client receives the DHCPNACK, it restarts the entire DHCP conversation with a new DHCPDISCOVER message.

The DHCPRELEASE Message

If the DHCP client no longer needs an assigned IP address, or if the LAN administrator would like to reassign an IP address, the DHCP client can send a DHCPRELEASE message to the DHCP server (see Figure 3-7). This will release the IP address, which is then available when the DHCP server receives a DHCPREQUEST from another client.

Although the use of broadcasts throughout the DHCP conversation makes DHCP seem like a chatty protocol, in actuality it is very efficient. Because of the use of lease durations and the T1 and T2 timers, DHCP clients need to broadcast only during initial lease negotiation and during the rebinding phase. Another reason for the heavy use of broadcasts is the potential problem BOOTP suffers from, discussed in Chapter 2, *In The Beginning: RARP and BOOTP*, where a server needs to respond to a client that does not yet have an IP address. Using a broadcast solves this problem.

The DHCP Relay Agent

As noted earlier, the entire DHCP conversation takes place using broadcast messages. When a DHCP client requests an IP address, it sends a broadcast DHCPDISCOVER message to the local subnet. DHCP servers, in turn, respond to the request by broadcasting DHCPOFFER messages. The client receives these messages and

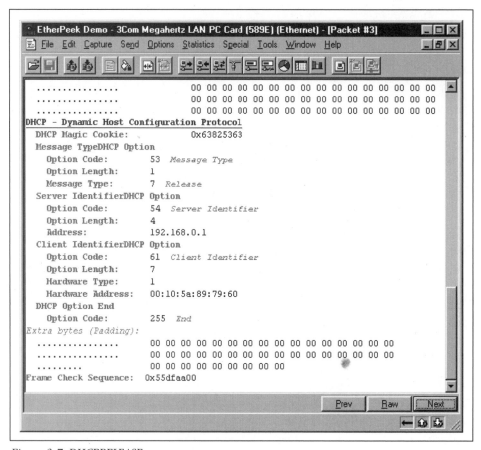

Figure 3-7. DHCPRELEASE message

accepts one of them. The client then responds with a broadcast DHCPREQUEST message, in which the DHCP server that was selected is identified. The DHCP server, upon receiving the DHCPREQUEST message, allocates the IP address in its database and responds with a DHCPACK message to the client.

So what happens if the network environment is not a single subnet, but a routed environment containing multiple subnets? In a routed environment, separate segments are connected via routers. A *router* is a hardware component that contains two or more interfaces that connect the router to the multiple physical segments. The router directs traffic between the subnets by examining the destination IP addresses in the packet headers. If a packet is destined for another subnet, the router examines its routing table to determine if a route to that subnet is available. If one is available, the router sends the packet out the interface that is the next hop to the subnet. If a route is not available, the router drops the packet and sends an ICMP message to the sending computer stating that the destination is not available.

Besides routing packets, another role a router plays is containing broadcast traffic to a single subnet. Broadcast traffic can take many forms, such as ARP requests, DHCP requests, NetBIOS name resolution requests (B-Node), etc. If broadcast traffic like this was permitted to travel throughout the network, the network would come to a grinding halt. By containing these broadcasts, routers create what is known as a broadcast domain (see Figure 3-8).

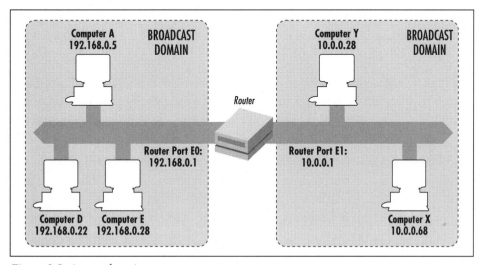

Figure 3-8. A routed environment

Because broadcasts cannot travel beyond the local subnet, DHCP conversations are impossible in a routed environment unless the DHCP server and DHCP client are on the same subnet. Having seen this problem, the IETF identified a solution.

Defined in RFC1542, the DHCP relay agent is a software program that runs on a computer or router. Its sole purpose is to forward DHCP or BOOTP requests to the DHCP server on behalf of the client. It accomplishes this by turning the broadcast requests into unicast messages sent directly to the server. The server then replies to the relay agent using a unicast message, and the relay agent forwards the message to the client.

How the DHCP Relay Agent Operates

DHCP broadcast messages sent from a DHCP client to a DHCP server have their UDP destination port set to 67. On a host running the relay agent software, the relay agent listens to port 67 for any DHCP messages.

As mentioned in Chapter 2 and earlier in this chapter, BOOTP and DHCP packets use a field called op to identify whether the message is a BOOTPREQUEST or a BOOTPREPLY. This is true for the entire DHCP conversation, i.e., all requests from the DHCP client are BOOTPREQUEST messages and all replies from the DHCP server are BOOTPREPLY messages. The relay agent responds differently depending on the message type.

The BOOTPREQUEST message

When a DHCP relay agent receives a BOOTPREQUEST message, it checks a number of the fields in the packet to determine how to handle the message.

First, the relay agent checks the value of the hops field. The hops field determines the number of routers, or "hops," between the client and the server. According to RFC1542, the relay agent must discard BOOTPREQUEST messages with a hops value exceeding 16. This is to keep BOOTPREQUEST messages from continuously traveling throughout the network. The default threshold setting for this field should be set to 4 hops. If the hops field is less than the configured threshold, the relay agent should increment the hops field by one and process the packet for forwarding.

Next, the relay agent must examine the giaddr field in the BOOTPREQUEST message. The giaddr field contains the IP address of the gateway or router that first received this BOOTPREQUEST message. If the giaddr field is zero, the relay agent must enter the IP address of the interface that received the request. If the giaddr field is not zero, the relay agent must not modify or change the IP address in the field.

Once the giaddr and hops fields have been examined and modified if necessary, the relay agent forwards the BOOTPREQUEST as a unicast message to the DHCP server. The DHCP relay agent is configured with the DHCP server's IP address.

The BOOTPREPLY message

When the DHCP server receives the BOOTPREQUEST message from the DHCP relay agent, the server processes the request just like any other request.

The DHCP server examines the giaddr field in the BOOTPREQUEST to determine which scope the server should use to offer an IP address from. After it selects a scope, it reserves an IP address in that scope.

In a routed environment, the DHCP server examines the ciaddr field in the BOOTPREQUEST. The ciaddr field contains the client's current IP address. If the ciaddr field is non-zero, the DHCP server sends the BOOTPREPLY as a unicast message to the client's IP address. If the ciaddr field is zero, the DHCP server examines the giaddr field in the BOOTPREQUEST to determine the IP address of the gateway by which the message was originally received. The server then creates a BOOTPREPLY (a DHCPOFFER) message and sends it to the gateway IP address.

The relay agent, upon receiving the BOOTPREPLY message, examines the following fields:

giaddr

The `giaddr` field is used to determine the interface that the BOOTPREPLY message must be sent with. If the `giaddr` does not match any of the relay agent's interfaces, the relay agent discards the message.

yiaddr

The `yiaddr` field is the IP address assigned to the DHCP client by the DHCP server.

chaddr

The `chaddr` field identifies the hardware or MAC address of the DHCP client.

htype

The `htype` field identifies the hardware type of the DHCP client, i.e., Ethernet.

hlen

The `hlen` field specifies the length of the hardware address.

flag

The `flag` field is used to determine whether the BOOTPREPLY message should be sent as a broadcast or unicast message. If the `flag` field is set to 1, the message should be broadcast. If it is set to 0, the message should be unicast to the IP address specified in `yiaddr` and the hardware address specified in `chaddr`.

Once the relay agent examines these fields, the relay agent forwards the message out of the interface specified in the `giaddr` field.

Summary

In this chapter, I described the differences between BOOTP and DHCP. Although they share many traits, there are significant differences in their operation. The BOOTP conversation is very simple, comprising a request and a reply. Because BOOTP uses static configuration files, and a client's MAC address must be listed in the file to receive an IP address, only one BOOTP server can be operational on a network at a time. The DHCP conversation in which a DHCP client broadcasts a request that multiple DHCP servers can receive is more robust. All DHCP servers that receive the request can respond. The DHCP client can then select a lease offer.

Also covered were the reasons why DHCP was developed and is currently being used in today's TCP/IP-based networking environments. Next I went step by step through the DHCP conversation, detailing the data that is supplied by each type of message. Finally I covered how the DHCP relay agent operates. When the DHCP client requests an IP address, it broadcasts the request. In a routed environment, routers do not route broadcasts. The DHCP relay agent provides a method for DHCP to function in a routed environment by intercepting DHCP requests and forwarding the request as a unicast message directly to the DHCP server.

4

Designing a DHCP Infrastructure

DHCP can quickly become an essential piece of an organization's data network. Once set up, DHCP is usually hardly noticed, silently and faithfully performing its duties day in and day out. Unfortunately, the hardest thing with DHCP is getting it to that point.

This chapter discusses the reasons an organization would want to use DHCP, along with the many different issues that need to be considered when designing a DHCP infrastructure.

Some of these considerations include planning for IP address use. An organization needs to determine how their existing environment is used as well as what types of users and workstations exist, such as mobile users and network devices.

The needs of a DHCP client must be considered, including which DHCP options are supported by the client's operating system and which options and their values need to be assigned.

In large-scale DHCP implementations, the topology of the network becomes a very important factor. The network topology dictates where DHCP servers and/or relay agents must be placed.

A final consideration is planning for fault tolerance. Once DHCP is implemented, it quickly becomes a service that the entire network is dependent on. Steps can be taken to ensure that DHCP will be available at all times.

Who Needs DHCP?

The Internet Engineering Task Force (IETF) created this new protocol, DHCP, to dynamically distribute IP addresses and configurations to clients. But what types of organizations would benefit from using DHCP?

Some administrators believe that having to administer yet another network service and the additional traffic it creates is an unnecessary burden. Administrators with this philosophy believe that it is easier to set up workstations and servers with static configurations that do not need to be maintained or administered.

In reality, however, any organization that wants to save the time and aggravation of manually maintaining the allocation of IP addresses would want to use DHCP. DHCP allows an administrator to standardize the IP address configurations for the entire network while dynamically maintaining the address table in a database.

Small companies benefit from DHCP because of the lower administrative burden. Most small companies cannot afford a full time network administrator who knows the ins and outs of IP addressing. Typically they delegate network administration to the one person in the office who is the most computer-savvy, whether or not he or she has technical training or experience with networking. By utilizing DHCP, the day-to-day administration of IP addressing and associated configuration details is handled automatically without any intervention from office personnel.

The biggest problem for small companies is the initial implementation of DHCP. Small companies may have to use a consultant for the initial implementation, during which the designated administrator is trained in the administration of DHCP. Alternatively, the administrator can attempt the DHCP implementation through trial and error, although this is not recommended.

Larger enterprises benefit from DHCP on two fronts: lower administrative burden and standardized IP configurations throughout the organization.

The benefit of lower administrative burden is similar to the benefit reaped by a small company, with the addition of the time saved from administering an IP address table. The next section about static IP addressing discusses some of the problems with manually maintaining the IP address table.

Larger enterprises also benefit from standardized IP configurations. Using standardized configurations minimizes connectivity problems relating to incorrect IP addresses, subnet masks, and default gateways. It also diminishes name resolution errors resulting from incorrect DNS and WINS addresses.

DHCP can also benefit organizations with a mobile workforce. With valid IP addresses in short supply, assigning static addresses to users with laptops would be both inefficient and foolish. The very nature of mobile users dictates that they will be connecting to the corporate network intermittently. Thus they do not require the constant exclusive use of an IP address. By using DHCP, an administrator can configure the DHCP server to reclaim these IP addresses after a short period of time. For example, for a company with 500 mobile users and 200 valid IP addresses to allocate, the administrator can set up the DHCP server to allocate these 200 IP addresses to mobile users. The administrator configures the lease time for the mobile users scope to a short duration, say one day. When a mobile user connects to the network, the DHCP client on the user's laptop negotiates an IP address lease from the DHCP server. The mobile user then proceeds to access network resources, such as email and file services. When the user is finished, he disconnects from the network. The DHCP server then reclaims the IP address once the one-day lease period expires.

Another option for a mobile workforce is to utilize a DHCP User Class. This is a new feature found in the Windows 2000 DHCP server. It allows you to assign additional configuration data to a particular set of users. Let's continue the example above. Instead of configuring a separate scope for the 200 IP addresses, the administrator could create a DHCP User Class for the mobile users. The user class would specify a lease period that is shorter in duration than the rest of the scope. The administrator would then configure each laptop's DHCP client to specify that the laptop is a member of this user class.

Creating an IP Addressing Plan

Before deciding to implement DHCP, an administrator must first decide on an IP addressing plan. There are many different ways to create an IP addressing plan, and in some cases they may need to be combined. This is a critical step because it is the foundation of the entire DHCP infrastructure. This section looks into each of the different methods, describing their benefits, how they may be implemented, and some of their limitations.

Static IP Addressing

In an environment that uses static IP addressing, when an administrator installs a new workstation, she looks up an available IP address and the corresponding subnet mask in the IP address table. This table may be written in a notebook or saved on a computer in a spreadsheet. Once she finds the IP address, she needs to determine the correct DNS and WINS server addresses for the workstation to use. In addition, in a routed environment, the administrator needs to ascertain the correct default gateway address for the workstation's subnet. Then she manually configures the workstation with the proper TCP/IP information. For small networks or networks that do not experience many changes, this may be fine.

One of the downsides to this method of administering IP addresses is human error. If the administrator mistypes the IP address or subnet mask, the workstation may not have connectivity to the resources it requires. If the DNS or WINS server IP addresses are mistyped, the workstation will not be able to perform name resolution. If the default gateway is incorrect, the workstation will not be able to connect to remote subnets and resources.

Another downside is maintaining the IP address table. The administrator must continually spend time viewing and searching the address table for available addresses. Once she finds an available address, the administrator must note in the table that the IP address is now in use. Also, by storing the address table in a notebook, the table could easily be lost. Even storing the address table in a spreadsheet does not lessen the chance that it will become corrupted or lost.

Moreover, if the network is large and its users move about often, using static IP configurations can be frustrating and inefficient. Problems such as the ones described earlier are compounded with larger networks. Incorrect configurations have a much larger effect on connectivity, as the workstation routinely needs access to resources on different subnets. Maintaining the IP address table centrally becomes nearly impossible. In all likelihood, the address table would need to be divided along subnets and individually maintained by the local administrator.

Static IP addressing can also be a huge liability if the organization needs to redesign their entire addressing structure. Factors that cause organizations to change their addressing structure include mergers and acquisitions, changing Internet service providers (ISPs), or network growth. Changing IP address configurations enterprise-wide requires an administrator to visit each workstation, server, and network device. In the end, it costs the organization a lot of time and money.

In short, as the network's capacity and scope grows in size, static IP address administration becomes unwieldy and inefficient.

Dynamic IP Addressing

There are four methods of dynamically allocating IP addresses: automatic, dynamic, roaming, and manual. Three of these methods, dynamic, roaming, and manual, use DHCP to allocate the IP addresses.

Automatic allocation

Automatic IP addressing utilizes the client's operating system to allocate a private IP address. Microsoft's Windows 2000 and Windows 98, along with the Apple MacOS 8.5 and later, are operating systems that support Automatic Private IP Addressing (APIPA).

The theory behind APIPA is that small ad hoc networks will be able to achieve basic connectivity without the need for intervention by the administrator.

An example of an ad hoc network would be a dentist's office. The dentist has 5 separate computers. One night at a dinner party, a friend tells him of all the benefits she is reaping from her new computer network. The dentist decides that he too could benefit from a network. He buys the necessary cabling and hooks everything together. Typically at this point things start getting difficult. It is likely that he doesn't have a deep understanding of the Windows 2000 operating system or the TCP/IP protocol. However, with APIPA, the computers will be automatically configured. In the end, the dentist will have a functioning network.

APIPA allows a workstation to configure itself with an IP address in the absence of DHCP or any other IP addressing mechanism. Other networking protocols, such as IPX/SPX and Appletalk, already include this type of functionality.

Creating small ad hoc networks can be very useful in environments such as small businesses and homes that include only a few machines. In order for the machines to communicate, they must be configured with IP addresses.

Computers using APIPA must also be DHCP clients. This is because APIPA uses the DHCP client to determine whether a DHCP server is available.

Using the DHCP client, the computer requests an IP address by sending a DHCPDISCOVER message. After not receiving a response, the computer automatically configures itself with an IP address in the reserved Class B network 169.254.0.0 and a subnet mask of 255.255.0.0. The DHCP client then performs a duplicate address check by sending an ARP request for the IP address. If it receives a response, it determines that the address is in use. At this point it selects another address from the 169.254.0.0 subnet and again performs a duplicate address check. The client repeats this process for up to 10 addresses, after which the automatic addressing fails.

Automatic allocation is a quick and easy solution to the IP addressing problem, but is only useful in small networks that need basic connectivity without Internet access. Larger environments are typically subnetted to segment network traffic and increase performance. Since APIPA is limited to the 169.254/16 subnet, it cannot be utilized in those environments. The downside to using APIPA even in small networks is the difficulty it may cause in troubleshooting connectivity issues.

Dynamic allocation

Dynamic allocation uses DHCP as the mechanism to allocate IP addresses. The administrator assigns a range of addresses to the DHCP server. The DHCP server, in turn, assigns an IP address in the range to DHCP clients upon request. This range is known as a scope. For example, if an administrator has workstations on a network and wants to assign these workstations addresses in the 192.168.1.0/24 subnet, he creates a DHCP scope that consists of the IP addresses 192.168.1.1 through 192.168.1.254. When a DHCP client requests an address from the DHCP server, the server assigns one of these addresses.

The administrator, when defining a scope, also specifies the lease duration for any IP address assignments from the scope. A lease duration is the amount of time that a DHCP client has exclusive use of an IP address. With DHCP, the client has two

---

Internet Connection Sharing

Internet Connection Sharing (ICS) is a new feature found in Windows 2000 Professional and Windows 2000 Server that permits a single computer to host an Internet connection for a network.

For example, if you have a small network with 15 computers, only one of the computers (running Windows 2000 and ICS) requires a connection to the Internet. This computer, known as the ICS server, hosts the Internet connection via a dial-up line, cable modem, or xDSL. The remaining 14 computers are ICS clients that access the Internet via the ICS server.

ICS provides network address translation (NAT), IP address allocation via DHCP, and name resolution services via DNS for all ICS clients. Clients can use Internet applications (e.g., Internet Explorer and Outlook) just as though the computers themselves were connected to the Internet.

The ICS server can also be configured to terminate the Internet connection when not needed. If one of the ICS clients attempts access when the Internet connection is down, ICS automatically dials the ISP and establishes a connection. The client is then able to access the requested resource.

The ICS server needs two network connections: one for the internal network (i.e., the connection for ICS clients in the office) and one for the connection to the Internet.

By enabling ICS, the computer automatically becomes a DHCP server for the office network. DHCP automatically assigns IP addresses to the hosts on the office network along with TCP/IP configuration information such as DNS servers.

When ICS is enabled, the computer acting as the ICS server is configured with a static IP address 192.168.0.1 and subnet mask 255.255.255.0. ICS's internal DHCP server is configured with a scope of 192.168.0.2 through 192.168.0.254.

Note that these default settings cannot be modified, nor can any particular service such as DHCP or DNS Proxy be disabled. If you are already running a DHCP server on your network, the ICS internal DHCP server and your network DHCP server will both attempt to honor DHCP client requests, resulting in NACKs (negative acknowledgments). In this case you cannot utilize ICS on your network. Consider using Windows 2000's Network Address Translating (NAT) instead.

---

opportunities to extend the lease, first when the lease duration is 50% complete and then again when the lease duration is 87.5% complete. After the lease duration has expired, the DHCP client must request a new lease from a DHCP server.

The administrator, if needed, can also exempt certain addresses from the scope. These addresses may be network devices or hosts whose IP addresses should not change, for example, network printers, routers, and servers. The administrator can set aside a portion of the scope, say 192.168.1.1 through 192.168.1.25, for these devices. Now when a DHCP client requests an IP address, the DHCP server assigns an address between 192.168.1.26 through 192.168.1.254. Another option for network devices such as these would be to configure a DHCP reservation, where the DHCP server allocates the same IP address to the device's MAC address.

Roaming allocation

Roaming allocation can be used in situations where there are areas that users may visit temporarily with their laptops. Such areas may be libraries, classrooms, laboratories, or conference rooms where users will need a DHCP-allocated address for a brief period of time.

The basic configuration of the roaming allocation method is much like the dynamic allocation method, with the notable exception that the lease duration time is very short for the scopes that service these areas.

For example, a company may have a conference room where users want to utilize network resources via their laptops. For the roaming allocation method to work, the conference room LAN first needs to be segmented. This is required because a subnet can be serviced by only one scope at a time. The administrator then creates a scope for the conference room subnet. The scope is given a lease duration of about 45 minutes. When users connect to the conference room LAN, they receive an IP address from the conference room scope. Once they leave the conference room, the user can wait for the lease to expire, at which point the laptop will restart the DHCP conversation. They could also release the IP address and request a new one.

The roaming allocation method is useful in small, local implementations. Although it can be used on a larger scale, the short lease duration may cause excessive DHCP traffic and additional load on the DHCP servers.

If the RRAS server contains more than one LAN interface, by default it will choose the LAN interface randomly. You can override this action by unselecting the "Allow RAS to select adapter" checkbox under IP properties and selecting the desired interface. This setting can be found in the Routing and Remote Access Microsoft Management Console (MMC).

Manual allocation

Manual allocation is another method that can be used in situations where an administrator wants to know the MAC address of the DHCP client before assigning an IP address. An administrator may want to do this for security reasons, or

DHCP and Remote Users

Any organization that employs a mobile workforce, such as salespeople or field technicians, needs to consider how their remote connectivity strategy and DHCP interact. This section discusses how Windows 2000 supports remote users. If your organization utilizes a third-party solution such as Shiva or Cisco for remote access, please refer to that vendor's documentation to implement DHCP for remote access.

Windows 2000 utilizes Routing and Remote Access Service (RRAS) to provide remote connectivity. RRAS includes a number of components that deal with routing and remote access issues, such as routing protocols (Open Shortest Path First [OSPF], Routing Information Protocol 1 [RIP1], and Routing Information Protocol 2 [RIP2]), Lightweight Directory Access Protocol (LDAP), Remote Access Dial-up User Service (RADIUS), and Virtual Private Network (VPN).

When a remote access client connects to the RRAS server, the RRAS server assigns the client an IP address along with the IP addresses of DNS and WINS servers.

There are a couple of items that need to be considered when designing a remote access infrastructure using RRAS. The RRAS server can be configured to utilize DHCP to obtain IP addresses for remote clients. You can also configure the RRAS server to assign IP addresses from a static IP address pool.

If the RRAS server is configured to use DHCP, the DHCP client on the RRAS server allocates 10 IP addresses from a DHCP server. The first allocated IP address is assigned to the RRAS server interface. The remaining IP addresses are assigned to the remote clients as they connect. When the initial pool of 10 IP addresses is depleted, the RRAS server's DHCP client allocates an additional 10 IP addresses from a DHCP server.

You can change the size of the initial address pool by modifying the value of the InitialAddressPoolSize entry in the registry. This entry can be found at HKLM\System\CurrentControlSet\Services\RemoteAccess\Parameters\Ip.

If a DHCP server is not available when the RRAS server is started, the DHCP client will allocate the IP address pool using APIPA. In other words, it will allocate 10 IP addresses from the range 169.254.0.1 through 169.254.255.254 with a subnet 255.255.255.0. Note that remote clients receiving an APIPA-based address will only be able to connect to the RRAS server, unless of course the APIPA is in use throughout the rest of the network.

—*Continued*—

The remote access server found in Windows NT 4.0 recorded the IP addresses obtained via DHCP. It reused them when the RRAS server was restarted. Windows 2000, however, releases the entire IP address pool whenever it is restarted.

You can also configure the RRAS server to assign IP addresses for DNS and WINS servers to remote clients. You can implement one of the following ways to assign DNS and WINS addresses:

- Prohibit the RRAS server from assigning DNS and WINS addresses.

- Globally assign DNS and WINS addresses from values stored in RRAS server's registry.

- Utilize the IP configuration on the RRAS server's interface.

If you want to prohibit the RRAS server from assigning the DNS and WINS addresses, you must set the values of SuppressDNSNameServers and SuppressWINSNameServers entries to 1. These entries can be found at HKLM\System\CurrentControlSet\Services\RemoteAccess\Parameters\Ip.

If you want to globally assign DNS and WINS addresses, you must enter the IP addresses as values of the DNSNameServers and WINSNameServers entries. Again, these entries can be found at HKLM\System\CurrentControlSet\Services\RemoteAccess\Parameters\Ip.

If the DNS and WINS address assignments are not prohibited or globally configured, the RRAS server will determine their assignments via the IP configuration of its LAN interface. If the IP configuration is static, the interface's statically assigned DNS and WINS addresses will be assigned to remote clients. If the IP configuration was obtained via DHCP, the interface's DHCP-assigned DNS and WINS addresses will be assigned to remote clients.

may simply want to know who is utilizing network resources for billing purposes. Manual allocation is typically used in academic settings.

The manual allocation process begins when a user wants to install a new computer or device on the network. The user must submit a request to the administrator that includes his computer's MAC address and its physical location (i.e., building and room number). Once the administrator receives the request, she configures an IP address reservation on the DHCP server. This reservation is placed in the appropriate subnet scope (i.e., the user's physical location) using the user's MAC address (i.e., the user's computer). Once notified that everything has been set up, the user can then boot the workstation. The workstation then obtains the IP address from the DHCP server.

Manual allocation can also be used for network devices such as servers and network printers. In this case, the MAC address of the server is used to create a reservation. With reservations, changes can be made to the IP configurations of all servers in a particular scope or even the entire enterprise. For example, if an administrator wants all servers to point to another DNS server, she could simply change the Name Server option for the scope where the servers were located. When a server renews its address lease, it will receive the updated Name Server option.

As you can see, manual allocation is very time consuming and labor intensive. In essence, manual allocation is very similar to using BOOTP. It should only be used in environments that require knowledge of what devices are connecting to the network.

Combining dynamic addressing methods

Some of these methods can be combined and intertwined to create the DHCP solution an organization requires. The only one that cannot be combined is the automatic allocation method (unless your network is going to use the 169.254.0.0 subnet, of course).

For example, an organization may want to use static IP addressing for some network devices, such as network printers and file servers, while using the dynamic allocation method for the rest of their network. They can also create some subnets for conference rooms and libraries using the roaming allocation method.

Network Topology

When designing a DHCP infrastructure, it is important to take into account the topology of the network being serviced. By determining the topology, the designer will be able to anticipate where the load on the DHCP servers may be high and identify single points of failure that may cause DHCP services to be disrupted.

There are two different areas that need to be examined:

- The physical layout of the network
- The number of users in each physical location

By determining the physical layout of the network, the designer will be able to create a list of subnets that need to be serviced by DHCP. This information will be needed when scopes are created later.

Another important factor is the placement of DHCP relay agents. The physical layout of the network establishes which routers and subnets will need to be serviced by relay agents.

The number of users in each location helps determine the placement of DHCP servers. If there are a small number of users located in a single location, the DHCP server may be placed in a remote subnet with a DHCP Relay Agent set up on the router to listen for DHCP requests. This eliminates the need to place a server physically on the LAN where the users reside. If the WAN link goes down, the number of users disrupted is minimized.

If some of your DHCP clients at remote sites are Windows 2000 or Windows 98 systems and the WAN link goes down, they will not be able to contact a DHCP server. As mentioned earlier in this chapter, when these operating systems fail to contact a DHCP server, they resort to using APIPA to obtain an IP address. As a result, once the WAN link is restored, they will not be able to achieve network connectivity with the rest of the production network until the APIPA address is released. Connectivity is restored once a new address lease is obtained from the DHCP server. See Chapter 7, *Advanced DHCP*, for information about disabling APIPA in Windows 2000 and Windows 98.

In situations where the number of users is high, the DHCP server should be placed locally. In this case the loss of the WAN link will not disrupt DHCP service.

DHCP Client Needs

Before creating any scopes, an administrator must first determine the needs of the DHCP clients the scope will be servicing.

Besides receiving an IP address, subnet mask, and default gateway from a DHCP server, DHCP clients can receive DHCP options that supply many different configuration parameters. Deciding which DHCP options to include can be determined by asking the following questions:

- Which DHCP options do DHCP clients in this scope require?
- What DHCP clients are in use on the network?
- Which DHCP options do the DHCP clients support?

Determining which options are required is relatively simple, unless there are applications in use that have special needs. Besides determining which options to use, an administrator must determine the values of those options as well. For example, an administrator wants the DHCP clients to receive DNS server addresses. For load balancing, each subnet has a different secondary DNS server to service client requests. In this case, the administrator must supply the correct IP address for each subnet's DNS server.

Next, an administrator must determine which DHCP clients are in use on the network. Since Microsoft operating systems are the most prevalent on most corporate desktops and laptops, it can pretty much be said that almost every network includes some Microsoft DHCP clients.

But there may be other types of DHCP clients as well, such as Unix, Linux, or Macintosh. Although these operating systems can all be DHCP clients, their implementations of DHCP vary. For example, they may not support certain DHCP options, such as WINS servers. The DHCP server in Windows 2000 supports all DHCP options defined in RFC2132. If you have a non-Microsoft DHCP client, you can configure the Windows 2000 DHCP Server to supply any DHCP option that the client can support. Refer to your non-Microsoft DHCP client's documentation for a complete list of supported DHCP options.

There may also be network devices that support DHCP, such as network printers. Deciding whether or not to use DHCP for network printers is a matter of choice; most administrators prefer to assign static addresses to the printers. This way IP addresses for the printers are always known, thus simplifying management and troubleshooting. However, DHCP can be used with network printers by using the manual allocation addressing method. By creating an address reservation using the printer's MAC address, the printer can receive other configuration information that may change from time to time, such as name server addresses.

Determining the DHCP options that the DHCP clients support can be a bit trickier. I will briefly describe which options are supported by most of the major operating systems. An administrator should always refer to the operating system's documentation to ascertain which options are supported.

Microsoft-based clients request the following DHCP options, described in Chapter 3, *Making Life Easier: DHCP*, and defined as properties of the scope:

- Renewal Time Option (58)
- Rebinding Time Option (59)
- IP Address Lease Time Option (51)
- Server Identifier Option (54)
- Subnet Mask Option (1)

Microsoft-based clients will also request the following DHCP options:

- Routers Option (3)
- Domain Name Option (15)
- Domain Name Servers Option (6)
- NetBIOS Name Servers Option (44)

- NetBIOS Node Type Option (46)

- NetBIOS Scope Option (47)

It is important to remember that these are the only options supported by Microsoft DHCP clients. Any other DHCP options specified by the DHCP server will be ignored.

The appendix, *DHCP Options*, lists all currently available DHCP options. Third-party clients such as Unix, Linux, and MacOS may also support these DHCP options.

Defining Scopes

Now that the IP addressing plan, network topology, and DHCP client needs have been defined, it is time to start defining the various scopes.

Address Ranges

When defining a scope, the most important information to define is the address range of the scope. The address range will be used by the DHCP server to determine which IP address to assign to a DHCP client. The address range is defined by the subnet the scope will be servicing. For example, if the subnet is 10.64.0.0/11, the valid range of IP addresses for this scope is 10.64.0.1 through 10.95.255.254. For any statically configured network devices on that subnet, exemptions have to be created. An exemption designates an IP address not to be assigned to a DHCP client. If a static IP address was not exempted, the DHCP server may assign the IP address to a DHCP client. As a result, an IP address conflict could occur and cause connectivity problems for the two computers involved.

If the IP addressing plan calls for using dynamic address allocation for this subnet, simply assign the address range to the scope. If the IP addressing plan calls for using manual address allocation, reservations need to be created for each network device.

Lease Durations

Lease durations determine when the DHCP server can reclaim the allocated IP address. Usually the default time period, 8 days, is more than sufficient for most scopes. Setting the lease duration too long will cause IP addresses to be shown as allocated, thus unable to be reclaimed. Setting the lease duration too short may cause excessive DHCP traffic on the network as DHCP clients attempt to renew their address leases.

One situation that does call for a shorter lease duration is when the roaming address allocation method is being used on a scope. By specifying a short lease duration, the DHCP server will be able to reclaim IP addresses that are only in use for a short period of time, such as a conference room or library.

Options

Any options required by the DHCP clients being serviced by the scope need to be configured at this point. Options such as the Router Option (3) need to specify the IP address for the default gateway on the subnet. Other options should be specified as well, such as the IP addresses of the DNS servers that will be servicing the subnet.

Fault Tolerance

Since DHCP is a critical network service, it is important for the designer to take steps that will make it fault tolerant. DHCP does not have a built-in method of fault tolerance. DHCP servers do not communicate with each other, letting the other know which addresses are allocated and whether or not it is still in operation. To create a fault tolerant DHCP service, the designer needs to manually create a fault tolerant design using scopes and/or clustering.

Splitting Scopes

Splitting scopes is a method to create DHCP fault tolerance. It is the process of creating two scopes, one on each DHCP server. The two scopes both service the same subnet, but the range of addresses is divided. If one DHCP server becomes unavailable, the remaining DHCP server continues to service DHCP client requests using its portion of the address range. So where is the address range split? That is determined by the needs of the network implementation.

The 50/50 method

The 50/50 method of splitting scopes provides both fault tolerance and load balancing for DHCP servers. In this method, 50% of the available address range is given to one scope, and the remaining 50% is given to the other scope. Typically this method is used when both DHCP servers are centrally located on the same subnet. When a DHCP client requests an IP address, the request is received by both servers and both respond with an offer. The client then accepts one of the offers (i.e., the first offer received). The selected DHCP server allocates the address and sends the acknowledgement to the client.

The 50/50 method of splitting scopes can only be implemented where the number of available IP addresses is plentiful. This allows each scope to fully service the number of DHCP clients requesting addresses in the event that one of the DHCP servers fails.

The 80/20 method

The 80/20 method of splitting scopes provides fault tolerance in a subnetted environment. In the 80/20 method, two DHCP servers are configured. One DHCP server resides on the subnet the scope is servicing. The other DHCP server is on another remote subnet.

80% of the available address range is allocated to the local DHCP server. The remaining 20% is allocated to the remote DHCP server. The router connecting the subnets is configured with a DHCP relay agent that will forward DHCP requests to the remote DHCP server. When a DHCP client on the local subnet sends out a DHCP request, the local DHCP server responds first with an offer. The remote DHCP server's request arrives later since it needs to traverse the WAN. The DHCP client then accepts the offer from the local DHCP server. In the event that the local DHCP server fails, the client eventually receives a response from the remote DHCP server.

The downside of the 80/20 method is that the remote DHCP server, with only 20% of the available address space, will not be able to handle all DHCP requests from the subnet.

Clustering

In Windows 2000, Microsoft added a new capability to the DHCP service, called clustering. A cluster is a group of servers (typically two nodes) that work in unison. By working together, the nodes provide load balancing and fault tolerance for the services the cluster provides. To the rest of the network, the cluster looks like a single server. By combining the DHCP service and clustering, a type of DHCP failover can be achieved.

The DHCP Server included in Windows 2000 is a cluster-aware application. This means that in the event that one node in the cluster fails, the DHCP service can be restarted on the surviving node. This is accomplished because the DHCP database, which houses all current address leases, is shared between the nodes. When the second node takes over, it is completely aware of all outstanding IP address leases and will not give out duplicate IP addresses.

Since the cluster itself appears as a single entity to the network, DHCP clients continue to communicate with the cluster's IP address. They are completely unaware that the second node in the cluster is responding to their requests.

Clustering is Microsoft's recommended strategy for DHCP fault tolerance in Windows 2000.

Putting It All Together: DHCP Strategies

DHCP can be used in many different networking environments. Regardless of the networking environment, DHCP in itself operates fundamentally the same. In other words, the server is installed, scopes are created, options are configured, and DHCP clients start receiving address leases. However, depending on the network infrastructure, more planning and configuration may need to take place before DHCP can function efficiently and acceptably. Fortunately, DHCP is very flexible, and a designer can take many different design ideas to create the solution best suited for the environment.

Non-Routed Environment (Single Subnet)

DHCP operating on a single subnet is the simplest DHCP configuration. A single subnet does not include any routers or DHCP relay agents. By simply installing and configuring the DHCP server, DHCP clients can begin allocating dynamic IP addresses.

Designing a DHCP strategy for a non-routed environment consists of determining the hardware requirements of the DHCP server and then deciding which clients will be assigned dynamic addresses and which will be configured with static addresses (typically servers and network printers). Finally, the designer determines which DHCP options need to be used, such as the IP addresses for the DNS and WINS servers on the network.

The network shown in Figure 4-1 consists of a single subnet that includes a DHCP server and several DHCP clients. To begin servicing the clients, the DHCP server needs a single scope whose addresses fall within the range of the subnet. Usually, in this scenario, the default lease duration of 8 days is sufficient.

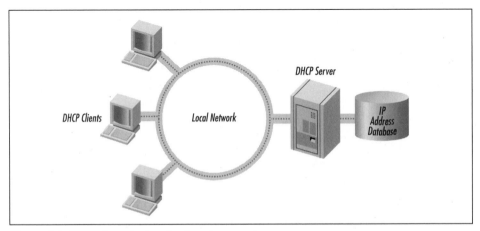

Figure 4-1. DHCP in a single subnet environment

Routed Environments (Multiple Subnets)

In a routed environment, more planning must be done in the design phase to create the appropriate DHCP infrastructure. The first step includes the layout of the subnets and deciding the placement of the DHCP servers. This step also includes deciding which fault tolerant strategies should be incorporated into the plan.

The layout of the subnets typically follows the physical layout of the network, such as remote sites or buildings in a campus. The subnet layout can also be determined by function or lines of business, e.g., the sales department and engineering department may be located on separate subnets, although they are both in the same building.

The placement of the DHCP servers can be a little bit trickier. In general, the placement of the DHCP servers should not be determined by the administrative structure of the network (i.e., domains or Active Directory), but by the number of users that need DHCP services. Placement of DHCP servers must also consider fault tolerance strategies so a particular subnet can continuously be serviced by DHCP.

Figure 4-2 shows one possible network topology. By using the data obtained from the network topology, the designer can create a table (see Table 4-1) listing the different sites, the number of users in each site, the subnets that service the site, and the number of addresses available in each subnet.

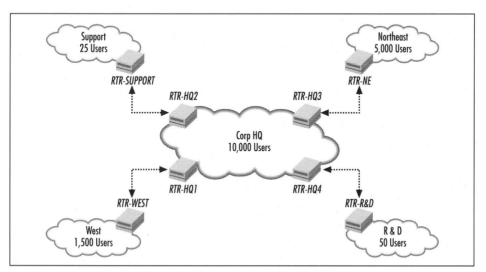

Figure 4-2. Routed network topology example

Table 4-1. Network Topology Requirements

Site	Number of Users	Subnet Address	Number of Hosts
Corp HQ	10,000	168.3.4.0	1022
		168.3.8.0	1022
		168.3.12.0	1022
		168.3.16.0	1022
		168.3.20.0	1022
		168.3.24.0	1022
		168.3.28.0	1022
		168.3.32.0	1022
		168.3.36.0	1022
		168.3.40.0	1022
Northeast	5,000	168.3.44.0	1022
		168.3.48.0	1022
		168.3.52.0	1022
		168.3.56.0	1022
		168.3.60.0	1022
West	1,500	168.3.64.0	1022
		168.3.68.0	1022
R & D	50	168.3.72.0	1022
Support	25	168.3.76.0	1022

First, review the number of users that require DHCP in each site. The Corp HQ site, with 10,000 users, definitely needs local DHCP servers. The Northeast site and the West site also require local DHCP servers. The two smaller sites, R & D and Support, have few users. Therefore they can be serviced by one of the DHCP servers back in Corp HQ.

How many DHCP servers are needed? Well, according to Microsoft, the DHCP server in Windows 2000 can handle as many as 100,000 users. So in this case a single DHCP server could handle all user requests from Corp HQ as well as the two small remote sites. However, one reason to have more than one DHCP server is to create a fault tolerant design.

To create fault tolerance, two DHCP servers can be placed in the Corp HQ site and split using the 50/50 scope splitting method. The scopes for the R & D and Support remote sites can also be split 50/50. To complete the fault tolerance plan, the routers connecting the remote sites to Corp HQ need DHCP relay agents configured to point to the DHCP servers.

The remaining two sites, Northeast and West, need one local DHCP server each. The scopes servicing these sites can be split using the 80/20 scope splitting method, with 80% of the addresses assigned to scopes on the local DHCP server and the remaining 20% assigned to scopes located on the Corp HQ DHCP servers. In the event that the DHCP server goes down on either of these sites, the DHCP servers at Corp HQ will service the client requests.

Another option for fault tolerance is the use of DHCP clusters. By replacing all the DHCP servers with DHCP clusters, the design benefits from virtually guaranteed uptime, short of a major disaster such as a power failure or fire.

To take fault tolerance even further, the designer can combine clusters with scope splitting. This ensures that the DHCP service will be available at all times.

A major factor in designing a fault tolerant plan is cost. Each of the scope splitting situations calls for an additional DHCP server. Using clusters drives the costs up further still, since a cluster must contain a minimum of two nodes.

Once server placement and fault tolerance is completed, the designer must begin creating the scopes.

In this scenario, there are a total of 19 subnets. Through scope splitting, there are a total of 38 scopes. Table 4-2 lists the scopes that need to be created.

Table 4-2. Scope Table

Site Served	DHCP Server	Scope	Address Range	Number of Addresses
Corp HQ	DHCP-HQ1 (Cluster)	168.3.4.0 (50% Scope)	168.3.4.1 through 168.3.5.255	511
		168.3.8.0 (50% Scope)	168.3.8.1 through 168.3.9.255	511
		168.3.12.0 (50% Scope)	168.3.12.1 through 168.3.13.255	511
		168.3.16.0 (50% Scope)	168.3.16.1 through 168.3.17.255	511
		168.3.20.0 (50% Scope)	168.3.20.1 through 168.3.21.255	511
		168.3.24.0 (50% Scope)	168.3.24.1 through 168.3.25.255	511
		168.3.28.0 (50% Scope)	168.3.28.1 through 168.3.28.255	511
		168.3.32.0 (50% Scope)	168.3.32.1 through 168.3.33.255	511
		168.3.36.0 (50% Scope)	168.3.36.1 through 168.3.37.255	511

Table 4-2. Scope Table (continued)

Site Served	DHCP Server	Scope	Address Range	Number of Addresses
		168.3.40.0 (50% Scope)	168.3.40.1 through 168.3.41.255	511
	DHCP-HQ2 (Cluster)	168.3.4.0 (50% Scope)	168.3.6.0 through 168.3.7.254	511
		168.3.8.0 (50% Scope)	168.3.10.0 through 168.3.11.254	511
		168.3.12.0 (50% Scope)	168.3.14.0 through 168.3.15.254	511
		168.3.16.0 (50% Scope)	168.3.18.0 through 168.3.19.254	511
		168.3.20.0 (50% Scope)	168.3.22.0 through 168.3.23.254	511
		168.3.24.0 (50% Scope)	168.3.26.0 through 168.3.27.254	511
		168.3.28.0 (50% Scope)	168.3.30.0 through 168.3.31.254	511
		168.3.32.0 (50% Scope)	168.3.34.0 through 168.3.35.254	511
		168.3.36.0 (50% Scope)	168.3.38.0 through 168.3.39.254	511
		168.3.40.0 (50% Scope)	168.3.42.0 through 168.3.43.254	511
Northeast	DHCP-NE1 (Cluster)	168.3.44.0 (80% Scope)	168.3.44.1 through 168.3.47.49	818
		168.3.48.0 (80% Scope)	168.3.48.1 through 168.3.51.49	818
		168.3.52.0 (80% Scope)	168.3.52.1 through 168.3.55.49	818
		168.3.56.0 (80% Scope)	168.3.56.1 through 168.3.59.49	818
		168.3.60.0 (80% Scope)	168.3.60.1 through 168.3.63.49	818
	DHCP-HQ1 (Cluster)	168.3.44.0 (20% Scope)	168.3.47.50 through 168.3.47.254	204
		168.3.48.0 (20% Scope)	168.3.51.50 through 168.3.51.254	204
	DHCP-HQ2 (Cluster)	168.3.52.0 (20% Scope)	168.3.55.50 through 168.3.55.254	204
		168.3.56.0 (20% Scope)	168.3.59.50 through 168.3.59.254	204
		168.3.60.0 (20% Scope)	168.3.63.50 through 168.3.63.254	204

Table 4-2. Scope Table (continued)

Site Served	DHCP Server	Scope	Address Range	Number of Addresses
West	DHCP-W1 (Cluster)	168.3.64.0 (80% Scope)	168.3.64.1 through 168.3.67.49	818
		168.3.68.0 (80% Scope)	168.3.68.1 through 168.3.71.49	818
	DHCP-HQ1 (Cluster)	168.3.64.0 (20% Scope)	168.3.67.50 through 168.3.67.254	204
		168.3.68.0 (20% Scope)	168.3.71.50 through 168.3.71.254	204
R & D	DHCP-HQ1 (Cluster)	168.3.72.0 (50% Scope)	168.3.72.1 through 168.3.73.255	511
	DHCP-HQ2 (Cluster)	168.3.72.0 (50% Scope)	168.3.74.0 through 168.3.75.254	511
Support	DHCP-HQ1 (Cluster)	168.3.76.0 (50% Scope)	168.3.76.1 through 168.3.77.255	511
	DHCP-HQ2 (Cluster)	168.3.76.0 (50% Scope)	168.3.78.0 through 168.3.79.254	511

While creating the scope, the designer needs to calculate appropriate lease durations. For most of the scopes, the default lease duration of 8 days is appropriate. However, the lease durations for the two remote sites without local DHCP servers, R & D and Support, should be extended. By extending the lease duration, the designer guarantees that DHCP clients in those sites will continue to have valid IP address leases in the event of a WAN link failure. Double the default lease duration for these scopes to 16 days.

Lease durations may also need to be modified if the subnet utilizes the roaming allocation method. For example, if there is a group of conference rooms in the Corp HQ site, the designer can designate one subnet for these rooms. The scope servicing the subnet could have its lease duration set to 1 hour. This allows a user with a laptop in the conference room to obtain an IP address. When the user moves to another location, he can either release the IP address or wait for the address lease to expire. At that point the laptop restarts the DHCP conversation to obtain an IP address for the new location.

Finally, the designer must determine which DHCP options need to be specified, along with their correct values. This includes items such as the router address for each subnet, as well as DNS and WINS server addresses. The router address option needs to be defined as a scope level option. The DNS and WINS server options can be defined at the scope or global levels, depending on the DNS and WINS infrastructure. In other words, if there is a single DNS server for the entire network, the DNS server option should be specified at the global level, since all

DHCP clients need to utilize the same DNS server address. If there are multiple DNS servers, the option can be specified at the scope level. This allows load balancing to take place, since each scope will point to a different DNS server.

Summary

There are many different components that need to come together to create a sound DHCP design. DHCP can be designed cafeteria-style, implementing certain components while disregarding others. Designing DHCP in this way assures that the needs of the organization are met.

This chapter discussed what types of organizations benefit from DHCP and some of the alternative methods that can be utilized. It also described the different components that are part of a DHCP solution, including IP addressing strategies, network topology, and client needs. Finally, the chapter concluded with two different scenarios and how DHCP could be implemented in each.

5

The DHCP Server

During the last few chapters, I covered the nuts and bolts of TCP/IP, the earlier protocols relating to IP address allocation, RARP and BOOTP, and finally I delved into the operation of DHCP, including breaking down the conversation between a DHCP server and client.

This chapter covers the installation and configuration of Windows 2000's DHCP server. First there will be a brief introduction to the Windows 2000 operating system family. Then I will cover the features found in DHCP server, followed by a discussion on the various installation options. The chapter continues with an explanation of the utility used to manage DHCP in Windows 2000: the DHCP Console. Using the DHCP design previously outlined in Chapter 4, *Designing a DHCP Infrastructure*, I will walk through the configuration of a DHCP server. This will include the creation of DHCP scopes, including lease durations and client options.

Introduction to Windows 2000

Windows 2000 comes in four flavors: Professional, Server, Advanced Server, and Data Center Server.

Windows 2000 Professional is the workstation member of the Windows 2000 family. It builds upon its predecessor, Windows NT Workstation 4.0, by adding Plug and Play support, Remote Installation Services (RIS), Encrypting File System (EFS), Kerberos support, Recovery Console, Offline Folders and Files, Intellimirror, as well as many other new features. I will cover Windows 2000 Professional in more detail in Chapter 6, *DHCP Clients*.

Windows 2000 Server is meant for workgroup and departmental environments that need a server-based operating system to supply file and print services. Windows 2000 Server supports up to four processors and 4 GB of RAM.

Windows 2000 Advanced Server is targeted at web applications and e-commerce. Advanced Server includes all of the features found in Windows 2000 Server with the addition of two-node failover capability and 32-node network load balancing. Windows 2000 Advanced Server supports up to 8 processors and 8GB of RAM.

Windows 2000 Datacenter Server is targeted at the high-end data warehousing and online transaction processing (OLTP) areas of the marketplace. Since applications of these types require more processing power and have larger memory requirements, Datacenter Server includes all of the features found in Advanced Server, with the failover capability increased to four nodes. Windows 2000 Datacenter Server supports up to 32 processors and 64 GB of RAM.

Table 5-1 summarizes the hardware requirements for the members of the Windows 2000 family.

Table 5-1. Hardware Requirements for Windows 2000

Windows 2000 Professional	Windows 2000 Server	Windows 2000 Advanced Server	Windows 2000 Datacenter Server
133 MHz Pentium-compatible CPU	133 MHz Pentium-compatible CPU	133 MHz Pentium-compatible CPU	Pentium III Xeon or higher CPU
64 MB RAM	256 MB RAM	256 MB RAM	256 MB RAM
2 GB disk space	2 GB disk space	2 GB disk space	2 GB disk space
			Minimum 8-way capable server

DHCP Server in Windows 2000

DHCP Server, which comes with Windows 2000 Server, Windows 2000 Advanced Server, and Windows 2000 Data Center Server, is a robust implementation compliant with RFCs 2131 and 2132 and includes many enhanced features. Although it is still fundamentally the same as the version of DHCP Server that shipped with Windows NT 4.0, Windows 2000's DHCP Server supports some new and advanced features, including the following:

Integration of DHCP and DNS
   Domain Name System (DNS) provides host name to IP address resolution. DNS is typically a static database that requires an administrator to manually enter host names. A new version of DNS, Dynamic DNS (DDNS), is included with Windows 2000. DHCP has been integrated with DNS to allow DHCP clients to automatically register their host names with the DNS database, thus alleviating the administrative burden of manually updating DNS.

Multicast address allocation
   DHCP Server in Windows 2000 now includes the ability to assign multicast addresses as well as unicast addresses. A multicast address is shared by a

group of computers. Typical applications include audio and conferencing where the entire multicast group receives the multicast messages. By allowing DHCP to administer multicast addresses, a user can simply join a multicast group, such as a conference room, and participate in a multicast session.

Rogue DHCP server detection

Windows 2000's DHCP Server now includes a feature that detects and shuts down rogue DHCP servers handing out bogus or invalid IP addresses. A rogue DHCP server can wreak havoc in a network and can also be difficult to troubleshoot. DHCP servers must be authorized to provide the service in Windows 2000. If a server is not authorized, it gets shut down automatically.

Windows Clustering

Windows Clustering allows two nodes to operate as a single entity. Since DHCP is a network dependency, DHCP along with Windows Clustering provides a fault tolerant solution that keeps the DHCP service running even if one of the nodes in the cluster crashes. This maximizes DHCP uptime.

Improved Monitoring

Monitoring features in DHCP Server have been enhanced. One of the new features is notification if available IP addresses fall below a user-defined level.

Many of these advanced features will be covered in more detail in later chapters.

Installing DHCP Server in Windows 2000

Before installing DHCP, you should have already designed the DHCP strategy, as discussed in Chapter 4. During this installation, I will be referring to the DHCP design discussed in that chapter.

The first DHCP server I will install is in the Corp HQ site, DHCP-HQ1. First I need to determine the range of IP addresses to be used to create the scopes. These are the scopes that this DHCP server will serve to DHCP clients. Remember that we will split the scopes in this site 50/50 with the second DHCP server. Table 5-2 lists the scopes to be created.

Table 5-2. DHCP Scopes for DHCP-HQ1

Scope	Address Range
168.3.4.0	168.3.4.1 through 168.3.5.255
168.3.8.0	168.3.8.1 through 168.3.9.255
168.3.12.0	168.3.12.1 through 168.3.13.255
168.3.16.0	168.3.16.1 through 168.3.17.255
168.3.20.0	168.3.20.1 through 168.3.21.255

Table 5-2. DHCP Scopes for DHCP-HQ1 (continued)

Scope	Address Range
168.3.24.0	168.3.24.1 through 168.3.25.255
168.3.28.0	168.3.28.1 through 168.3.28.255
168.3.32.0	168.3.32.1 through 168.3.33.255
168.3.36.0	168.3.36.1 through 168.3.37.255
168.3.40.0	168.3.40.1 through 168.3.41.255

Next, I need to assign a static IP address to DHCP-HQ1. I am going to assign an IP address from the first scope, 168.3.4.10. I need to remember to exclude this IP address when I am creating the scopes later.

OK, I have the scopes planned out and I have a static IP address for the server. Let's get started on the install.

Installing DHCP Server can be accomplished in one of two ways:

• During the initial install

• Adding the DHCP component

For the sake of thoroughness, I will detail both installation types.

The Initial Install

The first method of installing DHCP Server is to install it during the initial build of the server. Please note that the DHCP Server service can be installed at a later time. However, if a new server is being installed, adding the DHCP service at this time may save a couple of reboots.

1. Once you enter the GUI phase of the installation, you will see the opening screen of the Windows 2000 Setup Wizard. Pick Next.

2. The next screen is Regional Settings. This is where system locale and keyboard layout settings are defined. By default, English (United States) is the system locale and the keyboard layout is US. If these settings need to be changed, select Customize and choose the appropriate system locale and keyboard layout. Otherwise, pick Next.

3. Next you are prompted to personalize your software. Enter your name and organization in the appropriate boxes and pick Next.

4. Now you need to select the correct Licensing Modes. There are two different licensing modes: Per Server and Per Seat. Please keep in mind that these licenses are connected to the Server Service, which provides file and print sharing. These licenses do not affect other services, such as web, FTP, or even DHCP.

Per Server

> This mode determines the number of concurrent connections that the server will allow. If your company has one server, this is the licensing mode you should use.

Per Seat

> This mode is where each computer connecting to the server must have a Client Access License. If your company has multiple servers, this is the mode you should use.

After selecting the correct mode, pick Next.

 If you are not sure which mode to choose, select Per Server and enter the approximate number of licenses you believe will be needed. If you need to at a later time, Microsoft allows you to switch modes (only once) by using the Licensing applet located in Administrative Tools.

---

5. The next dialog box is for providing the Computer Name and Administrator Password. The Computer Name, sometimes referred to as the NetBIOS name, is limited to 15 characters in length. The Administrator Password is the password for the Administrator account. The Administrator account has full access to the entire system, so it is important to choose a good password that is difficult to guess, yet easy for you to remember. Enter the computer name and administrator password. You need to confirm the password as well. Pick Next.

6. After the Computer Name and Administrator Password dialog box, there is a dialog box to install additional Windows 2000 Components (see Figure 5-1). In this dialog box, software components can be added or removed from Windows 2000. For example, if you did not want to install any of the games included in Windows 2000 (I know, I know, why in the world should I remove solitaire?! I haven't played solitaire with a real deck of cards in years!) select Accessories and Utilities from the selection list. Next pick the Details button located in the lower left corner of the dialog box. Another dialog box is displayed listing all the accessories and utilities. At this point you can uncheck Games, or if you wish to remove a particular game, select Details again and uncheck that game.

Enough talk about boring things like games. Let's get back to the task at hand, this exciting installation of DHCP! On the Windows 2000 Components page, select Networking Services. Pick Details. From the list of available services, select Dynamic Host Configuration Protocol (DHCP) (see Figure 5-2). Pick OK.

Another point I would like to mention here is that by default, Internet Information Services (IIS) and the Indexing Service are selected. IIS and Index

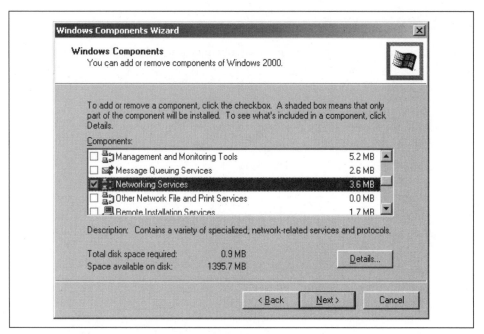

Figure 5-1. Windows 2000 Components Wizard page

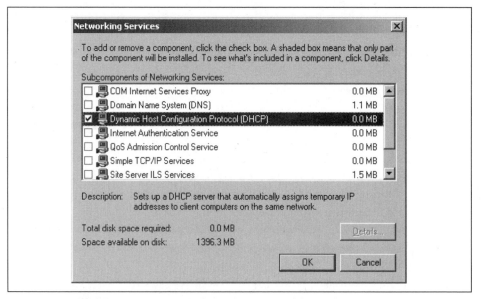

Figure 5-2. Adding Dynamic Host Configuration Protocol (DHCP)

Server supply web and FTP services to your server. If the server you are installing is not going to be hosting a web site or intranet, I strongly recommend unchecking these at this time. These services put additional load on the server. It is a potential security risk as well, not to mention the fact that IIS is quite large. By not selecting it you will save a good amount of time and disk space during the install.

Some applications may require the use of IIS and/or the Indexing Service. Verify the requirements of other applications you may be installing on the server.

After selecting the desired software components, pick OK to continue.

7. Now you must enter Modem Dialing Information. This is to configure Dial-Up Networking, where you will specify country/region and area code. Since this is not entirely important on a DHCP server, pick Next.

8. Make sure that the date and time settings for your system are correct. Remember that a DHCP lease is a duration of time. If the DHCP server and the DHCP client are not in sync, leases may expire prematurely. Also, make sure you select the correct time zone. Pick Next.

9. At this point, the Networking Settings dialog box is displayed. This is where you can either accept the default networking settings (by choosing Typical settings) or customize the settings. In this case we want to select Custom settings since we need to give the server a static IP address. Pick Next.

10. In the Networking Components list box, select Internet Protocol (TCP/IP) and pick Properties. By default, "Obtain an IP address automatically" is selected. This setting tells the system to obtain an IP address via DHCP. Since this server will be a DHCP server, this obviously will not do. Select "Use the following IP address" to give the server a static IP address. Enter the IP address for DHCP-HQ1, **168.3.4.10**. Enter the subnet mask **255.255.252.0**. Since this server is on a routed network environment, you must also supply the default gateway. For the subnet 168.3.4.0, the default gateway address is 168.3.4.1.

If you forget to specify a static IP address, the Windows 2000 Setup Wizard will prompt you to specify one during the final stage of the install.

You must also specify the IP addresses of DNS servers on the network. If you are not sure of the DNS servers' IP addresses, ask your network administrator. However, since you are installing DHCP, you probably are the network administrator. In this case, go to the Microsoft-based DNS server and at a command prompt type **ipconfig /all**. If the DNS server is Unix-based, refer to the operating system's documentation. From the output displayed, locate the IP address. Return to the server you are installing and select "Use the following DNS server addresses" and specify the preferred DNS server and the alternate DNS server IP addresses. Pick OK, then pick Next.

11. Finally, specify whether your server will participate in a workgroup or domain.

Whew! We made it. At this point the Windows 2000 Setup Wizard finishes installing the different components in Windows 2000. Go get a cup of coffee at this point, because it will be a while and frankly, you deserve it. The Wizard has a lot of work to do!

Adding the DHCP Server Component

If you are adding the DHCP Server component to an existing Windows 2000 server, the process is fairly simple.

Although there are a couple of different ways to accomplish this task, I will show you one method for adding DHCP Server to a Windows 2000 Server system. As you explore Windows 2000, you will notice that there are many different ways to do the same thing.

The first thing we need to do is give the server a static IP address:

1. Right-click on My Network Places and select Properties.

2. A window will be displayed called Network and Dial-up Connections. Right-click on the Local Area Connection icon and select Properties (see Figure 5-3). If the server has two or more network adapters (also known as multihomed), there will be an icon for each network adapter.

3. In the Networking Components list box, select Internet Protocol (TCP/IP) and pick Properties. Select "Use the following IP address" to give the server a static IP address and a subnet mask (see Figure 5-4). Enter the IP address for DHCP-HQ1, **168.3.4.10**. Enter the subnet mask **255.255.252.0**.

   Select "Use the following DNS server addresses" and specify the preferred DNS server and the alternate DNS server IP addresses. Pick OK, then pick OK to close the Local Area Connection Properties.

With that now accomplished, we need to add the DHCP Server component:

1. Right-click on My Network Places and select Properties

2. The Network and Dial-up Connections window is displayed. Select the Advanced pull-down menu. Choose "Optional Networking Components . . . "

3. On the Windows 2000 Components dialog box, select Networking Services. Pick Details. From the list of available services, select Dynamic Host Configuration Protocol (DHCP). Pick OK.

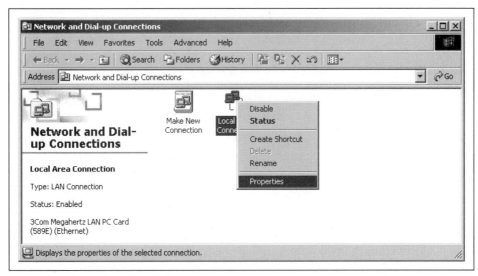

Figure 5-3. Network and Dial-up Connections

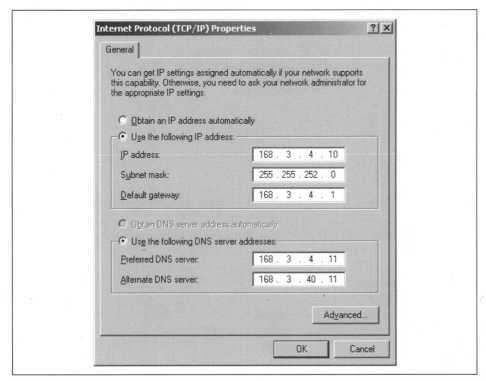

Figure 5-4. Internet Protocol (TCP/IP) Properties dialog box

Windows 2000 now copies the files necessary to install the DHCP Server components.

As you can see, installing the DHCP Server component is relatively simple. In fact it is one of the simplest steps in configuring DHCP.

Removing the DHCP Server Component

Remember earlier when I said that there are many different ways to accomplish the same task in Windows 2000? Well, I'm going to show you another way.

Removing the DHCP Server component can be simply accomplished by following the same steps as installing the component, but instead of checking the box next to DHCP, you remove the check. When you pick Next, Windows 2000 removes DHCP.

Now I promised you another way, so here it is:

1. Go to the Control Panel. This can be found by going to Start → Settings → Control Panel.

2. With the Control Panel displayed, select the Add/Remove Programs applet.

3. When the Add/Remove Programs window is displayed, choose Add/Remove Windows Components. It takes a few seconds for the Windows 2000 Setup Wizard to be displayed. This is the same dialog box that is displayed during the initial build of the server.

4. Scroll down through the list box and select Networking Services. Pick Details.

5. The Networking Services dialog box is displayed. Simply uncheck the box next to Dynamic Host Configuration Protocol (DHCP). Pick OK and Windows 2000 removes DHCP.

6. When the Windows 2000 Setup Wizard is done removing the component, pick Finish to close the wizard.

The DHCP Console

The DHCP Console, the utility used to manage the DHCP server in Windows 2000, can be found under Start → Programs → Administrative Tools → DHCP.

 If the Administrative Tools folder is not present, right-click on the Taskbar and select Properties. From the Taskbar and Start Menu Properties dialog box, select the Advanced tab. Under Start Menu Settings, select Display Administrative Tools.

If you are familiar with the DHCP Manager in Windows NT 4.0, you will notice a significant change. Like most of the management utilities found in Windows 2000, the DHCP Console is a snap-in to the Microsoft Management Console (MMC).

The Microsoft Management Console (MMC)

The MMC was first introduced with IIS4. It provides a common interface that can be customized by users, allowing them to "snap in" whichever utilities they may want to use. For example, in Windows NT 4.0, there were separate utilities to do domain administration. User Manager for Domains, Server Manager, and Event Viewer are all separate and distinct utilities, although collectively they are all essential for domain management. With the MMC, these three utilities can be snapped in to the MMC to create one single user interface.

The following steps illustrate how to add snap-ins to the MMC:

1. Click Start → Run. Type **MMC** and press Enter. A new MMC opens. This is a blank MMC (see Figure 5-5). There are no snap-ins present. There is one window displayed, called the Console Root. Now let's add some snap-ins.

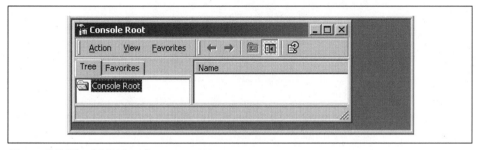

Figure 5-5. Blank MMC without snap-ins

2. Click Console → Add/Remove Snap-in. The Add/Remove Snap-in dialog box is displayed.

3. Click Add. The Add Standalone Snap-ins dialog box is displayed (see Figure 5-6). This displays the list of available snap-ins. A snap-in provides for the configuration of the different services and applications found in Windows 2000. Some snap-ins are supplied by third-party vendors, while the majority are supplied by Microsoft. Let's select the snap-ins that we want for our customized MMC.

4. Select Computer Management and click Add. A prompt is displayed, asking you to select the computer the snap-in will manage. Accept the default, Local Computer, and click Finish. The Local Computer is the computer that the MMC is installed on.

5. Next, select Event Viewer and click Add. Select Local Computer, then click on Finish. This adds the Event Viewer snap-in to the MMC. The Event Viewer provides an interface to view the System, Application, and Security logs on the Local Computer.

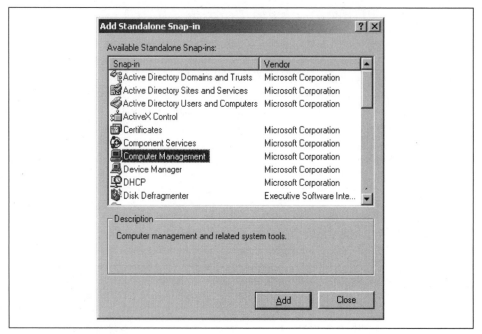

Figure 5-6. List of available snap-ins

6. Finally, select Local Users and Groups and click Add. Select Local Computer, then click Finish. The Local Users and Groups snap-in is the interface for creating, deleting, and modifying user accounts and groups. Click Finish.

7. Click Close to close the Add Standalone Snap-in dialog box.

8. Click OK to close the Add/Remove Snap-in dialog box.

Exploring the customized MMC, you will see that you now have the Windows 2000 equivalents of User Manager, Server Manager, and Event Viewer all under a single user interface (see Figure 5-7). In Windows NT 4.0, each of these utilities is a separate application. That is the beauty of the MMC: it is a common, expandable interface. A software vendor needs only to design a snap-in for their application and distribute the snap-in to their users. Users can then combine snap-ins to create their own custom MMC.

Exploring the DHCP Console

On the left-hand side of the DHCP Console is the tree pane, which displays the DHCP servers that are being managed by this MMC. DHCP is displayed at the top of the tree, with the DHCP servers listed below. The right-hand side displays the contents of the selected object (see Figure 5-8). For example, if the top of the tree (DHCP) is selected, the right-hand side displays the list of managed DHCP servers along with their current status (Running, Stopped, or Not Connected).

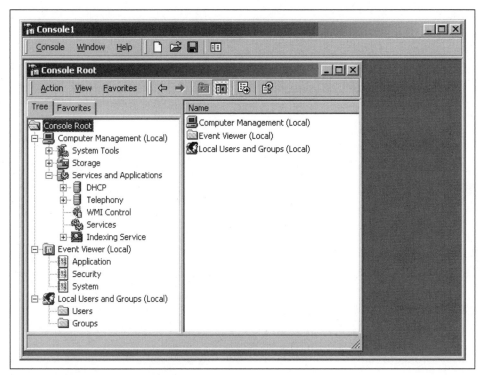

Figure 5-7. MMC with snap-ins

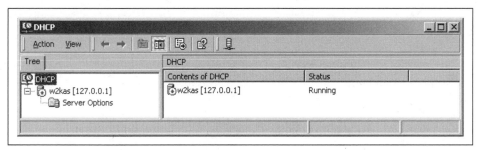

Figure 5-8. The DHCP Console

Selecting an object and right-clicking displays a menu listing the different activities that can be performed on the object. Another way to view this list is to select the object and pick the Action pull-down menu.

Add Server . . .

This item allows a DHCP server to be added to the list of servers displayed.

Manage authorized servers . . .

This item is used to authorize or unauthorize DHCP servers. An authorized DHCP server is a server that has been registered in Active Directory. Microsoft DHCP clients will only accept DHCP offers from authorized DHCP servers.

View

> This item can be used to manipulate and modify the display of the DHCP Console.

Export List . . .

> This item exports a tab-delimited text file that lists the managed DHCP servers and their current status (i.e., the output of the contents pane).

Help

> This item displays help relating to DHCP and the MMC.

In "Configuring a DHCP Server," later in this chapter, I will demonstrate some of the tasks that can be performed using the DHCP Console and the MMC.

Configuring a DHCP Server

When configuring a DHCP server in Windows 2000, there are some special configuration steps that need to be taken. Although some features may not be utilized in every situation, they nonetheless need to be considered and implemented.

Authorizing DHCP Servers

On networks running Active Directory, Windows 2000 provides a new feature that allows administrators to authorize DHCP servers. An authorized DHCP server can deliver IP addresses and TCP/IP configuration data on a Windows 2000–based network. If Active Directory detects an unauthorized DHCP server, it prevents the server's DHCP service from starting.

 Authorization of DHCP servers is available only in Windows 2000 Active Directory–based networks.

Why would an administrator need to authorize a DHCP server? As shown in Chapter 3, *Making Life Easier: DHCP*, when a DHCP client makes a request for an IP address, it sends a DHCPDISCOVER message. This message is a broadcast message that any DHCP server could receive and therefore respond to with an offer for an IP address. The DHCP client has no way of confirming the identity of the offering DHCP server.

An unauthorized or badly configured DHCP server could wreak havoc on a network. It could lease incorrect IP addresses that cause the DHCP client to be unable to connect to the network. Another possibility is that the DHCP server could send negative acknowledgments to the clients when they attempt to renew their current IP address leases. As a result, the client loses IP connectivity.

This situation is really not that hard to imagine. A user playing around and trying to learn DHCP could prevent a group of clients from logging on to the network and utilizing network resources. All the user needs to do is get a copy of Windows NT 4.0 and install the DHCP service and they are in business (and your network is in trouble!). A situation like this would be difficult to troubleshoot and track down. A network engineer would need to use a packet sniffer to analyze the DHCP packets. By analyzing the packets, they could locate the unauthorized DHCP server via its IP address.

Luckily, Windows 2000 will do this detection for us. So how does Windows 2000 detect an unauthorized DHCP server? Windows 2000 follows an ordered process to determine if the server is authorized to provide DHCP services.

When the DHCP service starts, it sends a broadcast message known as a DHCPINFORM message. The DHCP informational message is used to obtain information from a DHCP server. The information the server is looking for is the root domain where other DHCP servers are installed.

When other DHCP servers receive the DHCPINFORM, they respond with a DHCPACK that acknowledges the request and sends the root domain information. The requesting server compiles a list of DHCP servers that have responded and the root domain used by each of those servers.

After the list has been compiled, the initializing DHCP server checks to see if Active Directory is available.

When the first Windows 2000 domain controller is installed on the network, Active Directory is present.

If the directory is not available, the server can start the DHCP service as long as no other authorized DHCP servers are servicing the network. The server continues to send out DHCPINFORM broadcasts every five minutes and collect information about other DHCP servers.

If the directory is available, the server queries Active Directory for the list of authorized servers. The server searches the list for its IP address and if found, will initialize the DHCP service. If it is not found, the server does not initialize the service.

Although authorizing DHCP servers is a great thing to do, it is only useful on networks running Windows 2000. DHCP servers found in Windows NT 4.0 or other operating systems do not support server authorization. In cases like this, the network engineer needs to resort to the packet sniffer.

Well, now we know how Windows 2000 ferrets out unauthorized DHCP servers. But how do you authorize a Windows 2000 DHCP server? The following steps illustrate the authorization process:

1. To authorize a DHCP server in Windows 2000, you must be a member of the Enterprise Administrators group. If you are not a member of this group, log on with a user account that is a member, or have an Enterprise Administrator add you to that group. Another option is to have an Enterprise Administrator delegate control to your account. This is covered in detail later in this chapter.

2. Open the DHCP Console (Start → Programs → Administrative Tools → DHCP).

3. In the tree pane, pick DHCP.

4. Right-click on DHCP and select "Manage authorized servers . . . " The Manage Authorized Servers dialog box is displayed (see Figure 5-9).

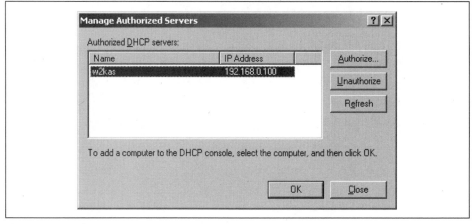

Figure 5-9. Authorizing DHCP servers

5. Pick Authorize and enter the name or IP address of the DHCP server you want to authorize.

 Please note that this procedure is required only if the server that is running the DHCP service is not a domain controller. If the DHCP server is installed on a domain controller, the DHCP server will automatically be authorized when it is added to the DHCP Console.

Authorizing DHCP servers is a powerful way to control the DHCP services that are active on the network.

Scopes

In order for DHCP clients to receive even a single IP address from the DHCP server, a DHCP scope needs to be created. A DHCP scope is a range of IP addresses to be distributed by the DHCP server. The range consists of contiguous IP addresses from the same subnet.

Scope design considerations

The range of IP addresses used to create the scope should not contain any static IP addresses of existing computers. If there are any static addresses in use, there are several choices available to fix the problem:

- Convert them into DHCP clients.
- Use address reservations.
- Use address exclusions.
- Shorten the scope's range of IP addresses.

The first option, converting the computers into DHCP clients, is the easiest solution. Once converted, the computer can request an IP address via DHCP. This may not be the ideal solution if the computer needs a static IP address, such as a web or FTP server. In this case, we would need to choose one of the remaining options.

The second option, using address reservations, enhances the first solution by adding IP address reservations in the scope. These address reservations contain the MAC address of the DHCP client. When a DHCP client requests an IP address, the DHCP server examines the MAC address from the DHCPREQUEST packet and looks for a reservation that matches it. As you can see, this is a more elegant solution. The computer always gets the same IP address, while any DHCP options that may change, such as DNS server addresses, are automatically updated. I will discuss reservations in greater detail later in this chapter.

Another option is to use address exclusions. Exclusions are IP addresses that are not to be leased to DHCP clients. Exclusions work great when a server or network device must use a static IP address or when the device does not support DHCP.

The final option is shortening the scope's range of IP addresses. For example, take a subnet of 192.168.0.0/24. This yields 254 host addresses. Since there are 25 servers on this subnet, you want to shorten the DHCP scope by removing the first 25 IP addresses in the range. As a result, the scope range of valid IP addresses is 192.168.0.26 through 192.168.0.254. I don't recommend doing this because it may be difficult to support and administer. In this example, the scope 192.168.0.0

looks like it includes the entire range. In actuality it doesn't, and the administrator who configured the scope is the only person aware of that. Another administrator or new employee would have a difficult time supporting this.

Another item to remember is that the DHCP server itself requires a static IP address. Therefore it too must be excluded from the scope. In this situation, an administrator should use an address exclusion.

So, why an address exclusion and not one of the other options discussed previously? The reason you need to use an address exclusion is because the DHCP server cannot be a DHCP client. Once the DHCP Server service is installed, the option to assign an IP address via DHCP is disabled. Since the DHCP server cannot be a DHCP client, the first two options are simply not possible. The final option, shortening the scope, is a possibility. But again, I do not recommend it.

The DHCP scope also contains other information, such as lease duration and DHCP options that will be distributed along with the IP address. Let's take a few moments to decide what these items should be.

First, let's consider the lease duration. The lease duration is the amount of time that a DHCP client can use an IP address before being required to renegotiate the lease.

As discussed in Chapter 4, the lease duration can have several functions. For example, if the subnet has an abundance of available IP addresses, the lease duration can be set to a longer length of time. This cuts down on DHCP traffic. On the other hand, if the subnet has a limited supply of IP addresses that need to be reclaimed more often, the lease duration can be set to a shorter length of time.

For the scopes I am creating, the main subnets have an abundance of IP addresses. In this case, I am going to leave the lease duration at the default setting of 8 days. Later in this chapter I will demonstrate how to change an existing lease duration.

Next, I need to consider the DHCP clients and the DHCP options they support and require. For example, let's say that the first scope I am creating contains Windows 95 workstations. The Windows 95 workstations support the following DHCP options:

Subnet Mask Option (1)
    This option specifies the subnet mask to be used by the client.

Routers Option (3)
    This option specifies the default gateway.

Domain Name Option (15)
    This option specifies the domain name to be used by the client.

Domain Name Servers Option (6)

This option lists the DNS servers to be used for host name resolution by the client.

NetBIOS Name Servers Option (44)

This option lists the WINS servers to be used for NetBIOS name resolution by the client.

NetBIOS Node Type Option (46)

This option determines the NetBIOS node type to be used by the client.

NetBIOS Scope Option (47)

This option specifies the NetBIOS scope ID to be used by the client.

Taking into account the current network infrastructure, a DHCP designer needs to determine which options are required and what are the correct values for these options.

According to my fictional network design, here are the DHCP option values for this subnet:

Option	Value
Subnet Mask	255.255.252.0
Routers	168.3.4.1
Domain Name	helpandlearn.com
Domain Name Servers	168.3.4.11, 168.3.40.11
NetBIOS Name Servers (WINS)	168.3.4.12, 168.3.40.12
NetBIOS Node Type	0x8 (H-node)
NetBIOS Scope Option	Not used

Now let's get started creating the first scope.

Creating a Scope

Creating a DHCP scope is very simple once the design criteria is decided. Just as with every other function in Windows 2000, Microsoft was nice enough to create a wizard that walks you through the DHCP scope creation process.

To create a DHCP scope, follow these steps:

1. In the DHCP Console, right-click on the DHCP server that will contain the scope. Select "New Scope . . . " from the menu.

2. The New Scope Wizard starts. Click Next on the Welcome screen.

3. Enter a name and description for the new scope. This name is used to identify the scope. For the scope I am creating, I enter 168.3.4.0 for the name and Corp-HQ for the description (see Figure 5-10). You can use more descriptive

names, such as the physical location of the scope (e.g., Building 411 – Third
Floor) if you prefer. Click Next.

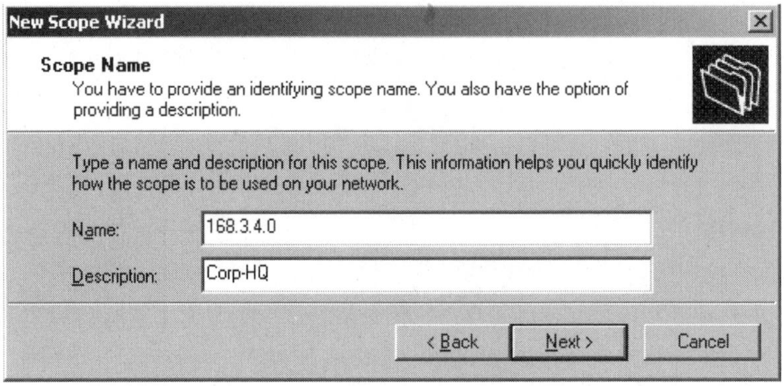

Figure 5-10. Scope name

4. Now define the scope address range. The range must be a set of contiguous
   IP addresses belonging to a single subnet (see Figure 5-11). Since I am defining the scope for subnet 168.3.4.0, I enter the starting IP address, 168.3.4.1,
   and the ending IP address, 168.3.4.254. Next enter the subnet mask traditionally (i.e., 255.255.252.0) or as a length (i.e., the number of bits that comprise
   the network address, 22).

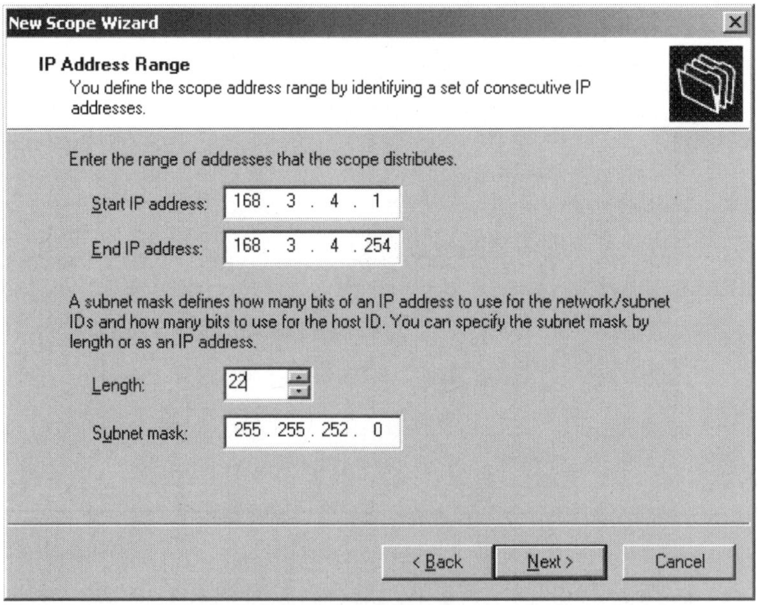

Figure 5-11. Specifying the scope address range

Note that the starting IP address cannot be the first address in the subnet. For example, if the scope being created was for the 192.168.0.0 subnet, the first address on that subnet is 192.168.0.1. Recall from Chapter 1, *TCP/IP Overview*, that any IP address with all zeros is invalid. All zeros in the host portion of the address designates the address as the subnet address. If you enter an invalid IP address, an error message will be displayed (see Figure 5-12).

Figure 5-12. Invalid IP address error message

If you enter a range of IP addresses that is bigger than the subnet mask provides, another dialog box will be displayed asking if you would like to create a superscope. Superscopes are covered later in this section. Click Next.

5. Next, enter any address exclusions (see Figure 5-13). An address exclusion is an IP address that is included in the scope range but which the DHCP server is not to distribute.

In the scope I am creating, I want to exclude the first 25 addresses in the scope. Therefore, I need to enter a range of IP addresses to be excluded. I enter 168.3.4.1 through 168.3.4.25. If you want to specify a single IP address, use that address in the starting address field only. Click Add to add the range of IP addresses to the exclusion list.

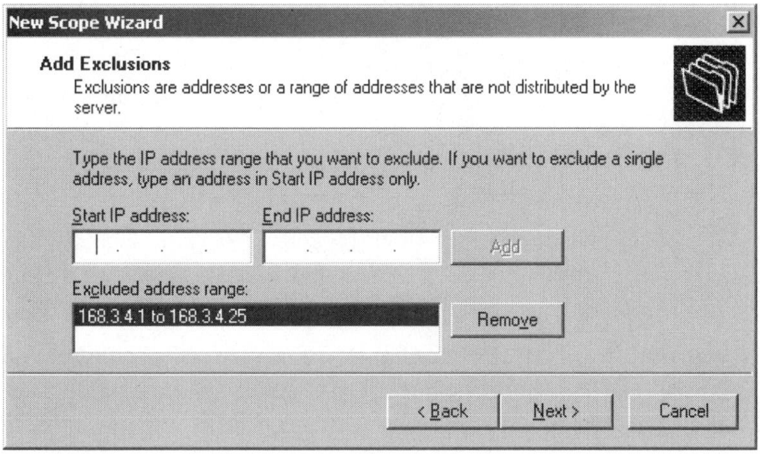

Figure 5-13. Specifying address exclusions

Also be sure to add the address of the DHCP server to the exclusion list. Remember that the DHCP server requires a static IP address. Since the IP address I used for the DHCP server (168.3.4.10) was within the exclusion range I defined, I do not need to create a separate exclusion. Click Next.

6. Next, specify the lease duration to be used for this scope (see Figure 5-14). Lease durations are used to allow the DHCP server to reclaim IP addresses. Lease durations and strategies in their use were covered in detail in Chapter 4. Use the up and down arrows to specify the duration in days/hours/minutes. For this subnet I am accepting the default value of 8 days. Click Next.

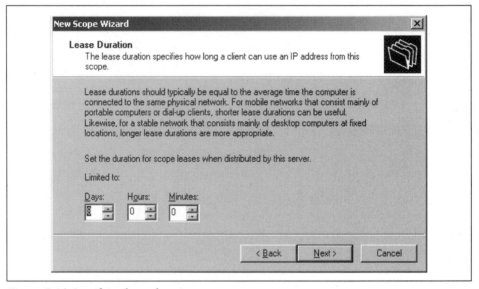

Figure 5-14. Specifying lease duration

7. Now you have a choice of configuring DHCP options now or later (see Figure 5-15). DHCP options are settings distributed to DHCP clients when they lease an IP address from this scope. These options can include information such as default gateway or DNS server addresses. Since I already determined which DHCP options to configure, select "Yes, I want to configure these options now" and click Next.

8. The New Scope Wizard prompts you to enter a Router (Default Gateway) IP address. For the subnet 168.3.4.0, the router address is 168.3.4.1. Enter the IP address for the router and click Add. Click Next.

9. Next you need to enter DNS configuration data. These configuration settings will allow the DHCP clients to query DNS servers for host name to IP address resolution. First, enter the parent DNS domain. The domain name that I am using for this example is *helpandlearn.com*. Next, enter the IP addresses for

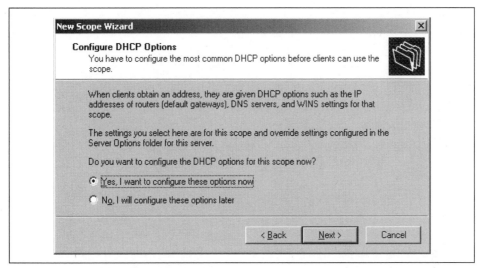

Figure 5-15. Configure DHCP Options page

the DNS servers. If you are not sure of the IP address but you do have the host name of the DNS server, you can enter the server's name and click Resolve to find the IP address. Enter 168.3.4.11 and 168.3.40.11. When finished, click Next.

10. Now it's time for WINS configuration. WINS servers resolve NetBIOS names to IP addresses. Enter the IP addresses for the WINS servers, or enter the WINS server's name and click Resolve. Enter 168.3.4.12 and 168.3.40.12 for my example. Click Next.

11. Next you are prompted to activate the scope. Activating the scope allows DHCP clients to obtain IP addresses from the scope. For this example, select "No, I will activate the scope later." (There may be situations where you want to wait before activating a scope, such as when you are converting from one IP addressing scheme to another.) Click Next.

12. Click Finish to create the scope.

13. Notice the red down arrow on the scope icon. This designates that the scope is not active. This is why I didn't want you to activate the scope yet. To activate the scope, right-click on the scope and select Activate from the menu. The red down arrow disappears and the scope is active.

After the scope has been created, additional items can be configured, such as more DHCP options, exclusions, and reservations.

Adding exclusion ranges

Any devices that are statically configured should be excluded from the scope. Devices such as DHCP servers, non-DHCP clients, or RAS clients should be defined and added to the exclusion list. During the New Scope Wizard, I created one exclusion range: 168.3.4.1 through 168.3.4.25. Let's say there is a web server on the 168.3.4.0 subnet that requires a static IP address. Its IP address, 168.3.5.45, is not within the exclusion range I previously created. I need to create another exclusion for this server.

1. To add additional exclusions, right-click on Address Pool and select "New Exclusion Range . . . "

2. If you want to exclude only a single address, enter only the starting IP address 168.3.5.45 in the Add Exclusion dialog box (see Figure 5-16). Click Add.

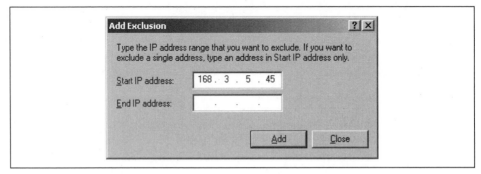

Figure 5-16. Add Exclusion dialog box

In the Address Pool, the exclusion just added is included in the list along with the address pool and all other exclusions for this scope.

 An exclusion range cannot be created if there is an active lease in that range. Delete the active lease and try to create the exclusion again.

Adding reservations

A reservation is used for a DHCP client that will always be assigned the same IP address. Reservations may be used for printers or other devices that are DHCP clients but require the same IP address continuously.

Note that the DHCP client does not automatically use the IP address being reserved. The DHCP server has no mechanism to notify the client to begin using the new reserved IP address. The DHCP client must issue a DHCPREQUEST to use the reservation. This can be done at a Windows 2000 client by using the `ipconfig /release` command. When the DHCP server gets the DHCPREQUEST, it reads the `chaddr` field that contains the client's MAC address. If there is a reservation for that MAC address, the DHCP server continues the process using the information found in the reservation.

1. To add a reservation, right-click on the Reservations folder listed under the selected scope and select "New Reservation . . . " (see Figure 5-17).

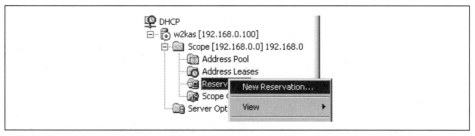

Figure 5-17. Adding reservations

2. The New Reservation dialog box will be displayed (see Figure 5-18). Enter the following information:

Reservation name
> The name for this reservation. This is displayed in the DHCP console under Reservations.

IP address
> The IP address being reserved. This IP address is given to the DHCP client.

MAC address
> The MAC address of the DHCP client. The DHCP server uses the MAC address to identify the DHCP client and honor the reservation.

Description
> A description of the reservation. This is displayed in the Address Leases view.

Supported types: Both, DHCP only, BOOTP only
> Specifies whether BOOTP clients, DHCP clients, or both can use this reservation.

 To change the IP address of a reservation, the reservation must be deleted and recreated.

Adding BOOTP support

The version of DHCP Server found in Windows 2000 responds to requests from both DHCP clients and BOOTP clients. Windows 2000 DHCP Server supports

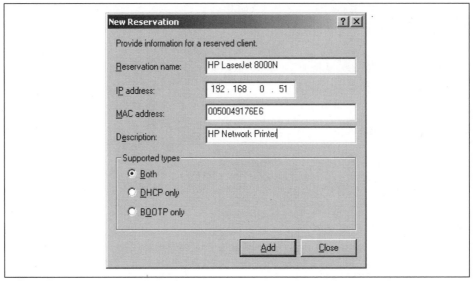

Figure 5-18. Configuring a new reservation

BOOTP clients by providing dynamic IP address allocation as well as providing boot file information. The BOOTP client uses the boot image file to complete its initialization. The file is located on a Trivial File Transfer Protocol (TFTP) server.

TFTP is said to be "trivial" because it is faster and has less functionality than its big brother, File Transfer Protocol (FTP). TFTP is faster than FTP because it uses UDP, which does not acknowledge data transfer, instead of TCP, which sends acknowledgments. TFTP has less functionality because it does not support features such as authentication and directory browsing.

Setting up the DHCP server to provide boot file information requires two steps:

1. For each BOOTP client, add a client reservation within an active DHCP scope (see "Adding reservations" earlier in this section).

2. In the BOOTP table, add BOOTP entries for each BOOTP client's operating system and hardware platform.

   To view the BOOTP table, right-click on the DHCP server. Select Properties. The Properties page of the DHCP server will be displayed. Check "Show the BOOTP table folder" and click OK.

   Right-click on the BOOTP table folder and select Add BOOTP Entry. In the dialog box, enter the BOOTP image filename and the TFTP server name. Click Add, then click Close.

To set up a scope to support BOOTP clients, follow these steps:

1. In the DHCP Console, right-click on the desired scope. Select Properties.

2. On the Advanced tab, designate whether this scope will assign IP addresses to DHCP clients, BOOTP clients, or both. Set the desired lease duration here as well.

Removing a Scope

If you want to remove a scope because the subnet is no longer in use or you want DHCP clients to use a new scope, you must follow a particular procedure:

1. First, create a replacement scope. The replacement scope must be on the same subnet that the existing scope is servicing. Activate the new scope.

2. Next, deactivate the existing scope. Deactivating the scope allows clients using that scope to renew their leases with the replacement scope. If the existing scope were simply deleted, the clients would lose their leases.

3. When there are no active leases in the existing scope, the scope can be deleted.

Reconciling a Scope

Reconciling a scope is the process of detecting and fixing discrepancies that relate to client information, such as who owns which IP address or showing an IP address as leased when it may not be. The DHCP server accomplishes this by comparing scope information stored in the DHCP database with scope information found in the registry. If any discrepancies are found, the DHCP server either creates a temporary reservation for the address or restores IP addresses to the original owner.

 Although reconciling fixes some errors in a scope, it is not meant to be a replacement for the normal backup and restore procedures discussed in Chapter 7, *Advanced DHCP*.

To reconcile a scope:

1. Right-click on the scope to be reconciled. Select "Reconcile . . . "

2. Click Verify to begin the reconciliation.

3. On the Reconcile dialog box, any inconsistent IP addresses are listed. These are IP addresses known to be leased in the registry, but not in the DHCP database. Click Reconcile to fix the discrepancies.

For the remainder of this chapter, I will discuss the different configuration items relating to DHCP scopes, such as leases, options, and reservations.

Leases

A lease is a length of time that the DHCP server agrees to let a DHCP client use an assigned IP address. When a client is using a lease, the lease is considered *active*. During the duration the client holds a lease, the client must attempt to renew the lease. These times are known as T1, which occurs at 50% of available lease time remaining, and T2, which occurs at 87.5% of available lease time remaining. If the lease is not renewed and expires, the lease is considered *inactive*.

Lease Duration Strategies

By default, when a scope is created, the lease time is set to 8 days. Usually 8 days is plenty of time. However, you may want to adjust the lease duration to improve performance of DHCP servers or to reclaim IP addresses more quickly.

- If there are a large number of IP addresses available and the environment is very stable, i.e., there are not many changes being made, the lease duration could be increased. By increasing the lease duration, DHCP traffic is decreased because clients do not have to attempt to renew their lease as often.

- If the number of IP addresses is limited and/or there are many remote users, the lease duration should be decreased. With a decreased lease duration, IP addresses are reclaimed at a faster rate.

Viewing Client Leases

To view a client's lease, follow these steps:

1. In the DHCP Console, expand the scope that contains the client lease. Click on Address Leases.

2. In the Details pane, find the client lease to view. View the information contained in the pane.

Deleting Client Leases

To delete a client's lease, follow these steps:

1. In the DHCP Console, expand the scope that contains the client lease. Click on Address Leases.

2. In the Details pane, find the client lease you want to delete.

3. Right-click on the client lease and select Delete. Answer Yes to the confirmation dialog box.

4. If you do not want that IP address to be used by a DHCP client, create a Reservation or Exclusion as discussed earlier in the chapter.

5. Go to the client that holds the release and force it to release the IP address. In Windows 2000, typing the command **ipconfig /release** accomplishes this.

6. If the client needs another IP address, type **ipconfig /renew**.

Options

DHCP options are used to pass TCP/IP configuration information from the DHCP server to the DHCP client. By using DHCP to configure these options, the administrator can centrally control and distribute configurations that would otherwise need to be manually set at the client.

DHCP options are standardized and defined in RFC2132. In Windows 2000, all DHCP options are predefined and available for use. Non-standard options can also be defined on the DHCP server. This should only be done in special cases where a particular software package requires them.

Please note that not all DHCP clients support all standard DHCP options. For example, the Microsoft-based DHCP clients are designed to request only a small subset of the options. The only exception is the Windows 2000 DHCP Client, which can also support the Perform Router Discovery (31) and Static Route (33) options.

Microsoft-based clients request the following options, which are defined as properties of the scope, such as lease duration time:

- Renewal Time Option (58)
- Rebinding Time Option (59)
- IP Address Lease Time Option (51)
- Server Identifier Option (54)
- Subnet Mask Option (1)

Microsoft-based clients will also request the following options:

- Routers Option (3)
- Domain Name Option (15)
- Domain Name Servers Option (6)
- NetBIOS Name Servers Option (44)

- NetBIOS Node Type Option (46)

- NetBIOS Scope Option (47)

Options in Windows 2000's DHCP Server can be defined in five different ways: Predefined Options, Server Options, Scope Options, Class Options, and Reservation Options.

 Options are applied on the DHCP client from most specific to most generic. In other words, they are applied in the following order: Reservation Options, Class Options, Scope Options, Server Options, and finally Predefined Options.

Predefined Options

Predefined Options are set at the DHCP server level. An administrator can add or remove options and set their default value. Predefined Options are available to any of the other option levels (i.e., Server Options, Scope Options, Class Options, or Reservation Options), but they are not assigned to clients until the administrator configures them for a scope.

Assigning Predefined Options

In the following example, I will predefine the Router (3) option to use a particular IP address:

1. In the DHCP console, right-click on the DHCP server where the predefined options will be located. Select "Set Predefined Options . . . "

2. The Predefined Options and Values dialog box is displayed. From the Option Name dropdown list, select 003 Router (see Figure 5-19). Click "Edit Array . . . "

3. The IP Address Array Editor is displayed (see Figure 5-20). Enter 192.168.0.1 in the IP address field and click Add. You can also enter a server or router name into the Server name field. Click Resolve and DNS resolves the name to an IP address. The resolved IP address is displayed in the IP address field, where you can add it to the list. Click OK.

4. Click OK on the Predefined Options and Values dialog box when you are finished.

Now when the 003 Router option is selected in any scope, it will already have the default IP address of 192.168.0.1. Of course, this can be deleted at the scope level and changed to another IP address.

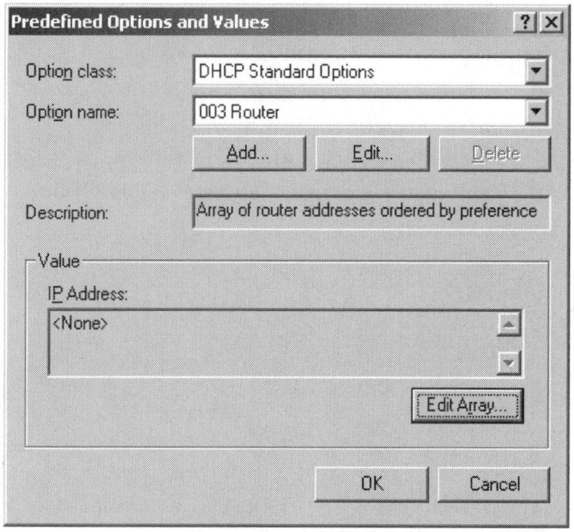

Figure 5-19. Predefined Options and Values dialog box

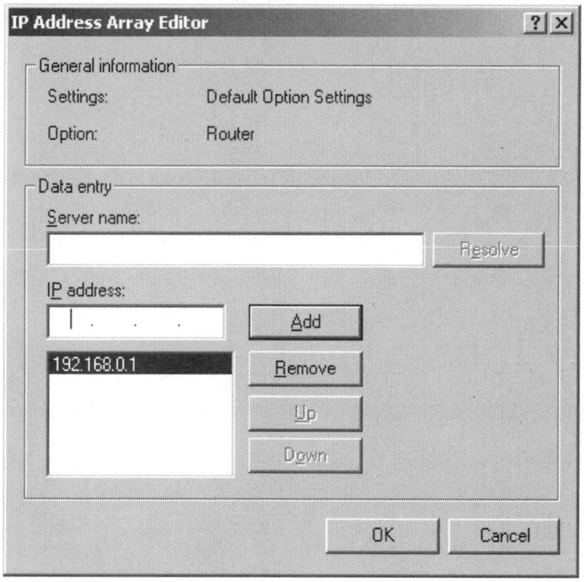

Figure 5-20. The IP Address Array Editor

You can also add a custom predefined DHCP option, but this should only be done if it is required by a software application. DHCP clients that are not designed to support the custom option ignore it. Just be careful: a poorly designed DHCP client may not handle it very well and could cause the operating system to crash.

Server Options

Server Options are options that are applied to all scopes and clients of the DHCP server. Options assigned here are typically used throughout the entire organization. For example, if the company has a single DNS server, the Domain Name Servers Option (6) can be defined here, and all clients in the company will receive the IP address of the DNS server. Scope Options, Class Options, and Reservation Options override Server Options.

Assigning Server Options

To assign Server Options, follow these steps:

1. In the DHCP Console, right-click on Server Options listed below the desired DHCP server. Select "Configure Options . . . "

2. The Server Options dialog box is displayed. Scroll through the Available Options windows and view the options available to be assigned (see Figure 5-21). Remember that DHCP clients only support certain options. Click the checkbox next to 003 Router. Remember when I predefined this option earlier in this section? The IP address 192.168.0.1 is already defined. Select 192.168.0.1 and click Remove. Add another IP address as the default gateway. Click OK when finished or assign additional Server options.

Scope Options

Scope Options are applied to all clients that have leases from a particular scope. In most environments, this is the level where options will be applied.

Assigning Scope Options

To assign Scope Options, follow these steps:

1. In the DHCP Console, expand the scope where Scope Options are to be assigned. Right-click on Scope and select "Configure Options . . . "

2. The Scope Options dialog box is displayed. Scroll through the Available Options windows and view the options available to be assigned. Click OK when finished or assign additional Server Options.

Class Options

Class Options are a new feature found in Windows 2000. Class Options can be used to identify a particular set of DHCP clients that have needs different from other clients found in the environment.

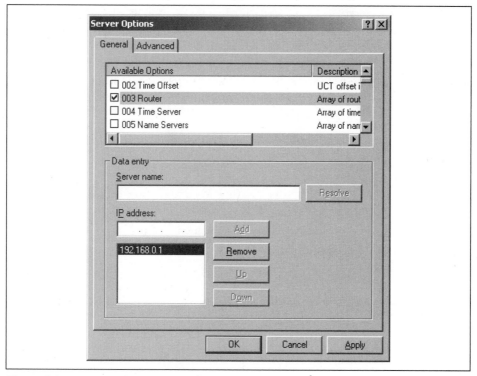

Figure 5-21. Assigning Server Options

A good example of this is Windows 2000. Besides the options listed earlier in this section, Windows 2000's DHCP Client can use two additional options:

Perform Router Discovery (31)

This option specifies whether the DHCP client can use ICMP to discover Routers by sending Router Solicitation messages.

Static Route (33)

This option specifies a list of static routes to be installed into the client's routing table.

Since other Microsoft clients will not support these options, a Class Option can be created for the Windows 2000 DHCP clients.

Windows 2000 supports the use of two types of class options: User Classes and Vendor Classes.

User Classes

User Classes are supported with the use of the User Class (77) Option. This option is not part of the DHCP standard and is proposed in a draft RFC called "The User Class Option for DHCP" (*http://www.ietf.org/internet-drafts/draft-ietf-dhc-userclass-10.txt*).

For example, users in separate departments might require the use of different DHCP options, even though they both use the same scope. Users in the accounting department may use a third-party application that requires a database server to be specified via DHCP options. By using User Class IDs, the DHCP server is able to differentiate between users in the accounting department and other users. Only users in the accounting department receive the DHCP option for the database server.

The User Class Option is simply ASCII text used to identify a DHCP client as a member of a particular User Class. Windows 2000 has several predefined User Classes (see Table 5-3).

Table 5-3. Predefined User Classes

Class Name	Class Data	Description
Default User Class	(none)	This class is used for clients that do not identify themselves as members of any User Class. Windows 2000 DHCP clients with user classes unknown to the DHCP server are placed in this class.
Default Remote Access Class	RRAS.Microsoft	This class is used to identify clients that are connected to the network via a RAS server.
Default BOOTP class	BOOTP.Microsoft	This class is used to identify BOOTP clients.

When a Windows 2000 DHCP server receives a DHCPREQUEST that contains the User Class Identifier, it sends options assigned to that User Class if available.

To use User Classes, the User Class must be defined at the DHCP server and the DHCP clients.

To define a User Class at the DHCP server, follow these steps:

1. In the DHCP Console, right-click on the DHCP server where the User Class is to be defined. Select "Define User Classes . . . "

2. In the DHCP User Classes dialog box, click Add to add a new User Class.

3. In the New Class dialog box (see Figure 5-22), enter a name in the "Display name" field. The display name is used to display the User Class; it is *not* the actual name of the class. Enter a description in the Description field. To enter the name of the class, click in the area right below ASCII. Enter the name here. Click OK to add the User Class.

At this point you can begin assigning DHCP options to the new User Class:

1. Select the scope that will use the new User Class.

2. Right-click on Scope Options and select "Configure Options . . . "

3. Click on the Advanced tab.

4. Select the new User Class from the dropdown box and select the DHCP options that will be a part of this User Class. Click on OK.

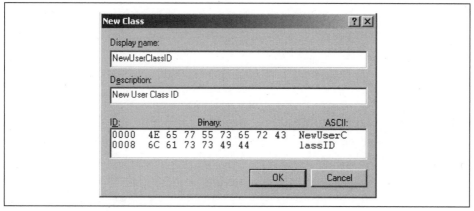

Figure 5-22. Configuring a new User Class

To assign a DHCP client to a User Class, use the following command at the client:

```
ipconfig /setclassid "Local Area Connection" NewUserClassID
```

To view which User Class the DHCP client belongs to, use this command at the client:

```
ipconfig /showclassid "Local Area Connection"
```

Vendor Classes

Vendor Classes are supported with two options that are part of the DHCP options standard, defined in RFC2132.

Vendor-specific options are used to exchange specific configuration options between a DHCP server and its clients. Servers that are not designed to handle vendor-specific options will ignore client requests for these options. Clients that do not receive the requested options should attempt to operate without them.

The vendor is identified by the Vendor Class Identifier Option (60). Clients use this option to identify their Vendor Class. When the Windows 2000 DHCP server receives a DHCPREQUEST that contains the Vendor Class Identifier, it sends vendor-specific information pertaining to that vendor, if available.

In Windows 2000's DHCP Server, there are several predefined DHCP Vendor Classes (see Table 5-4).

Table 5-4. Microsoft Vendor Classes

Class Name	Class Data	Description
Microsoft Windows 2000 Options	MSFT 5.0	This class is used to identify clients running Windows 2000.
Microsoft Windows 98 Options	MSFT 98	This class is used to identify clients running Windows 98. There are no options defined in this class.
Microsoft Options	MSFT	This class is used to identify all clients running either Windows 2000 or Windows 98.
DHCP Standard Options		This class is used to identify all clients that are not running Windows 2000 or Windows 98.

The Microsoft Options and Microsoft Windows 2000 Vendor Classes provide the following options:

Disable NetBIOS over TCP/IP (NetBT) Option

> This option disables NetBIOS over TCP/IP. With Windows 2000, NetBT is not required, and therefore it can be disabled. Earlier Microsoft operating systems required NetBT. A value of 2 disables NetBT.

Release DHCP Lease on Shutdown Option

> This option controls whether a Windows 2000 DHCP client releases its IP address lease upon shutdown. A value of 0 tells the client not to send a DHCPRELEASE message to the server. A value of 1 tells the client to send a DHCPRELEASE message.

Default Router Metric Base Option

> This option is used to set a base metric for all default gateway routes used on Windows 2000 DHCP clients. A metric is used to calculate the fastest and cheapest routes.

To define a Vendor Class at the DHCP server, follow these steps:

1. In the DHCP Console, right-click on the DHCP server where the Vendor Class is to be defined. Select "Define Vendor Classes . . . "

2. In the DHCP Vendor Classes dialog box, click Add to add a new Vendor Class.

3. In the New Class dialog box, enter a name in the "Display name" field. The display name is used to display the Vendor Class; it is *not* the actual name of the class. Enter a description in the description field. To enter the name of the class, click in the area right below ASCII. Enter the name here. Click OK to add the Vendor Class.

Assigning Class Options

Class Options can be assigned much like assigning options at the server and scope levels. Class Options can be found under the Advanced tab on the Server and

Scope Options dialog boxes (see Figure 5-23). Class Options assigned at the server level flow down to the scope and client levels.

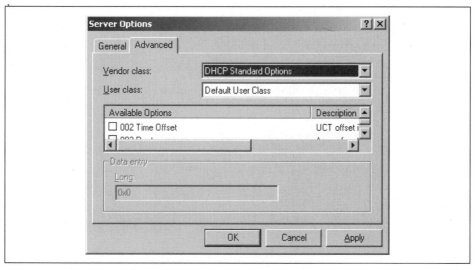

Figure 5-23. Assigning Class Options

Reservation Options

Reservation Options are used when a single client has special configuration needs. To assign Reservation Options, a reservation must first be created for the client.

Assigning Reservation Options

To assign Reservation Options, perform the following steps:

1. In the DHCP Console, expand the Reservations folder in the scope. Right-click on the client reservation where the options are to be assigned. Select "Configure Options . . . "

2. The Reservation Options dialog box is displayed. Scroll through the Available Options windows and view the options available to be assigned. Click OK when finished, or assign additional Reservation Options.

Well, by now you should have a fully functioning DHCP server. The DHCP server contains scopes that are servicing subnets with a range of IP addresses as well as excluding some IP addresses for servers and routers. The scopes' lease durations have been configured depending on the environment. If there are usually a lot of changes, the lease duration is short so the DHCP server can reclaim IP addresses. If it is a stable environment, the lease durations can be kept at the default of 8 days or increased further. Finally, DHCP options have been assigned so that DHCP clients are receiving configuration information such as default gateways and IP addresses of DNS and WINS servers.

Summary

Windows 2000's DHCP Server offers many new enhanced features that build upon a strong implementation based on RFCs 2131 and 2132. This chapter covered Windows 2000's DHCP Server starting with a brief introduction to the Windows 2000 operating system family.

In this chapter, I covered some of the features found in DHCP server, followed by a discussion on the various installation options. Next, I introduced the Microsoft Management Console (MMS) and explained the DHCP Console that is used to manage DHCP in Windows 2000. Walking you through the configuration of a DHCP scope, I explained the different configuration items and demonstrated how they need to be configured. Finally I discussed leases, options, and reservations and how they can be configured.

6

DHCP Clients

The DHCP server in Windows 2000 supports any RFC 2131-compliant DHCP client. In this chapter, I will be covering the Microsoft DHCP clients. In all reality, most of the Microsoft DHCP clients support the same DHCP options. However there are small differences, such as where additional DHCP options have been added or where the utilities used to support the DHCP client have changed. In this chapter I will be covering each DHCP client in detail, so, although it may seem redundant in areas, you will get to see the complete picture for each client.

Windows 2000 Professional

Windows 2000 Professional is the next generation of Microsoft's desktop operating system. This upgrade replaces Windows NT Workstation 4.0 in the product line.

Microsoft designed Windows 2000 Professional to provide a standard business desktop and notebook configuration for every size organization. It includes many new and enhanced features geared towards making the OS more reliable, easier to maintain, and suitable for mobile use. Windows 2000 Professional also includes support for Universal Serial Bus (USB) and Plug and Play.

Some of the features include the following:

Windows File Protection
> One of the biggest problems with the Windows NT and Windows 9x OS families is known as DLL-hell. Many applications install their own version of system files, some of which are incompatible with others. Trying to restore all the affected DLL files to functioning versions can be quite challenging, hence the name DLL-hell. Since neither OS family protects system files from being overwritten, something as simple as installing an application could introduce bugs or worse, crash the system. Windows 2000 corrects this by safeguarding system files. If a system file is overwritten, Windows File Protection restores the

original system file in its place. This feature eliminates many system-related problems associated with DLL-hell.

Microsoft Installer

Microsoft Installer packages applications so users can simply install and remove software without the risk of user error.

Remote OS Installation

This utility allows Windows 2000 Professional to be installed across the network. Note that Remote OS Installation requires the use of Windows 2000–based servers on the back end, however.

Encrypting File System (EFS)

EFS uses public key encryption technology to allow users to encrypt files.

IP Security (IPSec)

IPSec protects data being transmitted across the network. It also provides security for Virtual Private Networks (VPNs). VPNs are network connections that use the Internet as the transmission medium, while providing security for those connections.

Recovery Console

The Recovery Console is a command line interface that allows an administrator to start and stop services, access data on local drives, and perform other tasks.

Intellimirror

Intellimirror, based on group-level policies, allows users' settings, data, and applications to be accessible no matter where they have logged onto the network. Intellimirror can only be utilized using a Windows 2000–based backend with Active Directory.

Offline Files and Folders

The Offline Files and Folders feature allows a user to create mirrored copies of data stored on the network. The user can then access that data even when disconnected from the network.

Installing the Windows 2000 DHCP Client

Windows 2000 Professional has a DHCP client built into its TCP/IP stack. By default, Windows 2000 enables DHCP during installation. Previously, the default was to display a prompt asking the user whether she wanted to use DHCP. Microsoft changed this to make configuration easier for most users.

To install the DHCP client on Windows 2000 Professional, follow these steps:

1. Locate the network connection on which you want to enable DHCP. Select Start → Settings → Network and Dial-up Connections. Right-click on Local Area Connection and select Properties.

Although the default name for connection in Windows 2000 is Local Area Connection, it can be renamed. Also, if the workstation is multi-homed, there will be more than one connection displayed. Verify that you are configuring the correct connection by removing the network cable. The icon will change to show it has been disconnected. Once you have verified the connection, plug the network cable back in.

2. From the Local Area Connection Properties dialog box (see Figure 6-1), select Internet Protocol (TCP/IP), then click Properties.

3. On the Internet Protocol (TCP/IP) Properties dialog box (see Figure 6-2), select "Obtain an IP address automatically." If DNS addresses are assigned by the DHCP server, select "Obtain DNS server address automatically."

   If you do not want DHCP to assign DNS servers, simply select "Use the following DNS server addresses" and enter IP addresses for the Preferred and/or Alternate DNS Server.

4. Click OK to close the dialog box.

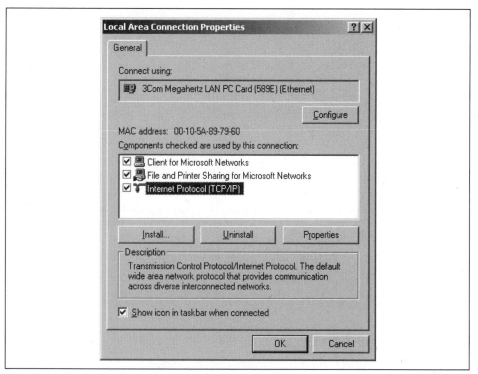

Figure 6-1. Local Area Connection Properties dialog box

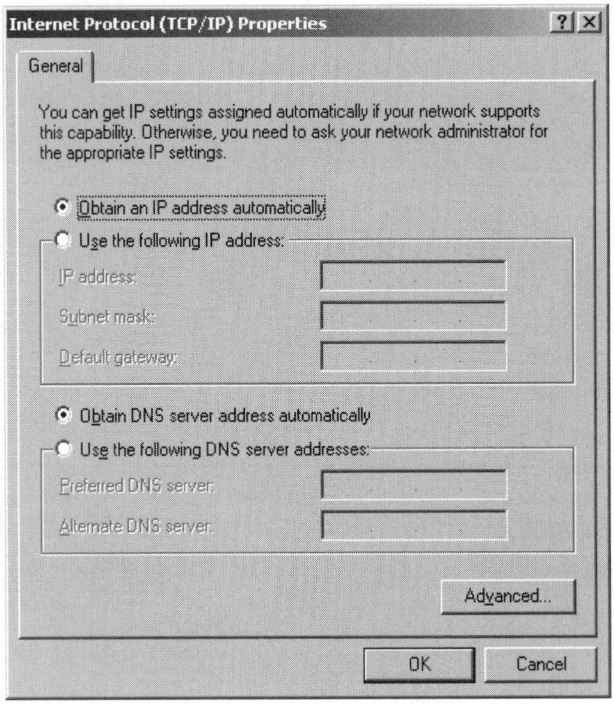

Internet Protocol (TCP/IP) Properties   ? X

┌─ General ┐

You can get IP settings assigned automatically if your network supports
this capability. Otherwise, you need to ask your network administrator for
the appropriate IP settings.

   ⦿ Obtain an IP address automatically
   ◯ Use the following IP address:

     IP address:

     Subnet mask:

     Default gateway:

   ⦿ Obtain DNS server address automatically
   ◯ Use the following DNS server addresses:

     Preferred DNS server:

     Alternate DNS server:

                   Advanced...

                  OK   Cancel

Figure 6-2. Internet Protocol (TCP/IP) Properties dialog box

One less reboot! Unlike Windows NT and Windows 9x, you do not
need to reboot after modifying the IP configuration in Windows 2000.

To configure the Windows 2000 DHCP client to not use DHCP, simply select "Use
the following IP address" and specify an IP address, subnet mask, and default
gateway.

DHCP Client Configuration Details

The following sections provide additional Windows 2000 DHCP client configuration information.

Supported DHCP options

The Windows 2000 DHCP client supports the following DHCP options:

Subnet Mask Option (1)
    This option specifies the subnet mask to be used by the client.

Routers Option (3)

This option specifies the default gateway.

Domain Name Option (15)

This option specifies the domain name to be used by the client.

Domain Name Servers Option (6)

This option lists the DNS servers to be used for hostname resolution by the client.

NetBIOS Name Servers Option (44)

This option lists the WINS servers to be used for NetBIOS name resolution by the client.

NetBIOS Node Type Option (46)

This option determines the NetBIOS node type to be used by the client.

NetBIOS Scope Option (47)

This option specifies the NetBIOS scope ID to be used by the client.

Perform Router Discovery (31)

This option specifies whether the DHCP client can use ICMP to discover routers by sending router solicitation messages (see RFC1256, "ICMP Router Discovery Messages," at *http://www.ietf.org/rfc/rfc1256.txt*).

Static Route Option (33)

This option specifies a list of static routes to be installed into the client's routing table.

Registry entries

The Windows 2000 DHCP client service stores its configuration information in the following registry key:

HKLM\SYSTEM\CurrentControlSet\Services\Dhcp

The TCP/IP configuration information, used to register TCP/IP parameters, is stored in two other locations:

HKLM\SYSTEM\CurrentControlSet\Services\Tcpip\Parameters\

HKLM\SYSTEM\CurrentControlSet\Services\Netbt\Parameters\Interfaces\
Tcpip_<ID for Adapter> (used to register NetBIOS over TCP/IP parameters)

The following registry entry is configurable from the Network Control Panel Applet:

EnableDhcp

Value type: REG_DWORD-(Boolean)

If this value is 1, the DHCP Client service attempts to contact a DHCP server and configure the NIC with a DHCP IP address. If this value is 0, the DHCP client service is disabled. This value is set to 1 by selecting "Obtain an IP address automatically" (see Figure 6-2).

Registry location: Tcpip\Parameters\Interfaces\<Adapter_Name>

The remaining registry entries are not configurable and are entered automatically by the DHCP Client service:

DhcpDefaultGateway

Value type: REG_MULTI_SZ (Multiple Strings)

This value specifies a list of IP addresses to be used as default gateways. A default gateway is used to route packets to a network that the system is not connected to (i.e., one not on the same subnet). Please note that if a Default-Gateway value is present, this parameter is overridden.

Registry location: Tcpip\Parameters\Interfaces\<Adapter_Name>

DhcpIPAddress

Value type: REG_SZ (String)

This value specifies the IP address obtained by a DHCP server. Please note that if the IPAddress value is other than 0.0.0.0, this parameter is overridden.

Registry location: Tcpip\Parameters\Interfaces\<Adapter_Name>

DhcpNameServer

Value type: REG_SZ (String)

This value specifies the IP addresses of DNS servers to be queried for host-name resolution. If the NameServer value is present, this parameter is overridden.

Registry location: Tcpip\Parameters\Interfaces\<Adapter_Name>

DhcpServer

Value type: REG_SZ (String)

This value specifies the IP address of the DHCP server that granted the IP lease address (found in the DhcpIPAddress parameter) to this DHCP client. The client uses this IP address to renew or release the lease.

Registry location: Tcpip\Parameters

DhcpSubnetMask

Value type: REG_SZ (String)

This value specifies the subnet mask to be used by the DHCP client with the IP address found in the DhcpIPAddress parameter.

Registry location: Tcpip\Parameters\Interfaces\<Adapter_Name>

Lease

Value type: REG_DWORD (Time in seconds)

This value specifies the amount of time that the lease on the IP address found in the DhcpIPAddress parameter is valid.

Registry location: Tcpip\Parameters\Interfaces\<Adapter_Name>

LeaseObtainedTime

Value type: REG_DWORD (Absolute time in seconds since midnight of 1/1/70)

This value specifies the absolute time that the lease was obtained.

Registry location: Tcpip\Parameters\Interfaces\<Adapter_Name>

LeaseTerminatesTime

Value type: REG_DWORD (Absolute time in seconds since midnight of 1/1/70)

This value specifies the absolute time at which the lease expires.

Registry location: Tcpip\Parameters\Interfaces\<Adapter_Name>

T1

Value type: REG_DWORD (Absolute time in seconds since midnight of 1/1/70)

This value specifies the time at which the DHCP Client service will attempt to renew the lease on the IP address found in the DhcpIPAddress parameter by contacting the DHCP server found in the DhcpServer parameter. This value is set to 50% of the time allocated by the Lease parameter.

Registry location: Tcpip\Parameters\Interfaces\<Adapter_Name>

T2

Value type: REG_DWORD (Absolute time in seconds since midnight of 1/1/70)

This value specifies the time at which the DHCP Client service will attempt to renew the lease on the IP address found in the DhcpIPAddress parameter by broadcasting a renewal request. T2 is used only if the DHCP Client service is unable to renew the lease at T1. This value is set to 87.5% of the time allocated by the Lease parameter.

Registry location: Tcpip\Parameters\Interfaces\<Adapter_Name>

DhcpNameServer

Value type: REG_SZ (String)

This value specifies the primary WINS server to be queried for NetBIOS name resolution. If the NameServer value is present, this parameter is overridden.

Registry location: Netbt\Parameters\Interfaces\Tcpip_<ID for Adapter>

DhcpNameServerBackup

Value type: REG_SZ (String)

This value specifies the secondary WINS server to be queried for NetBIOS name resolution. If the BackupNameServer value is present, this parameter is overridden.

Registry location: Netbt\Parameters\Interfaces\Tcpip_<ID for Adapter>

DhcpNodeType

> Value type: REG_DWORD (Number)
>
> This value (1, 2, 4, or 8) specifies the NetBIOS node type (see Chapter 1, *TCP/IP Overview* for a description of the various node types). If the NodeType value is present, this parameter is overridden.
>
> Value Range: 1 = B-node, 2 = P-node, 4 = M-node, 8 = H-node
>
> Registry location: Netbt\Parameters

DhcpScopeId

> Value type: REG_SZ (String)
>
> This value specifies the NetBIOS name scope. If the ScopeId value is present, this parameter is overridden.
>
> Registry location: Netbt\Parameters

Automatic Private IP Addressing

Windows 2000 uses Automatic Private IP Addressing (APIPA) to establish an IP address in the event that the workstation tries and fails to obtain an IP address from a DHCP server. This provides network connectivity to the client on a limited basis.

APIPA uses the IP address range of 169.254.0.1 through 169.254.255.254. The subnet mask is set to 255.255.0.0.

The difficulty with using APIPA is in troubleshooting potential DHCP problems. Normally, if the client does not find a DHCP server, the client does not have IP connectivity. Simple enough, right? Immediately you have an idea where the problem lies. However, what happens if a particular subnet loses DHCP? As leases expire and clients are unable to contact a DHCP server, they all obtain an IP address from the 169.254 range using APIPA. When the user or administrator investigates the problem, he will be able to see and connect to other systems in the 169.254 subnet. The administrator would need to know that this subnet is used for APIPA and that automatic addressing is taking place.

My recommendation is to disable APIPA on all workstations that will be DHCP clients. To disable APIPA, follow these steps:

1. Log on as Administrator or as a user that is a member of the Administrators group.

2. Open the Registry Editor.

3. In the Registry Editor, go to the following key:

   > HKLM\SYSTEM\CurrentControlSet\Services\Tcpip\Parameters\Interfaces\ <Adapter_Name>

   where Adapter_Name is the NIC that is bound to TCP/IP.

4. Create the following entry:

      IPAutoconfigurationEnabled: REG_DWORD

Assign a value of 0. This value disables Automatic Private IP Addressing on that NIC. A value of 1 enables APIPA.

5. If you need to disable APIPA on multiple adapters, add the IPAutoconfigurationEnabled: REG_DWORD entry with the value of 0 at the key:

      HKLM\SYSTEM\CurrentControlSet\Services\Tcpip\Parameters

6. Close the Registry Editor.

IPCONFIG

IPCONFIG is a command line utility that allows a user to diagnose the state of the TCP/IP network configuration. IPCONFIG also allows administrators to release and renew DHCP assigned IP addresses.

IPCONFIG was first introduced with Windows NT 3.5. The release of IPCONFIG in Windows 2000 includes several new options (`displaydns`, `flushdns`, and `registerdns`).

The IPCONFIG command has the following syntax:

```
ipconfig [/? | /all | /release [adapter] | /renew [adapter]
         | /flushdns | /registerdns]
         | /showclassid adapter
         | / setclassid adapter [classidtoset] ]
```

The IPCONFIG switches are described in the following list:

`/?`

    Displays command help.

`/all`

    Displays full TCP/IP configuration information for all bound network adapters.

`/release [adapter]`

    Releases the IP address for the specified network adapter.

`/renew [adapter]`

    Renews the IP address for the specified network adapter.

`/displaydns`

    Lists the contents of the local DNS resolver cache. Hostnames resolved by DNS are cached locally by the client.

`/flushdns`

    Purges the local DNS resolver cache.

/registerdns

Reregisters the client's dynamic DNS entries.

/setclassid

Modifies the DHCP User Class ID.

/showclassid

Displays all class IDs.

Using IPCONFIG to view current IP configuration

To check the current IP configuration for a Windows 2000 computer, simply type **ipconfig** at a command prompt. Output like the following is displayed:

```
D:\>ipconfig
Windows 2000 IP Configuration
Ethernet adapter Local Area Connection:
  Connection-specific DNS Suffix . :
  Autoconfiguration IP Address. . . : 169.254.203.218
  Subnet Mask . . . . . . . . . . . : 255.255.0.0
  Default Gateway . . . . . . . . . :
```

To check the entire current IP configuration for all connections on a Windows 2000 computer, simply type **ipconfig /all** at a command prompt. Output like the following is displayed:

```
D:\>ipconfig /all
Windows 2000 IP Configuration
  Host Name . . . . . . . . . . . . : W2KHOST
  Primary DNS Suffix. . . . . . . . : someco.com
  Node Type . . . . . . . . . . . . : Broadcast
  IP Routing Enabled. . . . . . . . : No
  WINS Proxy Enabled. . . . . . . . : No

Ethernet adapter Local Area Connection:
Connection-specific DNS Suffix . :
  Description . . . . . . . . . . : 3Com Megahertz LAN PC Card (589E) (Ethernet)
  Physical Address. . . . . . . . : 00-10-5A-89-79-60
  DHCP Enabled. . . . . . . . . . : No
  IP Address. . . . . . . . . . . : 192.168.0.10
  Subnet Mask . . . . . . . . . . : 255.255.255.0
  Default Gateway . . . . . . . . :
  DNS Servers . . . . . . . . . . : 192.168.0.10
Ethernet adapter Local Area Connection #2:
Connection-specific DNS Suffix . :
  Description . . . . . . . . . . : 3Com Megahertz LAN PC Card (589E) (Ethernet)
  Physical Address. . . . . . . . : 00-10-5A-9C-6D-6E
  DHCP Enabled. . . . . . . . . . : No
  IP Address. . . . . . . . . . . : 10.0.0.223
  Subnet Mask . . . . . . . . . . : 255.0.0.0
  Default Gateway . . . . . . . . :
  DNS Servers . . . . . . . . . . : 10.0.0.10
```

Using IPCONFIG to refresh hostname registration

A Windows 2000 client registers its hostname via DHCP with DNS. If the registration does not take place or is missing from the DDNS server zone file, an administrator can use IPCONFIG to refresh the DNS registration without restarting the computer.

To refresh the registration of computers with either static or dynamically assigned IP addresses, type **ipconfig /registerdns** at a command prompt.

Using IPCONFIG to assign a DHCP User Class

Windows 2000 DHCP clients support DHCP User Class ID options. You configure this feature by using IPCONFIG along with the `setclassid` switch.

To set and enable DHCP User Class ID on Windows 2000, type the following line at a command prompt:

```
ipconfig /setclassid ADAPTER_NAME USER_CLASS_ID_TO_SET
```

If the User Class ID or Adapter Name contains spaces, enclose it in quotation marks. For example:

```
ipconfig /setclassid "Local Area Connection" "Accounting Department"
```

To clear and disable DHCP Class ID, leave USER_CLASS_ID_TO_SET blank:

```
ipconfig /setclassid "Local Area Connection"
```

Using IPCONFIG to clear the DNS cache

Windows 2000 ships with a client-side DNS cache. Sometimes the client-side DNS caching may make it appear that DNS "round robin" is occurring between the DNS server and the Windows 2000 client.

Round robin is a method of load balancing. With round robin, multiple A resource records exist in a zone for the same hostname. Each A resource record points to the IP address of a different host. When a DNS client queries the DNS server, the DNS server responds with the IP address from one of the A resource records. On the next query for that hostname, the DNS server returns the next IP address, and so on. A very simple method for load balancing, round robin is typically used for web servers and other frequently queried servers.

You may experience a situation where pinging the same hostname may result in the client using the same IP address.

This occurs because the actual DNS request is being sent to the client's DNS cache. If the requested entry is in the DNS cache, Windows 2000 uses the entry and does not make the request to the DNS server. Entries in the DNS cache timeout and are removed after 24 hours.

You may also experience a situation where pinging a hostname results in the client not resolving the IP address, even if you verify that the appropriate resource records exist.

This occurs because Windows 2000 clients have the ability to cache both positive and negative responses returned from the DNS server. In other words, if the DNS server responded that the address could not be resolved, Windows 2000 creates an entry in the DNS cache so future queries regarding that host won't be sent to the DNS server.

To delete the entries in the DNS cache, type **ipconfig /flushdns** at a command prompt.

 You can lower the TTL for entries in the client-side DNS cache if you are experiencing name resolution problems or if you simply want them to be cleared quicker. Locate the MaxCacheEntryTtlLimit entry in the registry at HKLM\SYSTEM\CurrentControlSet\Services\Dnscache\ Parameters. This entry specifies the Time To Live in seconds for cached name requests. The default value for this entry is 86,400 seconds, or 24 hours. If, in essence, you want to disable the DNS cache, you can specify a very short Time To Live, such as one second. Although technically this does not disable the DNS cache, a one second timeout forces the DNS client to go to the DNS server for name resolution.

Windows NT Workstation 4.0

Windows NT Workstation 4.0 is the desktop member of the Windows NT 4.0 family. It combines the power and reliability of Windows NT with the ease of use found in Windows 95.

The major difference between Windows NT Workstation 3.51 and 4.0 is the user interface. As you will see, many of the new features found in Windows NT Workstation 4.0 relate to the GUI.

Some NT Workstation 4.0 features include:

Windows 95 User Interface
Users now benefit from a single common user interface across all Windows platforms.

Windows NT Explorer
Replacing File Manager, NT Explorer displays all computer contents, including network connections, as a single hierarchical tree.

Internet Explorer

Internet Explorer is built in to the OS to provide Internet functionality to users.

System Policies and User Profiles

System policies provide a way for administrators to standardize and enforce system configurations. User profiles allow users to obtain the same customized desktop wherever they log on from.

Installing the Windows NT Workstation 4.0 DHCP Client

Windows NT Workstation 4.0 has a DHCP client built into its TCP/IP stack. During installation, a dialog box is displayed asking the user whether they want to use DHCP.

To install the DHCP client on Windows NT 4.0, follow these steps:

1. Double-click My Computer.

2. Double-click Control Panel.

3. Double-click Network.

4. The Network control panel applet is now displayed (see Figure 6-3). From the tabs along the top of the applet, select the Protocols tab.

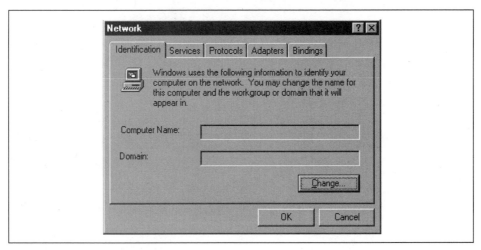

Figure 6-3. The Network applet

5. On the Protocols page, check to see if TCP/IP is installed (see Figure 6-4). If TCP/IP is not listed, you will need to install it.

   a. To install TCP/IP, select Add from the Protocols page. From the list of protocols, select TCP/IP (see Figure 6-4). A warning box is displayed asking if this computer should get TCP/IP information from a DHCP server (see Figure 6-5). Select Yes.

b. Select TCP/IP and pick Properties. The Microsoft TCP/IP Properties dialog box is displayed (see Figure 6-6). Click "Obtain an IP Address from a DHCP server" and click OK. A warning box is displayed asking if this computer should get TCP/IP information from a DHCP server (see Figure 6-5). Select Yes.

6. Windows NT now binds TCP/IP to the network interface cards. Once it is finished, it prompts you to restart the computer. Select Yes for the computer to restart.

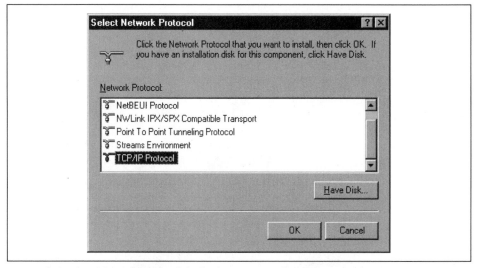

Figure 6-4. Select Network Protocol dialog box

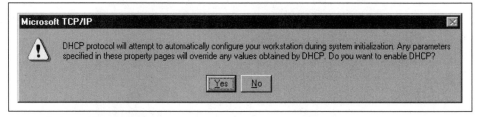

Figure 6-5. Enabling DHCP

Once the computer reboots, it obtains an IP address from an available DHCP server.

To configure the Windows NT Workstation 4.0 DHCP client to not use DHCP, simply select "Specify an IP address" and specify an IP address, subnet mask, and default gateway.

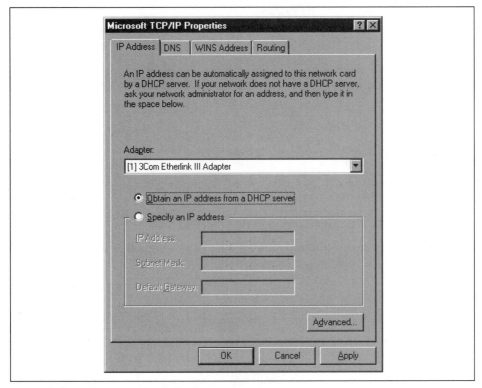

Figure 6-6. TCP/IP Properties dialog box

DHCP Client Configuration Details

The following sections provide additional Windows NT DHCP client configuration information.

Supported DHCP options

The Windows NT DHCP client supports the following DHCP options:

Subnet Mask Option (1)
   This option specifies the subnet mask to be used by the client.

Routers Option (3)
   This option specifies the default gateway.

Domain Name Option (15)
   This option specifies the domain name to be used by the client.

Domain Name Servers Option (6)
   This option lists the DNS servers to be used for hostname resolution by the client.

NetBIOS Name Servers Option (44)

This option lists the WINS servers to be used for NetBIOS name resolution by the client.

NetBIOS Node Type Option (46)

This option determines the NetBIOS node type to be used by the client.

NetBIOS Scope Option (47)

This option specifies the NetBIOS Scope ID to be used by the client.

Registry entries

The Windows NT DHCP Client service stores its configuration information in the following registry key:

HKLM\SYSTEM\CurrentControlSet\Services\Dhcp

The actual TCP/IP configuration information is stored in three other locations:

- HKLM\SYSTEM\CurrentControlSet\Services\Tcpip\Parameters\

  used to register system wide TCP/IP parameters

- HKLM\SYSTEM\CurrentControlSet\Services\<Adapter_Name>\
  Parameters\Tcpip

  used to register TCP/IP parameters bound to a specific network adapter

- HKLM\SYSTEM\CurrentControlSet\Services\Netbt\Parameters\Interfaces\
  Tcpip_<ID for Adapter>

  used to register NetBIOS over TCP/IP parameters

The following registry entry is configurable from the Network Control Panel Applet:

EnableDhcp

Value type: REG_DWORD (Boolean)

If this value is 1, the DHCP Client service will attempt to contact a DHCP server and configure the NIC with a DHCP IP address. If this value is 0, the DHCP Client service is disabled. This value is set to 1 by selecting "Obtain an IP address automatically."

Registry location: <Adapter_Name>\Parameters\Tcpip

The remaining registry entries are not configurable and are entered automatically by the DHCP Client service:

DhcpDefaultGateway

Value type: REG_MULTI_SZ (Multiple Strings)

This value specifies a list of IP addresses that are to be used as default gateways. A default gateway is used to route packets to a network that the system is not connected to (i.e., not on the same subnet). Please note that if a DefaultGateway value is present, this parameter is overridden.

Registry location: <Adapter_Name>\Parameters\Tcpip

DhcpIPAddress

Value type: REG_SZ (String)

This value specifies the IP address obtained by a DHCP server. Please note that if the IPAddress value is other than 0.0.0.0, this parameter is overridden.

Registry location: <Adapter_Name>\Parameters\Tcpip

DhcpNameServer

Value type: REG_SZ (String)

This value specifies the IP addresses of DNS servers to be queried for host-name resolution. If the NameServer value is present, this parameter is overridden.

Registry location: <Adapter_Name>\Parameters\Tcpip

DhcpServer

Value type: REG_SZ (String)

This value specifies the IP address of the DHCP server that granted the IP lease address (found in the DhcpIPAddress parameter) to this DHCP client. The client uses this IP address to renew or release the lease.

Registry location: Tcpip\Parameters

DhcpSubnetMask

Value type: REG_SZ (String)

This value specifies the subnet mask to be used by the DHCP client with the IP address found in the DhcpIPAddress parameter.

Registry location: <Adapter_Name>\Parameters\Tcpip

Lease

Value type: REG_DWORD (Time in seconds)

This value specifies the amount of time that the lease on the IP address found in the DhcpIPAddress parameter is valid.

Registry location: <Adapter_Name>\Parameters\Tcpip

LeaseObtainedTime

Value type: REG_DWORD (Absolute time in seconds since midnight of 1/1/70)

This value specifies the absolute time that the lease was obtained.

Registry location: <Adapter_Name>\Parameters\Tcpip

LeaseTerminatesTime

Value type: REG_DWORD (Absolute time in seconds since midnight of 1/1/70)

This value specifies the absolute time at which the lease expires.

Registry location: <Adapter_Name>\Parameters\Tcpip

T1

Value type: REG_DWORD (Absolute time in seconds since midnight of 1/1/70)

This value specifies the time at which the DHCP Client service will attempt to renew the lease on the IP address found in the DhcpIPAddress parameter by contacting the DHCP server found in the DhcpServer parameter. This value is set to 50% of the time allocated by the Lease parameter.

Registry location: <Adapter_Name>\Parameters\Tcpip

T2

Value type: REG_DWORD (Absolute time in seconds since midnight of 1/1/70)

This value specifies the time at which the DHCP Client service will attempt to renew the lease on the IP address found in the DhcpIPAddress parameter by broadcasting a renewal request. T2 will only be used if the DHCP Client service was unable to renew the lease at T1. This value is set to 87.5% of the time allocated by the Lease parameter.

Registry location: <Adapter_Name>\Parameters\Tcpip

DhcpNameServer

Value type: REG_SZ (String)

This value specifies the primary WINS server to be queried for NetBIOS name resolution. If the NameServer value is present, this parameter is overridden.

Registry location: Netbt\Adapters\<Adapter Name>

DhcpNameServerBackup

Value type: REG_SZ (String)

This value specifies the secondary WINS server to be queried for NetBIOS name resolution. If the BackupNameServer value is present, this parameter is overridden.

Registry location: Netbt\Adapters\<Adapter Name>

DhcpNodeType

Value type: REG_DWORD (Number)

This value (1, 2, 4, or 8) specifies the NetBIOS node type (see Chapter 1 for a description of the various node types). If the NodeType value is present, this parameter is overridden.

Value Range: 1 = B-node, 2 = P-node, 4 = M-node, 8 = H-node

Registry location: Netbt\Parameters

DhcpScopeId

> Value type: REG_SZ (String)
>
> This value specifies the NetBIOS name scope. If the ScopeId value is present, this parameter is overridden.
>
> Registry location: Netbt\Parameters

IPCONFIG

IPCONFIG is a command line utility that allows a user to diagnose the state of the TCP/IP network configuration. IPCONFIG also allows administrators to release and renew DHCP-assigned IP addresses.

The IPCONFIG command has the following syntax:

```
ipconfig [/? | /all | /release [adapter] | /renew [adapter]
```

The IPCONFIG switches are described in the following list:

`/?`

> Displays command help.

`/all`

> Displays full TCP/IP configuration information for all bound network adapters.

`/release [adapter]`

> Releases the IP address for the specified network adapter.

`/renew [adapter]`

> Renews the IP address for the specified network adapter.

More examples of using IPCONFIG can be found earlier in this chapter.

Windows 9x

Windows 95 and its sister upgrades, Windows 98 and Windows Me, provide users with a stable OS platform that supports 32-bit applications as well as older 16-bit Windows 3.x and MS-DOS applications.

The Windows 9x family contains many features, including the following:

New User Interface

> With Windows 95, Microsoft revamped the GUI, providing an interface that is easier to use and customize to the user's needs.

Windows Explorer

> Replacing File Manager, Windows Explorer displays all computer contents, including network connections, as a single hierarchical tree.

Internet Explorer

> Internet Explorer is built into the OS to provide Internet functionality to users.

System Policies and User Profiles
> System policies provide a way for administrators to standardize and enforce system configurations. User profiles allow users to obtain the same customized desktop wherever they login from.

Windows 98 introduced even more new features:

FAT32
> A new file system, FAT32 allows Windows 98 machines to store more data on a physical disk by providing a smaller cluster size (4 KB) than the previous file system, FAT (where the cluster size was 32 KB).

More Devices Supported
> Windows 98 includes better driver support for newer devices, such as USB and DVD.

Internet Connection Sharing (ICS)
> ICS allows multiple networked computers to share a single Internet connection.

Installing the Windows 9x DHCP Client

Before installing the Windows 95 DHCP client, obtain the Windows Sockets 2.0 upgrade. Note that this is for Windows 95 only; Windows 98 ships with the upgraded components. The Windows Sockets 2.0 upgrade fixes a few bugs and provides support for several new features:

- TCP large windows (TCPLW) and timestamps
- Selective acknowledgments
- Fast retransmission and recovery
- DHCP release on shutdown
- DHCP decline
- Per-adapter WINS servers

The Windows Sockets 2.0 upgrade can be found at *http://www.microsoft.com/windows/downloads/bin/W95ws2setup.exe*. Once downloaded, simply double-click the executable to begin installation.

To install the DHCP client on Windows 95/98, follow these steps:

1. Double-click My Computer.

2. Double-click Control Panel.

3. Double-click Network.

4. The Network control panel applet is now displayed (see Figure 6-7). Scroll through the list of components to see if TCP/IP is installed. If TCP/IP is not listed, you will need to install it. To install TCP/IP:

a. Select Add. The Select Network Component Type dialog box is displayed (see Figure 6-8). Select Protocol from the list of components. From the Select Network Protocol dialog box, select Microsoft in the Manufacturers pane, then select TCP/IP from the Network Protocols pane (see Figure 6-9).

b. Select TCP/IP and pick Properties. The Microsoft TCP/IP Properties dialog box will be displayed (see Figure 6-10). Click "Obtain an IP address automatically" and click OK. A warning box will be displayed asking if this computer should get TCP/IP information from a DHCP server. Select Yes.

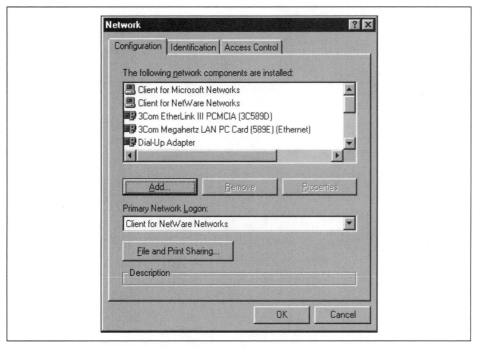

Figure 6-7. Windows 95 Network control panel

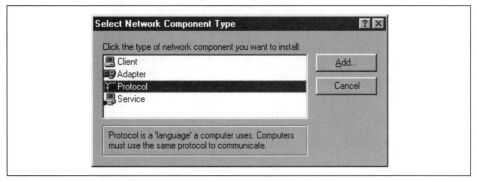

Figure 6-8. Select Network Component Type dialog box

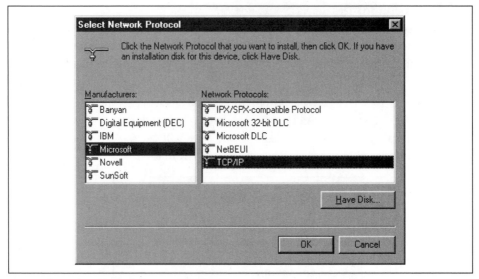

Figure 6-9. Select Network Protocol dialog box

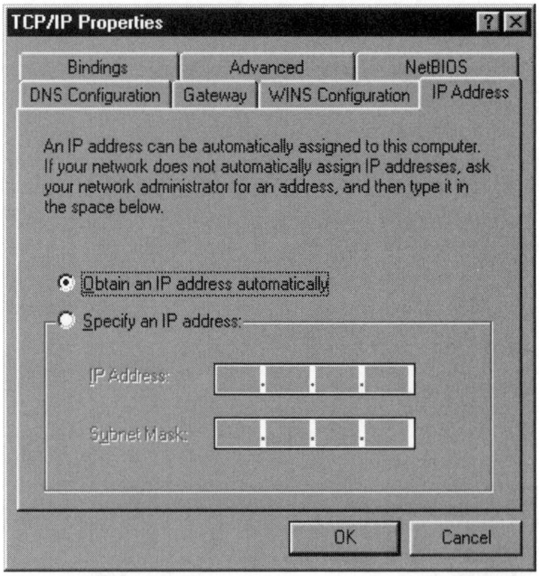

Figure 6-10. TCP/IP Properties dialog box

DHCP Client Configuration Details

The following sections provide additional information about DHCP client configuration for Windows 9x.

Supported DHCP options

The Windows 9x DHCP client supports the following DHCP options:

Subnet Mask Option (1)
> This option specifies the subnet mask to be used by the client.

Routers Option (3)
> This option specifies the default gateway.

Domain Name Option (15)
> This option specifies the domain name to be used by the client.

Domain Name Servers Option (6)
> This option lists the DNS servers to be used for hostname resolution by the client.

NetBIOS Name Servers Option (44)
> This option lists the WINS servers to be used for NetBIOS name resolution by the client.

NetBIOS Node Type Option (46)
> This option determines the NetBIOS node type to be used by the client.

NetBIOS Scope Option (47)
> This option specifies the NetBIOS scope ID to be used by the client.

Registry entries

The Windows 9x DHCP Client service stores its configuration information in the following registry key:

> HKLM\System\CurrentControlSet\Services\VxD\DHCP

Unlike Windows 2000 and Windows NT, there are not many DHCP items found in the Windows 9x registry. Some of note are:

PopupFlag
> This value determines whether the warning that the client was unable to contact a DHCP server is displayed. A value of 1 causes the warning not to be displayed. A value of 0 causes the warning to be displayed.
>
> Registry location: VxD\DHCP

NodeType
> This value (1, 2, 4, or 8) specifies the NetBIOS node type (see Chapter 1 for a description of the various node types). If the NodeType value is present, this parameter is overridden.
>
> Registry location: VXD\MSTCP\NodeType

WINIPCFG

WINIPCFG is a graphical utility for diagnosing the state of the TCP/IP network configuration, much like IPCONFIG in Windows 2000 and Windows NT. It also allows administrators to release and renew DHCP-assigned IP addresses:

1. To start WINIPCFG, select Start → Run, enter WINIPCFG in the Run dialog box, and click OK (see Figure 6-11).

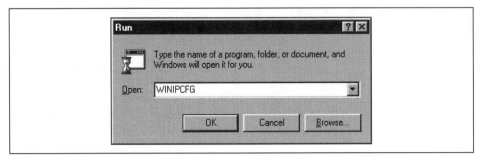

Figure 6-11. Starting WINIPCFG

2. The WINIPCFG dialog box is displayed (see Figure 6-12). By default it displays basic configuration information for the selected adapter, such as the adapter (MAC) address, IP address, subnet mask, and default gateway. You can also release and renew the IP address of the selected adapter, or release and renew all IP addresses for all installed adapters.

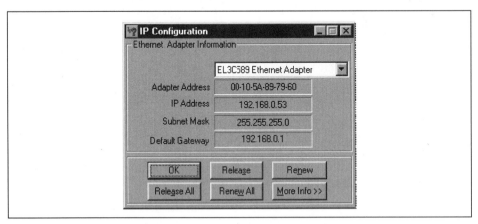

Figure 6-12. WINIPCFG utility

3. To show more configuration information, click the "More Info >>" button (see Figure 6-13).

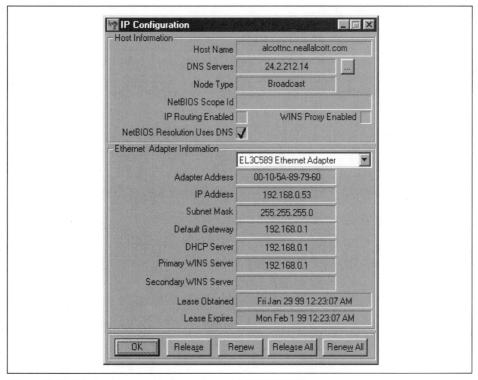

Figure 6-13. Displaying more information with WINIPCFG

Windows for Workgroups

While no longer in wide use, Windows for Workgroups can still be found in corporations that haven't migrated to Windows 9x or Windows NT. It can also be found in smaller companies that don't have the capital to upgrade or are using a 16-bit software package that has not been ported to a 32-bit Windows platform.

Installing the Windows for Workgroups DHCP Client

Before installing the Windows for Workgroups DHCP client, you need to obtain the TCP/IP-32 protocol stack. Windows for Workgroups did not ship with a TCP/IP protocol stack, so it needs to be added. TCP/IP-32 Version B can be found on the Windows NT Server Installation CD or downloaded from Microsoft's web site.

To retrieve TCP/IP-32b from the Windows NT Server CD, go to the *Clients\ TCPIP32WFW* directory. There you will find two subdirectories, *Disks* and *Netsetup*. The *Disks* directory is for making diskettes while the *Netsetup* directory is for network installations. If you look at the two directories, they both contain the same information. It takes exactly one diskette to make the installation disk.

To download TCP/IP-32b from Microsoft's web site, enter the following link in your web browser: *http://www.microsoft.com/downloads*. Next, select Windows for Workgroups as the operating system and click on Search. After the list is returned, look for Windows for Workgroups 3.11 TCP/IP-32 Update Version 3.11b (*Tcp32b.exe*).

To install the DHCP client on Windows for Workgroups, follow these steps:

1. In the Program Manager, pick the File pull-down menu and select Run. In the Run dialog box, enter the command **WINSETUP /Z**.

2. In the Network Setup dialog box (see Figure 6-14), click Drivers.

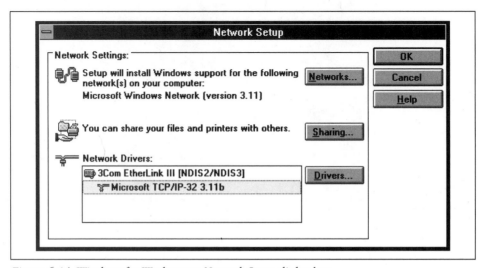

Figure 6-14. Windows for Workgroups Network Setup dialog box

3. In the Network Drivers dialog box, select Microsoft TCP/IP-32 (see Figure 6-15). Pick Setup.

4. The Microsoft TCP/IP Configuration dialog box is displayed. Select "Enable Automatic DHCP Configuration" (see Figure 6-16).

5. A dialog box is displayed asking you if you want to enable DHCP (see Figure 6-17). Select Yes.

6. At the Microsoft TCP/IP Configuration dialog box, click OK.

7. At the Network Drivers dialog box, click Close.

8. At the Network Setup dialog box, click OK.

9. Restart the computer.

Once the computer restarts, it receives an IP address from an available DHCP server.

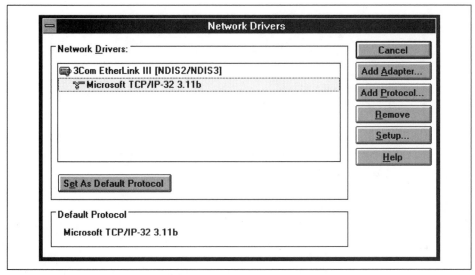

Figure 6-15. Windows for Workgroups Network Drivers dialog box

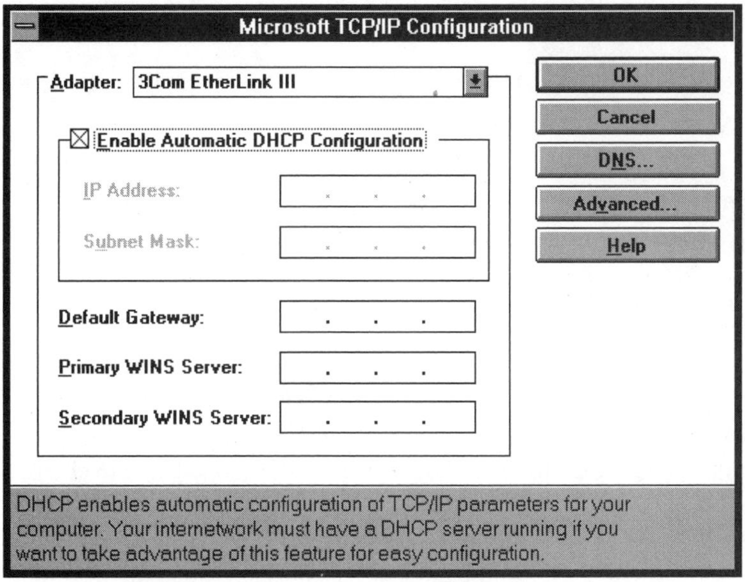

Figure 6-16. Microsoft TCP/IP Configuration dialog box

DHCP Client Configuration Details

The following sections provide additional DHCP client configuration information for Windows for Workgroups systems.

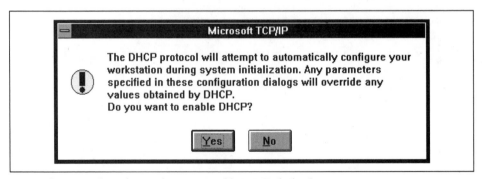

Figure 6-17. Windows for Workgroups Enable DHCP dialog box

Supported DHCP options

The Windows for Workgroups DHCP client supports the following DHCP options:

Subnet Mask Option (1)
 This option specifies the subnet mask to be used by the client.

Routers Option (3)
 This option specifies the default gateway.

Domain Name Option (15)
 This option specifies the domain name to be used by the client.

Domain Name Servers Option (6)
 This option lists the DNS servers to be used for hostname resolution by the client.

NetBIOS Name Servers Option (44)
 This option lists the WINS servers to be used for NetBIOS name resolution by the client.

NetBIOS Node Type Option (46)
 This option determines the NetBIOS node type to be used by the client.

NetBIOS Scope Option (47)
 This option specifies the NetBIOS scope ID to be used by the client.

Configuration files

Configuration settings in Windows for Workgroups are stored in two files, *SYSTEM.INI* and *PROTOCOL.INI*. *SYSTEM.INI* contains system configuration settings, while *PROTOCOL.INI* contains network configuration settings.

DHCP configuration settings are stored in a hidden binary file called *DHCP.BIN* located in the Windows directory.

IPCONFIG

IPCONFIG is a command line utility that allows a user to diagnose the state of the TCP/IP network configuration. IPCONFIG also allows administrators to release and renew DHCP-assigned IP addresses.

The IPCONFIG command has the following syntax:

```
ipconfig { /all | /release | /renew }
```

The IPCONFIG switches are described in the following list:

/all

 Displays full TCP/IP configuration information for all bound network adapters.

/release

 Releases the IP address for the specified network adapter.

/renew

 Renews the IP address for the specified network adapter.

MS-DOS

A DHCP client is included with the Microsoft Network Client v3.0 for MS-DOS. If you need DHCP support for a DOS-based workstation, this is what you will need to make it happen.

Install the Microsoft Network Client v3.0 for MS-DOS, which can be found on the Windows NT Server Installation CD.

To retrieve the Microsoft Network Client v3.0 for MS-DOS from the Windows NT Server CD, go to the *Clients\MSCLIENT* directory. There you will find two sub-directories, *Disks* and *Netsetup*. The *Disks* directory is for making diskettes while the *Netsetup* directory is for network installations. It takes exactly two diskettes to make the installation disk set.

To install the Microsoft Network Client v3.0 for MS-DOS, follow these steps:

1. Change to the directory containing the installation files. Type **SETUP**. A welcome screen is displayed (see Figure 6-18). Press Enter to set up the Network Client.

2. Specify the location Setup will copy the Network Client files to, or select the default, *C:\NET.*

3. Specify the username that will identify you in your workgroup (see Figure 6-19).

4. The next screen lists the options you selected, such as username, setup options, and network configuration (see Figure 6-20). Using the arrow keys, highlight Change Network Configuration and press Enter.

```
Setup for Microsoft Network Client v3.0 for MS-DOS

            Welcome to Setup for Microsoft Network Client for MS-DOS.

            Setup prepares Network Client to run on your computer.

            * To get additional information about a Setup screen,
              press F1.

            * To set up Network Client now, press ENTER.

            * To quit Setup without installing Network Client,
              press F3.

ENTER=Continue  F1=Help  F3=Exit  F5=Remove Color
```

Figure 6-18. MS-DOS Network Client setup

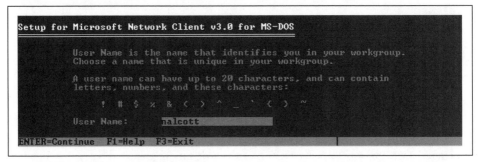

```
Setup for Microsoft Network Client v3.0 for MS-DOS

            User Name is the name that identifies you in your workgroup.
            Choose a name that is unique in your workgroup.

            A user name can have up to 20 characters, and can contain
            letters, numbers, and these characters:

                  ! # $ % & < > ^ _ ` < } ~

            User Name:      nalcott

ENTER=Continue  F1=Help  F3=Exit
```

Figure 6-19. Specifying username

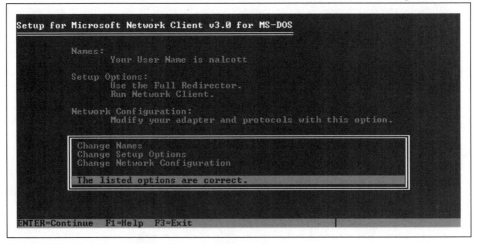

```
Setup for Microsoft Network Client v3.0 for MS-DOS

            Names:
                    Your User Name is nalcott

            Setup Options:
                    Use the Full Redirector.
                    Run Network Client.

            Network Configuration:
                    Modify your adapter and protocols with this option.

            ┌────────────────────────────────────────────────────┐
            │ Change Names                                         │
            │ Change Setup Options                                 │
            │ Change Network Configuration                         │
            │ The listed options are correct.                      │
            └────────────────────────────────────────────────────┘

ENTER=Continue  F1=Help  F3=Exit
```

Figure 6-20. Changing MS-DOS Network Client settings

5. In the Network Configuration screen, use the arrow keys to highlight Add
   Adapter. Select the correct network adapter for your computer and press
   Enter. Now highlight Add Protocol, select Microsoft TCP/IP, and press Enter
   (see Figure 6-21).

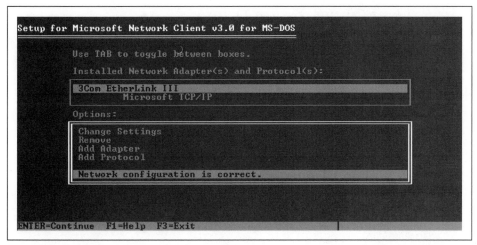

Figure 6-21. Adding and removing components

6. Using the Tab key, toggle to the "Installed Network Adapter(s) and Protocol(s)" box. Using the arrow keys, highlight Microsoft TCP/IP. Toggle to the Options box using the Tab key again, then highlight Change Settings.

A screen is displayed showing TCP/IP configuration settings (see Figure 6-22). By default, DHCP should be enabled. Verify that Disable Automatic Configuration is set to 0. If it is set to 1 (disabled), press Enter and select 0. Highlight "The listed options are correct" and press Enter.

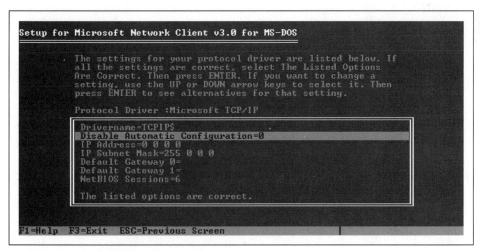

Figure 6-22. Specifying TCP/IP parameters

7. Continue pressing Enter until Setup begins copying the files. When complete, Setup prompts you to reboot your computer.

Once the computer restarts, it receives an IP address from an available DHCP server.

DHCP Client Configuration Details

The following sections provide additional DHCP client configuration information for MS-DOS systems.

Supported DHCP options

The DHCP client found in the Network Client for MS-DOS supports the following DHCP options:

Subnet Mask Option (1)
> This option specifies the subnet mask to be used by the client.

Routers Option (3)
> This option specifies the default gateway.

Domain Name Option (15)
> This option specifies the domain name to be used by the client.

Domain Name Servers Option (6)
> This option lists the DNS servers to be used for hostname resolution by the client.

NetBIOS Name Servers Option (44)
> This option lists the WINS servers to be used for NetBIOS name resolution by the client.

NetBIOS Node Type Option (46)
> This option determines the NetBIOS node type to be used by the client.

NetBIOS Scope Option (47)
> This option specifies the NetBIOS scope ID to be used by the client.

Configuration files

Configuration settings in the Network Client for MS-DOS are stored in two files, *SYSTEM.INI* and *PROTOCOL.INI*. *SYSTEM.INI* contains system configuration settings, while *PROTOCOL.INI* contains network configuration settings.

IPCONFIG

IPCONFIG in the Network Client for MS-DOS differs from the IPCONFIG that ships with Windows for Workgroups and Windows NT. It does not support any of the switches (`all`, `release`, and `renew`) and merely displays configuration information.

Summary

In this chapter, I covered the Microsoft DHCP clients, including brief overviews of each of the operating systems the DHCP client is from.

Windows 2000 Professional includes an improved DHCP client with support for additional DHCP options, such as the Perform Router Discovery (31) and Static Route (33) Options. Windows 2000 also includes Automatic Private IP Addressing (APIPA), which automatically assigns the workstation an IP address in the event that the workstation could not contact a DHCP server. The IPCONFIG utility in Windows 2000 is used to maintain and configure the DHCP client. It includes some new functions relating to the tight integration between DHCP and DNS in Windows 2000.

Windows NT Workstation 4.0 also includes a DHCP client with support for many basic DHCP options. Like Windows 2000, the IPCONFIG utility is used to maintain and configure the DHCP client.

Windows 9x, which includes Windows 95 and Windows 98, includes a DHCP client as well. It uses a graphical interface called WINIPCFG to maintain and configure the DHCP client.

Windows for Workgroups, while nowhere near as dominant as it once was, can still be found in some older networks. It did not ship with a DHCP client, but the client can be obtained from the Windows NT Server CD-ROM or the Microsoft web site. It includes basic DHCP functionality.

Finally, MS-DOS was the last DHCP client discussed. Again, like Windows for Workgroups, MS-DOS does not include DHCP support. A DHCP client can be obtained from the Windows NT Server CD-ROM or the Microsoft web site. And again, the client includes basic DHCP functionality.

7

Advanced DHCP

In the previous three chapters, I discussed the design of a DHCP infrastructure, the installation and configuration of the DHCP servers, and finally the installation and configuration of the DHCP clients.

This chapter is devoted to tidying up the remaining components that relate to the configuration of DHCP in Windows 2000.

In most situations, a basic DHCP implementation contains one or more DHCP servers, scopes, and exclusions, some reservations, and various DHCP options. There are special situations that require the use of some of these advanced DHCP tools, such as superscopes and the DHCP relay agent. This chapter explores these tools and adds them to your DHCP toolbox.

Superscopes

A superscope is a group of scopes that are managed as a single entity. Typically, a superscope is used where a DHCP server is being used to support DHCP clients on a single physical network that has multiple IP subnets in use. This is sometimes referred to as multinetting.

Why would there be multiple logical subnets in use on a single physical network? Sometimes this occurs when a subnet is being depleted of available IP addresses and more addresses need to be used. For example, if a company has a single Class C network address, the company has 254 IP addresses to use. If the company is growing and has used all of these addresses, the company needs to purchase another Class C network address and route the data between the two networks. Since these address ranges are not contiguous, they cannot belong to the same scope. By creating a superscope, the DHCP server is able to manage both Class C networks as a single entity.

Creating a Superscope

Since a superscope must contain multiple scopes, at least one scope must be defined before a superscope can be created. Once the superscope is created, scopes can be added and removed from it.

To create a superscope, follow these steps:

1. In the DHCP Console, right-click on the DHCP server that will contain the superscope. Select "New Superscope . . . " from the menu (see Figure 7-1).

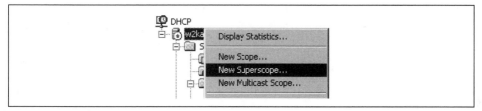

Figure 7-1. Creating a new superscope

2. The New Superscope Wizard starts. Click Next.

3. Enter a name for the new superscope (see Figure 7-2). Click Next.

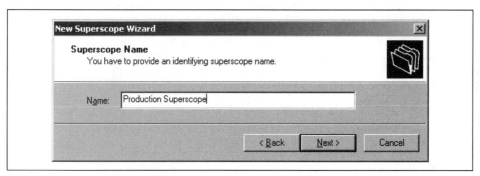

Figure 7-2. Naming the superscope

4. In the Select Scopes dialog box, select the scopes to be included in the Superscope (see Figure 7-3). Use the Ctrl or Shift key to select multiple scopes. Click Next.

5. The next dialog box displays the information you entered. Click Finish to create the superscope.

Adding Scopes to a Superscope

To add a scope to a superscope, select the scope to be added and right-click. From the menu, select Add To Superscope. In the dialog box, select the superscope that the scope should be added to.

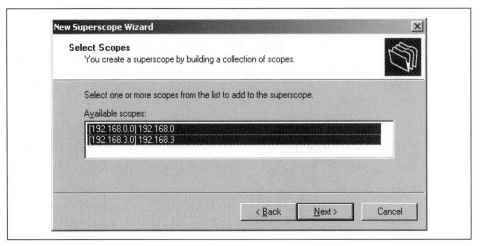

Figure 7-3. Selecting scopes

Activating and Deactivating a Superscope

It is important to remember that a superscope is simply a collection of scopes. It is more of an administrative tool than anything else. As such, when you deactivate a superscope, you are actually deactivating all scopes that are members of the superscope. Conversely, if you activate a superscope, all member scopes are activated.

To activate a superscope, simply right-click on the desired superscope and select Activate from the menu.

To deactivate a superscope, simply right-click on the desired superscope and select Deactivate from the menu.

You can also selectively activate, deactivate, or delete individual member scopes. Right-click on the individual member scope and select Activate, Deactivate, or Delete as desired.

If you delete the last member scope in a superscope, Windows 2000 deletes the superscope as well.

Removing a Superscope

Removing a superscope is simply a matter of right-clicking on the appropriate superscope and selecting Delete. When prompted, answer Yes to the confirmation message and the superscope is deleted.

Deleting a superscope does not affect the scopes that are members of it. They are not removed from the DHCP database.

Delegating Administration

In Active Directory, you can delegate administrative duties to particular users or groups. Delegating administrative control occurs at the organizational unit level. Of course, determining and creating organizational units should follow the structure of your organization.

By delegating administration, you eliminate the need for separate administrative accounts that may have authority over the entire domain. This allows you to limit control to specific areas of the directory for a small number of administrators.

Some organizations have separate teams responsible for administering different services. For example, a company may have a Windows 2000 team that is responsible for administering Active Directory and a network team responsible for administering network services such as DNS and DHCP. Because of their limited responsibilities, you would not want to add the network team to the Enterprise Administrators group. By delegating administration of DHCP servers to the network team, you avoid giving unnecessary rights.

To delegate the ability to authorize DHCP servers to a non-Enterprise Administrator, follow these steps:

1. Open Active Directory Sites and Services. You must be an Enterprise Administrator to do this.

2. From the View menu, select Show Services Node.

3. In the Sites and Services console's tree pane, select NetServices

4. Select the Action pull-down menu and select Delegate Control. This starts the Delegate Control Wizard.

5. Click Next, the click Add to display the users and groups.

6. Locate the group or user account that you want to permit access to the NetServices object.

7. Click Add, then OK.

8. On Tasks to Delegate, select "Create a custom task to delegate," and click Next.

9. Select "This folder, existing objects in this folder, and creation of new objects in this folder" and click Next.

10. Click Full Control for permissions, and click Next.

You have now delegated DHCP administration to the users or groups that you selected.

Using Netsh Commands for DHCP

Netsh is a utility that provides command-line and scripting abilities to Windows 2000. It can be used to manage many of the Windows 2000 networking components, such as routing, interfaces, RAS, DHCP, and WINS.

Netsh operates in three command modes:

Online

> In online mode, Netsh processes commands immediately as they are entered at the Netsh command prompt.

Offline

> In offline mode, commands are collected by Netsh. When the user issues the `commit` global command, Netsh executes the collected commands as a script. The user can also discard collected commands by issuing the `flush` command.

Script

> A script file containing Netsh commands can be executed by issuing the `exec` command at the Netsh command prompt or by using `netsh -f scriptfile`.

Netsh can support multiple Windows 2000 networking components through the use of Netsh helper DLLs. These helper DLLs extend the functionality of Netsh by providing commands that are specific to a particular networking component. These commands allow Netsh to be used in monitoring or configuring the networking component.

To view the currently loaded helper DLLs, enter the following command at the Netsh command prompt:

```
netsh> show helper
```

A list like the following is displayed:

```
Command      Helper GUID  DLL Filename
-------------------------------------------------------------------------------
routing      {65EC23C0}   IPMONTR.DLL
interface    {0705ECA1}   IFMON.DLL
ras          {0705ECA2}   RASMONTR.DLL
dhcp         {0F7412F0}   DHCPMON.DLL
wins         {BF563723}   WINSMON.DLL
aaaa         {1D0FA29B}   AAAAMON.DLL
```

The Netsh helper DLL that provides DHCP functionality is *DHCPMON.DLL*. This DLL provides an alternative to using the DHCP console to administer the DHCP environment in Windows 2000. More importantly, an administrator can create scripts that can be used repeatedly on many DHCP servers in an environment.

To use Netsh DHCP commands at the command prompt, follow these steps (see Figure 7-4):

1. Open a Command Prompt

2. Type **netsh**. You enter Netsh in online mode. Notice that the prompt now reads netsh>.

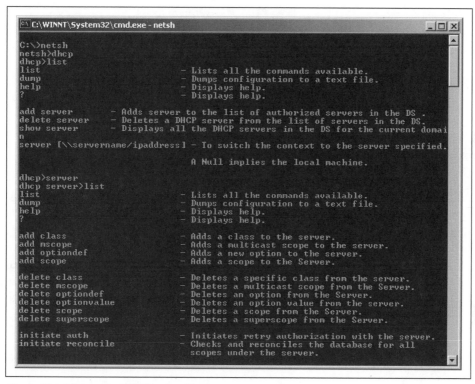

Figure 7-4. Managing DHCP using Netsh

3. At the netsh> prompt, type **dhcp**. Netsh enters the DHCP subcontext, and the prompt is now dhcp>.

4. Type list to display all commands available at that context level. The list of commands changes depending on the current context level. For example, at the DHCP context level, the available commands are add server, delete server, show server, and server \\<*servername*> or server <*ipaddress*>.

5. Type **server \\<*servername*>** or **server <*ip_address*>** to switch to the server you want to manage. If the server you want to manage is local, simply enter **server**.

6. Type **list** to display the commands available at this context level.

As you can see, the list of commands changed dramatically. See Table 7-1 for the complete list of Netsh DHCP first-level commands and descriptions of what they do.

Table 7-1. Netsh DHCP First-Level Commands

Command	Description
add server	Adds a DHCP server to the DHCP console.
delete server	Deletes a DHCP server from the DHCP console.
show server	Displays all DHCP servers currently added under the DHCP console.
server \\<*servername*> or server <*address*>	Shifts the current DHCP command-line context to the server specified by either its name or IP address.

Let's walk through a quick example of using Netsh to create a DHCP scope.

First open a command prompt and type **netsh** to enter the Netsh command mode. If you have ever configured a Cisco router, you will quickly realize that Netsh is very similar to the Cisco IOS command language.

After you start Netsh, you are placed in the main Netsh context. To configure and administrate the DHCP server, you need to switch to the dhcp subcontext. Type **dhcp** at the Netsh command prompt to enter the dhcp subcontext. At this point you are located at the equivalent to the DHCP console, where you can configure and manage the local DHCP server or remote DHCP servers. To switch to the local DHCP server context, you can simply enter **server** and press Enter. If you want to configure a remote DHCP server, type **server** followed by either the DHCP server's name or IP address. For example, to switch to the remote DHCP server, DHCP1, type **server DHCP1**.

Now at the DHCP server context, you can create a new scope. The command is the following:

    add scope <scope ID> <subnet mask> <scope name> <scope description>

where <*scope name*> and <*scope description*> are optional.

For example, I want to create a scope for a production subnet that is located on the first floor of my building. Here is the command I must enter:

    dhcp server>add scope 192.168.1.0 255.255.255.0 "Production Subnet
    192.168.1.0" "Main Production Subnet for 1st Floor"
    Command completed successfully.

As you can see, when Netsh completes the creation of the scope, it reports that the command completed successfully. If there were any problems, Netsh returns a message stating that the command failed due to an incorrect command or another reason such as the server was not available.

Now that the scope itself has been created, I still need to specify the IP address range as well as any exclusions and options I want to configure. To start this, I need to switch to the scope's context in Netsh:

```
dhcp server>scope 192.168.1.0
Changed the current scope context to 192.168.1.0 scope.
```

Once in the scope's context, I can begin to configure the scope. Notice how the Netsh command prompt now says dhcp server scope to let me know that my current context is within a scope:

```
dhcp server scope>add iprange 192.168.1.1 192.168.1.254
Command completed successfully.
```

This specifies that the IP address range will be 192.168.1.1 through 192.168.1.254. Since I have some network devices such as servers and network printers on this subnet, I want to exclude the first 50 IP addresses from the range:

```
dhcp server scope>add excluderange 192.168.1.1 192.168.1.50
Command completed successfully.
```

Also, there is one DHCP client on this subnet that requires a specific IP address at all times. The format of the reservedip command is reservedip <IP address> <MAC address>. Using this command, I can enter the DHCP reservation:

```
dhcp server scope>add reservedip 192.168.1.125 0c001003451c
Command completed successfully.
```

Finally, what is a DHCP scope without some DHCP options? Using the set optionvalue command, you can enter DHCP options. The format of the command is set optionvalue <option ID> <option element type> <option element value>. For this subnet, I want to specify two DNS servers and a default gateway:

```
dhcp server scope>set optionvalue 006 ipaddress 192.168.1.10 192.168.1.11
Command completed successfully.
dhcp server scope>set optionvalue 003 ipaddress 192.168.1.1
Command completed successfully.
```

By using the show optionvalue command, I can confirm that I entered the option values correctly:

```
dhcp server scope>show optionvalue
Options for Scope 192.168.1.0:
 DHCP Standard Option :
 General Option Values:
 OptionId : 51
 Option Value:
 Number of Option Elements = 1
 Option Element Type = DWORD
 Option Element Value = 691200
 OptionId : 3
 Option Value:
 Number of Option Elements = 1
```

```
Option Element Type = IPADDRESS
Option Element Value = 192.168.1.1
OptionId : 6
Option Value:
Number of Option Elements = 2
Option Element Type = IPADDRESS
Option Element Value = 192.168.1.10
Option Element Value = 192.168.1.11
Command completed successfully.
```

Now, when all is said and done . . . or maybe typed and done, you can open the DHCP console and see all of the items that were just configured in Netsh, much like those shown in Figure 7-5.

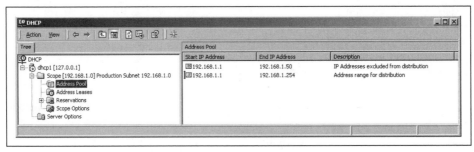

Figure 7-5. DHCP console following Netsh configuration

You can also create a Netsh script. This helps automate many tasks. For example, if you are implementing DHCP on a network that is primarily using static IP addresses, you can create a Netsh script that automatically changes a computer's IP configuration from static to DHCP. Say the network also uses static addresses for DNS and WINS servers, and you want to switch these to DHCP as well. You could execute the Netsh script either manually or from a logon script:

1. First, create a text file called *switchdhcp.scp*. Enter the following commands:

```
interface ip
set address "Local Area Connection" dhcp
set dns "Local Area Connection" dhcp
set wins "Local Area Connection" dhcp
```

 Although the default name for the connection in Windows 2000 is Local Area Connection, it can be renamed. Also, if the workstation is multihomed, there is more than one connection displayed. Verify that you are configuring the correct connection by removing the network cable. The icon changes to show it has been disconnected. Once you have verified the connection, plug the network cable back in.

2. Save the text file.

3. Create a batch file called *switchdhcp.cmd*. This batch file will be called from a logon script to execute the Netsh script. It maps a drive (Z:) to a DHCP server named DHCP1. It also writes a flag file to the workstation. If the flag file is present, the script will not be executed. This keeps the script from executing unnecessarily once the configuration change has been made. The following commands should go in the *switchdhcp.cmd* batch file:

```
if not exist %systemroot%\switchdhcp.flg
    net use z: \\dhcp1\switchdhcp
    netsh -f z:\switchdhcp.scp
    copy z:\switchdhcp.flg %systemroot%\switchdhcp.flg
    net use z: /delete
```

4. Copy the script *switchdhcp.scp* to a common network share, such as *SysVol* in Windows 2000 or *Netlogon* in Windows NT. Add the following command to the logon script:

```
switchdhcp.cmd
```

When a user logs on to the workstation, the workstation executes the logon script, which in turn calls the *switchdhcp.cmd* batch file. The batch file looks for the flag file, *switchdhcp.flg*. If the flag file exists, the Netsh script is not executed. If it is not present, the batch file maps Z: to a network share called *SWITCHDHCP* on the server DHCP1. Next, it executes the Netsh script found on Z:. After the Netsh script is executed, the batch file copies the flag file from Z: to *%systemroot%* (usually *C:\WINNT*) and disconnects from the network share.

To have the user execute a Netsh script, you need to give them the appropriate rights to modify the IP configuration. You can do this by adding them to an administrators group (not recommended) or via Group Policy.

Thanks to the addition of a Telnet Server service to Windows 2000, you can also utilize Netsh to administer remote DHCP servers. Simply start the Telnet Server service on the DHCP server. From a remote workstation, open a command prompt and enter the command **telnet <dhcp server name>**. This will start a telnet session on the DHCP server. At this point, you can use Netsh or execute a Netsh script as though you are at a command prompt on the DHCP server.

To create a Telnet session, you must be a member of the Administrators group on the Telnet server.

Netsh is a powerful utility that can be used to manage many different network components, from a single DHCP server to an entire DHCP infrastructure. Although it may seem like more work to configure a DHCP server with Netsh because of the typing, it gives administrators the option of automating and scripting tasks that may be very time consuming using the GUI interface. Hopefully Microsoft and third-party vendors will continue to add more helper DLLs, extending this functionality.

Configuring Multihomed DHCP Servers

A multihomed server is a computer that is attached to more than one physical network. This requires the installation of multiple network cards in the server.

A multihomed DHCP server is a server that may be providing the DHCP service on multiple physical networks. Although I personally would not recommend the use of a multihomed DHCP server, it can be used in situations where there are two or more network segments that are not connected via a router, or where the network segments are connected with a router but the router does not have any DHCP relay agent functionality. Both of these situations are extremely unlikely, however. The most likely situation is that where the Windows 2000 server is functioning as both a router and a DHCP server.

By default, when DHCP first starts on a multihomed server, the service binds to the first network interface. If this first network interface has a static IP address (which is required to run a DHCP server), the service binds to that card as normal. However, if the first network interface is using a dynamically assigned IP address, the service does not bind to that interface.

In this case, an administrator needs to either assign static IP addresses or selectively bind the DHCP service to an interface with a static IP address.

I will take a moment to describe another situation where the administrator needs to selectively bind the DHCP service to an interface. Let's say that there is a network with two segments. Both of these segments are connected to a Windows 2000 server that is acting as both an IP router and a DHCP server. The first segment contains Windows 2000 Professional workstations. These workstations are using the DHCP service to obtain their IP address configurations. The second segment contains network devices that rely on a BOOTP server. The BOOTP server is located on the second segment. By default, the DHCP service is bound to both network segments. Since both BOOTP and DHCP use the same UDP ports for their conversations (67 and 68), they cannot both be running on the same segment. If they did, some of the network devices would get their configurations from the BOOTP server and the others from the DHCP server. In this case, the administrator should unbind the DHCP service from the network interface that is connected to the BOOTP segment.

You can use the following Netsh command to view the binding on a multihomed DHCP server:

```
D:\>netsh dhcp server show bindings
Binding information : 0
========================================================================
Bound To Server : TRUE
Adapter Primary Address : 10.0.0.10
Adapter Subnet Address : 255.0.0.0
Interface Description : Local Area Connection 2
Interface ID : E3665B450D7DAC4B8633D464055B5352
========================================================================
Binding information : 1
========================================================================
Bound To Server : TRUE
Adapter Primary Address : 192.168.0.10
Adapter Subnet Address : 255.255.255.0
Interface Description : Local Area Connection
Interface ID : C4D2C67C6DC86A4DADE24D9EABDA00F3
========================================================================

Command completed successfully.
```

To modify the bindings, follow these steps:

1. Open the DHCP console.

2. Right-click on the DHCP server. Select Properties.

3. The Properties dialog box is displayed. Select the Advanced tab.

4. On the Advanced page, click on the Bindings button.

5. The Bindings dialog box is displayed (see Figure 7-6). Any connections selected (or checked) are interfaces that are bound to the DHCP server. Uncheck an interface to remove the binding from that network segment.

6. Click OK to apply the settings.

7. Click OK to close the Properties dialog box.

Once finished, you can use the same Netsh command (**netsh dhcp server show bindings**) to verify that the bindings have been changed.

Using a multihomed DHCP server may be more trouble than it's worth. It can be difficult to troubleshoot and maintain. However, if cost is an issue and you are planning to use Windows 2000 as an IP router, this gives you a low cost alternative. Just remember that you have options when it comes to binding the DHCP service to the network segments you desire.

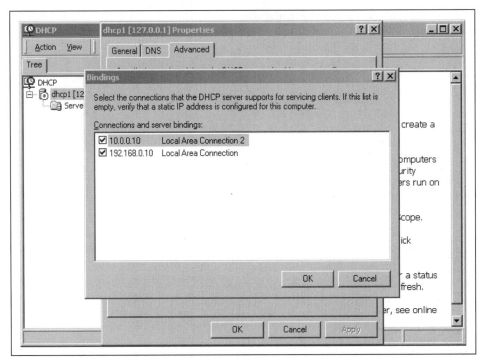

Figure 7-6. Modifying the bindings on a DHCP server

The DHCP Database

The DHCP database is the most critical component in a DHCP infrastucture. Each DHCP server maintains its own database. This database contains the server's current configuration, such as scopes, reservations, exclusions, options, and so on, as well as active leases.

The DHCP database found in Windows 2000 uses the Exchange Server Storage engine v4.0. The files that make up the DHCP database are located in the directory *%systemroot%\system32\dhcp*. They are listed and described in Table 7-2.

Table 7-2. DHCP Database Files

File	Description
DHCP.MDB	The DHCP database file.
DHCP.TMP	A swap file used by the database during maintenance operations.
J50.LOG	A transaction log detailing database activity. These log files are used to recover the database in the event of a failure.
J50.CHK	A checkpoint file.

The DHCP database is backed up automatically every 15 minutes by default. By editing the following registry key, this interval can be changed:

HKLM\SYSTEM\CurrentControlSet\Services\DHCPServer\Parameters\
BackupInterval

The location of the backup copy of the DHCP database located in the directory *%systemroot%\system32\dhcp\backup* by default. The location can be changed by editing the following registry key:

HKLM\SYSTEM\CurrentControlSet\Services\DHCPServer\Parameters\
BackupDatabasePath

You can force a backup copy of the database to be created by stopping and restarting the DHCP service.

Compacting the DHCP Database

The size of the DHCP database is proportional to the number of DHCP clients that the DHCP server is servicing. As such, there is no limitation on the number of entries the database may contain. The database will continue to grow as DHCP clients activate and release leases.

Since the database continues to grow and not contract, the DHCP database must be compacted periodically to recover unused space. This unused space occurs as DHCP clients release their leases or their leases expire.

There are two methods of compacting the DHCP database: dynamic and offline.

Dynamic compacting occurs automatically as a background process during idle time. When the DHCP server does not have any updates to perform on the DHCP database, it starts to compact the database.

Offline compacting is more appropriate for DHCP databases on very large and busy networks. Since the database is constantly being updated, the DHCP server does not have the idle time available to do a dynamic compact. Offline compacting is recommended for DHCP databases that have grown beyond 30 MB in size. The utility that performs an offline compaction is called Jetpack.

The syntax for Jetpack is:

```
jetpack <database_name> <temporary_database_name>
```

database_name

Specifies the name of the original DHCP database file

temporary_database_name

Specifies the name of the file that Jetpack will copy the database information to during the compaction

For offline compacting, the DHCP service must be stopped. To stop the DHCP service, go to Start → Programs → Administrative Tools → Computer Management. In the left-hand pane, select Services and Applications, then double-click Services in the right-hand pane. In the list of services, find DHCP Server. Right-click on DHCP Server and select Stop. In a few seconds the DHCP Server service stops.

Another method of stopping the DHCP Server service is by opening a command prompt by selecting Start → Run and entering **cmd**. Type **net stop dhcpserver** to stop the service.

Next, change to the location of the DHCP database files. At the command prompt type **cd %systemroot%\system32\dhcp**.

Type **jetpack dhcp.mdb tmp.mdb**.

Jetpack now compacts the database. First, Jetpack copies the DHCP database information to the temporary file *tmp.mdb*. After copying the information, Jetpack deletes the original database file *dhcp.mdb*. Finally, it renames the temporary database file, *tmp.mdb*, to the original file, *dhcp.mdb*.

When Jetpack is finished, the DHCP Server service can be restarted.

At the command prompt type **net start dhcpserver**.

You have now performed an offline compaction of the DHCP database.

Offline compacting is usually very fast (within a minute or so), even on DHCP servers that service many DHCP clients. If you find that offline compacting is taking an extended period of time, you can create a batch file that stops the DHCP service, compacts the database, and restarts the DHCP service once complete. This batch file can then be scheduled to execute at a time when there is less network activity, such as 3:00 A.M.

Backing Up and Restoring the DHCP Database

If the DHCP database has been corrupted or lost, there are a few steps that can be performed to recover and restore the DHCP service.

First, determine whether data has been lost or corrupted. If data has been lost or corrupted, check to make sure that it is not related to a hardware or software fault, such as a disk drive failure. Another possibility is that the server may have run out of disk space. In that case, the server will not be able to write changes to the database as it services DHCP clients.

Data corruption can also be detected by examining the System event log for JET database errors. Table 7-3 lists the JET database errors that are generated when database corruption has occurred.

Table 7-3. Jet Database Errors

Event ID	Source	Description
1014	DhcpServer	The JET database returned the following error: -510.
1014	DhcpServer	The JET database returned the following error: -1022.
1014	DhcpServer	The JET database returned the following error: -1850.

Once it has been determined that corruption has taken place, perform an offline compaction using the Jetpack utility as demonstrated earlier in this chapter.

If the offline compaction fails to correct the data corruption, the database will need to be completely restored.

The first option in restoring the database is to restore the DHCP database files from an offline source, such as the latest tape backup.

Another option is to use the Netsh **set databaserestore flag** command. This flag tells the DHCP server to load the database files from the backup database location.

Supporting BOOTP Clients

The DHCP Server found in Windows 2000 responds to requests from both DHCP clients and BOOTP clients. Although the two protocols are similar, they differ in the way they initialize. (See Chapter 2, *In The Beginning: RARP and BOOTP* for more information on BOOTP.)

Besides requesting IP address information (IP address, subnet mask, default gateway), BOOTP clients can request the location of a boot image file. The file is located on a Trivial File Transfer Protocol (TFTP) server. The BOOTP client uses the boot image file to complete its initialization.

Windows 2000 DHCP Server supports BOOTP clients by providing dynamic IP address allocation as well as providing boot file information.

Dynamic IP address allocation is provided by configuring a BOOTP address pool within a DHCP scope on the server. This is covered in detail in Chapter 5.

Setting up the DHCP server to provide boot file information requires two steps:

1. For each BOOTP client, add a client reservation within an active DHCP scope. (see Chapter 5, *The DHCP Server*).

2. In the BOOTP table, add BOOTP entries for each BOOTP client's operating system and hardware platform.

Configuring Cisco Routers

In large routed network environments, routers are used to direct IP packets between different subnets. As such, routers are perfect candidates to be DHCP relay agents.

In this section, I will explain how to configure a Cisco router to act as a DHCP relay agent. Although there are other manufacturers of routing equipment, I am describing this configuration because Cisco is the de facto standard in routers. To configure other routers, please refer to the product documentation.

 There are many aspects to correctly configuring a Cisco router. This book describes the configuration of the DHCP relay agent. Please see other O'Reilly books for more information on configuring Cisco routers.

The following configuration is based on a Cisco Systems 2500 router using the Cisco IOS Release 12.0:

1. Using either Telnet or terminal emulation, establish a connection with the router.

2. If prompted for a password, enter it now.

   At this point, the router is in user mode. User mode can be used to get basic information about the router.

3. Next, enter privileged mode by entering the following command at the console prompt:

   ```
   Router> Enable
   ```

4. If prompted for the enable password, enter it now. The prompt now looks like the following:

   ```
   Router#
   ```

5. To enter configuration mode, the `config terminal` command must be used. The `config terminal` command executes commands entered at the router prompt. Enter **config terminal** at the prompt:

   ```
   Router# config terminal
   Enter configuration commands, one per line. End with CTRL/Z.
   Router (config)#
   ```

6. Enter the following commands:

   ```
   Router (config)# ip forward-protocol udp 67
   Router (config)# ip forward-protocol udp 68
   ```

7. These commands specify that the router will forward broadcast packets from these two ports (67 and 68). If these commands were not entered, all broadcasts would be forwarded.

8. Now the DHCP Relay Agent needs to be started. At the prompt, enter the following commands to change to the router interface that runs the relay agent:

```
Router (config)# interface ethernet 0
```

9. The command ip helper-address <*ip address of dhcp server*> causes the router to act as a DHCP relay agent. Enter the following command at the prompt:

```
Router (config-if)# ip helper-address 192.168.0.1
```

10. Now enter the following commands to exit and save the changes to the router's NVRAM:

```
Router (config-if)# exit
Router (config)# exit
Router# copy running-config startup-config
Building configuration...
[OK]
```

At this point the router has been configured with the IP helper address (or DHCP relay agent). The router immediately forwards any broadcast packets sent to UDP ports 67 and 68 to the IP address specified in the IP helper command.

Configuring Windows 2000 as a DHCP Relay Agent

Windows 2000 ships with a fully RFC1542-compliant DHCP Relay Agent. The DHCP Relay Agent is considered part of RRAS.

Enabling RRAS

To enable RRAS, perform the following steps:

1. Click Start → Programs → Administrative Tools → Routing and Remote Access.

2. In the Routing and Remote Access console, right-click on the computer that will run the DHCP Relay Agent. Select Configure and Enable Routing and Remote Access.

3. If the computer is not listed, right-click on Routing and Remote Access and select Add Server to select another computer.

4. The Routing and Remote Access Server Setup wizard starts. Click Next.

5. On the Common Configurations screen, select Network router and click Next.

6. The Routed Protocols screen is displayed. This screen is used for selecting which protocols are to be routed by this computer. Verify that TCP/IP is selected. Select "Yes, all of the available protocols are on this list." Click Next.

7. On the Demand-Dial Connections screen, select No and click Next.

8. Click Finish to close the Routing and Remote Access Server Setup wizard.

Adding the Windows 2000 DHCP Relay Agent

To add the Windows 2000 DHCP Relay Agent, perform the following steps:

1. Click Start → Programs → Administrative Tools → Routing and Remote Access.

2. In the Routing and Remote Access console, click the plus sign to expand the computer that will run the DHCP Relay Agent. Expand IP Routing, then right-click on General and select "New Routing Protocol" (see Figure 7-7).

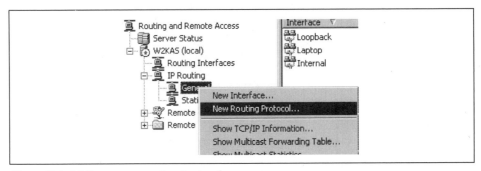

Figure 7-7. Adding a new routing protocol

3. In the New Routing Protocol dialog box, select DHCP Relay Agent and click OK (see Figure 7-8).

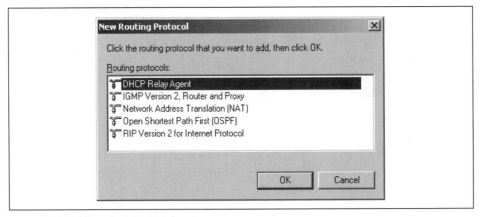

Figure 7-8. Adding the DHCP Relay Agent

4. The DHCP Relay Agent will now be listed below IP Routing. Right-click on DHCP Relay Agent and select Properties.

5. The DHCP Relay Agent Properties dialog box is displayed (see Figure 7-9). Enter the IP address of the DHCP server the relay agent is to forward BOOTP requests to. Click Add to add the IP address to the list. Click OK to close the dialog box.

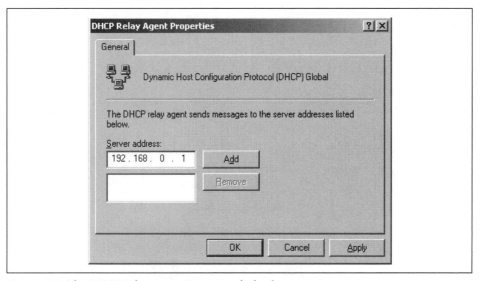

Figure 7-9. The DHCP Relay Agent Properties dialog box

6. Next, enable the DHCP Relay Agent on an interface.

   Right-click on DHCP Relay Agent and select "New Interface . . . "

7. The New Interface for DHCP Relay Agent dialog box is displayed. Select the interface that the DHCP relay agent is to run on (see Figure 7-10). This should be the interface where remote DHCP clients are located. Click OK to close the dialog box.

8. The DHCP Relay Properties are displayed for the interface (see Figure 7-11). Verify that "Relay DHCP packets" is checked.

   "Relay DHCP packets" designates that any BOOTP requests from DHCP clients on the subnet that this interface services will be forwarded to the DHCP server.

   There are two other items listed, "Hop-count threshold" and "Boot threshold." The hop-count threshold designates the maximum number of DHCP relay agents that will handle BOOTP traffic. The boot threshold is used to allow a local DHCP server on the segment to respond before the DHCP relay agent forwards the message. Click OK to start the DHCP Relay Agent.

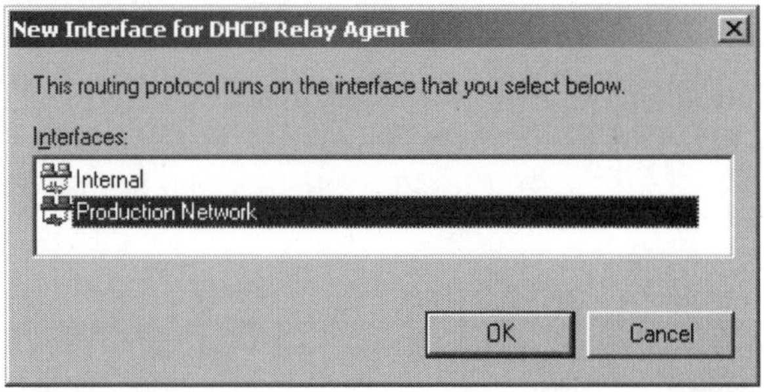

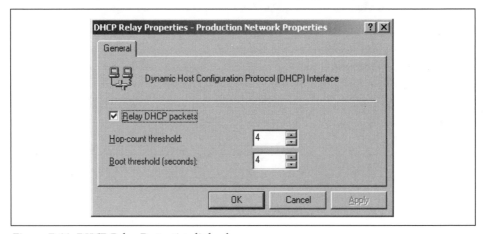

Figure 7-10. Selecting an interface for the DHCP Relay Agent

Figure 7-11. DHCP Relay Properties dialog box

It's important to note that you should never install the DHCP Relay Agent on a Windows 2000 server that is also a DHCP server. Any requests from clients being sent to the DHCP server will be captured by the DHCP relay agent, and they will never get to the DHCP server.

Summary

This chapter discussed some the advanced features found in the Windows 2000 DHCP Server. Although not all of these features would be used in a typical DHCP implementation, it is important to realize and understand all of the different tools that are in your Windows 2000 DHCP toolbox.

The DHCP Server in Windows 2000 includes the ability to create superscopes. Superscopes are a group of scopes that are managed as a single entity, typically used where a single DHCP server is supporting multiple IP subnets on a single physical network.

In Windows 2000, an administrator can delegate the task of administering DHCP servers to a particular user or group. This can help ease the administrative burden on an Enterprise Administrator.

Netsh is a command-line utility that operates a lot like the Cisco IOS command language found in Cisco routers and switches. It is a powerful utility that can be used to configure a DHCP server without the use of the DHCP console. It can also be used by administrators to create batch files and scripts to help ease redundant administrative tasks.

When using DHCP Server on a multihomed Windows 2000 server, an administrator has the capability of selectively binding the DHCP service to particular network interfaces.

The DHCP database is a critical element in a DHCP server that contains all aspects of the server's configuration, such as scopes and active leases. The database found in the Windows 2000 DHCP Server is based on the Exchange Server Storage Engine v4.0. This is a transaction logging database engine. The DHCP Server contains a utility called Jetpack that helps maintain the database.

The Windows 2000 DHCP Server contains support for BOOTP clients. The DHCP Server provides dynamic IP address allocation as well as boot file information.

Finally, the chapter concluded with a discussion of the configuration of a couple of DHCP relay agents found in Cisco routers and Windows 2000.

8

Multicasting: Using MADCAP

With the introduction of Windows 2000, Microsoft added a number of advanced features to the DHCP Server. Many of these features have been discussed in earlier chapters. The new DHCP Server in Windows 2000 also includes the ability to automatically assign multicast IP addresses to DHCP clients. This chapter is dedicated to discussing multicast address allocation via DHCP.

Multicast Address Allocation

Administrators can benefit from having a service, much like DHCP, that automatically assigns multicast addresses to clients. This new service is known as Multicast Address Dynamic Client Allocation Protocol (MADCAP). MADCAP is currently defined in RFC2730 (*http://www.ietf.org/rfc/rfc2730.txt*).

But before I dive into MADCAP, let's take a moment to define what multicasting is.

Most communication that occurs on a network is in the form of unicast messages. A unicast message is a single point-to-point message between a sender and a receiver (see Figure 8-1). TCP and UDP use this method of communication.

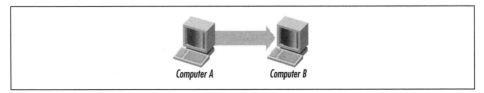

Computer A   Computer B

Figure 8-1. Unicasting

Another type of message is the broadcast message. A broadcast message is sent from a sender to all computers on the network (see Figure 8-2). As noted in earlier chapters, DHCP relies on this form of communication.

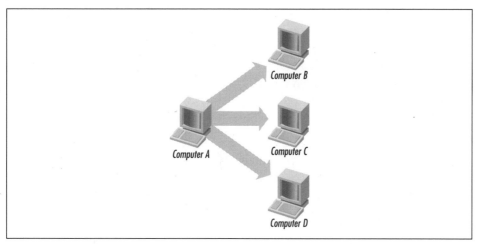

Figure 8-2. Broadcasting

A multicast message is a combination of the unicast and broadcast messages. It provides a bridge between unicasting and broadcasting. Multicasting allows a computer to send a single message to a group of computers. Only computers that are in that group listen for and receive the multicast message (see Figure 8-3). With unicasting, if a computer wants to send messages to a group of computers, it needs to replicate the messages and address each individually to each destination. With broadcasting, all computers receive the message, even though some computers may not want to receive it. As you can see, multicasting is more efficient for both the sender and potential receivers in the conversation.

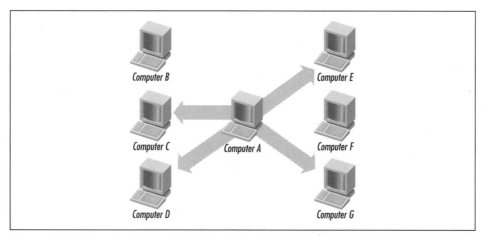

Figure 8-3. Multicasting

Multicast addresses are typically used for applications such as real-time audio and video conferencing. Members of the multicast group are identified by their group membership, also known as the multicast IP address. Group membership, as it pertains to multicasting, is a method of determining which multicast transmissions the client should receive. For example, a company has two separate groups communicating via a multicast application. The users' computers in the first meeting are in the multicast group 224.0.0.10. The users' computers in the second meeting are in the multicast group 236.1.15.12. All computers with the multicast address 224.0.0.10 will receive the transmissions for the first group. Those with the multicast address 236.1.15.12 would receive the other transmission.

Multicast addresses are defined by RFC1112, "Host Extensions for IP Multicasting" (*http://www.ietf.org/rfc/rfc1112.txt*). Multicasting uses a best effort form of delivery, where packets are not guaranteed to arrive and may not arrive in the correct order.

Multicast addresses are identified as Class D IP addresses. Therefore, the first 4 bits in a Class D address are 1110 (see Chapter 1, *TCP/IP Overview*, for more information on IP addressing). Since multicasting is used by a group of computers, it is more accurate to think of multicast addresses as multicast group addresses. Multicast group addresses can range from 224.0.0.0 to 239.255.255.255. An individual multicast address can service many hosts, since transmissions are multicast, not unicast. Therefore all computers in a group need the same multicast IP address to communicate. The only exceptions are that the group address 224.0.0.0 cannot be used, and 224.0.0.1 is considered a permanent group for all IP hosts.

So, in a complex environment like the Internet where there are many different subnets, how does a computer that wants to receive multicast messages do so, and a computer that does not wish to receive the messages avoid getting them?

If a computer is configured to be part of a multicast group, the computer must notify its nearest router that it is a member of the group and wishes to receive multicast messages. The router keeps a list of multicast groups on each attached physical network. Note that this is simply a list of multicast groups, not a list of group members. The routers share this list with other routers using Internet Gateway Multicast Protocol Version 2 (IGMP), defined in RFC2236 (*http://www.ietf.org/rfc/rfc2236.txt*). This allows the routers to form a chain from the members of the multicast group back to the sending computer.

In Windows 2000, Microsoft added MADCAP support to the DHCP Server. Although DHCP and MADCAP are combined into a single service, it is important to remember that they are quite independent of one another. DHCP is strictly used for dynamically allocating unicast addresses, while MADCAP is strictly used for dynamically allocating multicast addresses.

The MADCAP Conversation

Much like DHCP, multicast address allocation uses a client/server architecture. The server side delivers multicast addresses to clients, while the client side is implemented as an API that applications can use to request, renew and release the addresses.

As such, there are two main components in the MADCAP conversation: the client piece and the server piece.

The INFORM message

The MADCAP conversation begins when the multicast client sends an INFORM message. The INFORM message is used by the client to request configuration information, such as a list of multicast scopes. This message can be unicast if the client knows the address of the MADCAP server, or it can be multicast to the MAD-CAP server multicast address if an address is not known. This multicast address is determined by subtracting one from the last address of the local scope or 239.255. 0.0/16. Therefore the MADCAP server multicast address is 239.255.255.254.

The local scope multicast address is defined in RFC2365, "Administratively Scoped IP Multicast" (*http://www.ietf.org/rfc/rfc2365.txt*), and is used as a private multicast address space. In other words, if an organization wants to take advantage of multi-casting technology but does not need to connect to other sites or the Internet, it can use the local scope.

The INFORM message includes an option request list (see the next section in this chapter for a list of all available MADCAP options). The list typically includes the multicast scope list (see Figure 8-4).

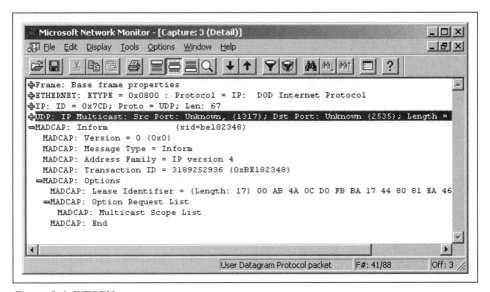

Figure 8-4. INFORM message

The ACK message

If a MADCAP server receives an INFORM message, it must send a unicast ACK message back to the client (see Figure 8-5). The MADCAP server should also attempt to include the options requested by the client (the multicast scope list).

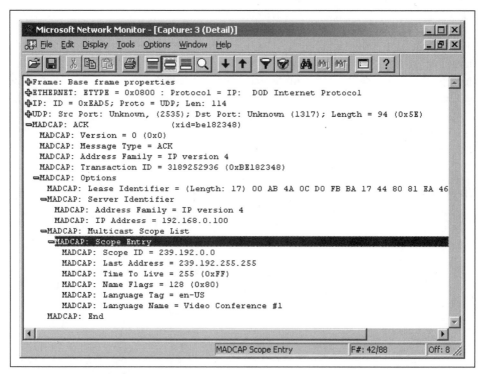

Figure 8-5. ACK message

The DISCOVER message

The DISCOVER message is used by a client to look for an available MADCAP server (see Figure 8-6). It is important to note that clients are not required to use the DISCOVER message. They can use an INFORM message as well.

The DISCOVER message includes MADCAP options such as Multicast Scope, Lease Time, Minimum Lease Time, and Maximum Lease Time. These options are used to notify the MADCAP server what the client wants to receive. Other options that must be included in the DISCOVER message are Current Time and Lease Identifier.

The client sends the DISCOVER message to the MADCAP server multicast address, as defined earlier.

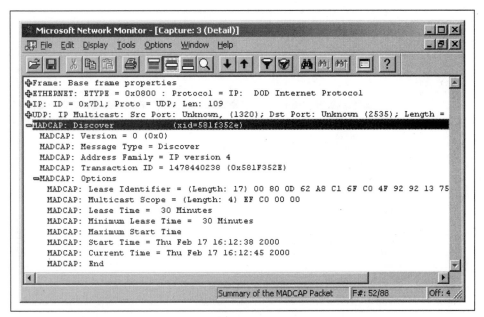

```
Microsoft Network Monitor - [Capture: 3 (Detail)]                    _|□|×|
File   Edit   Display   Tools   Options   Window   Help                _|8|×|

⊞Frame: Base frame properties
⊞ETHERNET: ETYPE = 0x0800 : Protocol = IP:  DOD Internet Protocol
⊞IP: ID = 0x7D1; Proto = UDP; Len: 109
⊞UDP: IP Multicast: Src Port: Unknown, (1320); Dst Port: Unknown (2535); Length =
⊟MADCAP: Discover            (xid=581f352e)
  MADCAP: Version = 0 (0x0)
  MADCAP: Message Type = Discover
  MADCAP: Address Family = IP version 4
  MADCAP: Transaction ID = 1478440238 (0x581F352E)
⊟MADCAP: Options
  MADCAP: Lease Identifier = (Length: 17) 00 80 0D 62 A8 C1 6F C0 4F 92 92 13 75
  MADCAP: Multicast Scope = (Length: 4) EF C0 00 00
  MADCAP: Lease Time =  30 Minutes
  MADCAP: Minimum Lease Time =  30 Minutes
  MADCAP: Maximum Start Time
  MADCAP: Start Time = Thu Feb 17 16:12:38 2000
  MADCAP: Current Time = Thu Feb 17 16:12:45 2000
  MADCAP: End

                          Summary of the MADCAP Packet    F#: 52/88        Off: 4
```

Figure 8-6. DISCOVER message

The OFFER message

The OFFER message is sent by the MADCAP server. It is a unicast message sent to the client that sent the DISCOVER message (see Figure 8-7). The OFFER message must include the Lease Time and Multicast Identifier options. These options describe the multicast addresses the server can distribute. Also included are the Server Identifier and Lease Identifier options.

The REQUEST message

Once the client has received OFFER messages from one or several MADCAP servers, the client selects an offer (see Figure 8-8). After it selects the offer, it must multicast a REQUEST message to the MADCAP server multicast address. This is done to notify all MADCAP servers that sent OFFER messages that the client's request has been satisfied.

Again, much like the DISCOVER message, the REQUEST message includes MADCAP options such as Multicast Scope, Lease Time, Minimum Lease Time, and Maximum Lease Time. These options describe the multicast addresses that the client wants to receive.

Once the MADCAP server receives the REQUEST message from the client, the MADCAP server enters the lease and sends an ACK message back to the client.

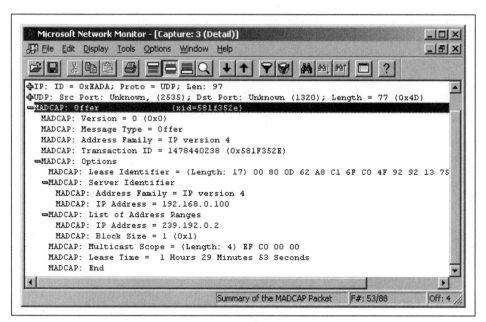

Figure 8-7. OFFER message

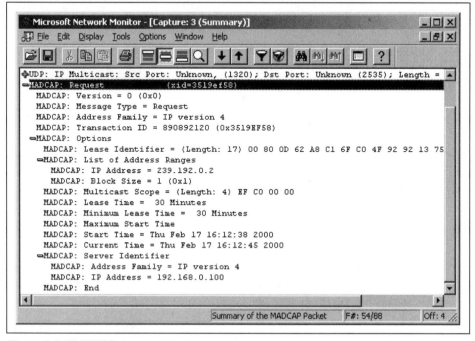

Figure 8-8. REQUEST message

The NAK message

The NAK message, which stands for Negative AcKnowledgment, is used by a MADCAP server to respond negatively to an INFORM, DISCOVER, REQUEST, or RENEW message. In this case, the MADCAP server being contacted is not able to respond to the request.

The RENEW message

The RENEW message is a unicast message sent from the client to the MADCAP server that currently holds its lease. This message is used by the client to renew a lease or change the lease time or starting time.

The RELEASE message

The RELEASE message is a unicast message sent from the client to the MADCAP server that currently holds its lease. This message is used by the client to release its multicast addresses.

MADCAP Options

All MADCAP messages include a field that is used to define MADCAP options. This section describes the available MADCAP options:

End

> The End option is used to designate the conclusion of options found in the options field.

Lease Time

> The Lease Time option is used in client messages (DISCOVER, REQUEST, or RENEW) to request a lease time duration for a multicast address. In server messages (OFFER or ACK), this designates the lease time duration that the server is offering.

Server Identifier

> The Server Identifier option holds the IP address of the MADCAP server. Messages sent by a MADCAP server include this option. A client includes this option in a REQUEST message to designate which MADCAP server it is accepting a lease from.

Lease Identifier

> The Lease Identifier option is used to designate which lease a client or server is referring to.

Multicast Scope

> The Multicast Scope option is used to indicate which multicast scope the client is requesting. This option is used in DISCOVER and REQUEST messages.

Option Request List

The Option Request List is used by the client in an INFORM message to request certain options from the server. The server includes these options when it responds with an ACK message.

Start Time

The Start Time option designates the starting time of a multicast address lease.

Number of Addresses Requested

The Number of Addresses Requested option designates the number of multicast addresses the client would like to lease.

Requested Language

This option is specifies the language to be used in items such as time zones.

Multicast Scope List

This option lists the available multicast scopes from which the client can choose.

List of Address Ranges

This option is used by the MADCAP server to list the range of addresses allocated to the client.

Current Time

This option specifies the sender's current time. It is used to determine if the two systems' clocks are out of sync.

Feature List

This option is used to specify any options supported, requested, or required by the sender.

Retry Time

This option specifies when a client can retry a REQUEST or RENEW message.

Minimum Lease Time

This option is used when a client makes a request to a MADCAP server. It is used to specify a minimum lease time. If the MADCAP server cannot supply a lease with this minimum lease time, the server cannot send an OFFER message.

Maximum Start Time

This option designates the absolute latest starting time that the client will accept for a multicast address lease.

Installing the MADCAP Service

To install the MADCAP service, follow these steps (assuming DHCP is not installed):

1. Double-click My Computer, then double-click Control Panel.

2. Double-click Add/Remove Programs, then click Add/Remove Windows Components (see Figure 8-9).

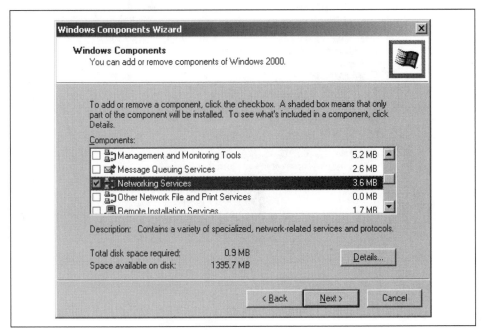

Figure 8-9. Adding Windows components

3. In the component list, select Networking Services, then click Details.

4. Check Dynamic Host Configuration Protocol (DHCP) and then click OK (see Figure 8-10).

5. Click Next in the Windows Component Wizard dialog box.

6. Click Finish, then click Close to close Add/Remove Programs.

Creating Multicast Scopes

Multicast scopes, much like regular DHCP scopes, define the IP address range of the scope, including the lease durations and any exclusions.

Now that the MADCAP service is installed, follow these steps to create multicast scopes:

1. In the DHCP console, right-click on the DHCP server that will contain the scope. Select "New Multicast Scope . . . " from the menu (see Figure 8-11).

2. The New Multicast Scope Wizard starts. Click Next on the Welcome screen.

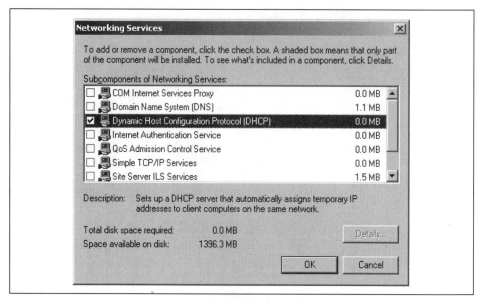

Figure 8-10. Installing DHCP

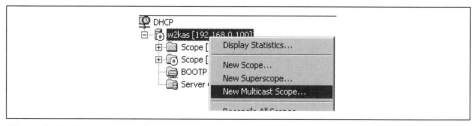

Figure 8-11. Creating a multicast scope

3. Enter a name and description for the new multicast scope. This name will be used to identify the scope (see Figure 8-12). Click Next.

4. Now define the multicast scope address range (see Figure 8-13). The range must be within the valid address range for multicasting (224.0.0.0 to 239.255. 255.255). Enter the starting IP address and the ending IP address. Next enter the Time to Live (TTL) value. The TTL value can be used to limit the propagation of multicast packets throughout an internetwork. This value determines the number of routers that the multicast traffic is permitted to pass through. Each time a multicast packet passes through a router, the TTL value is decremented by one. Once the multicast packet's TTL reaches zero, it is no longer permitted to propagate through the network and is dropped. It is possible to enter 255, which is the maximum value for TTL.

5. Next, enter any address exclusions. An address exclusion is an IP address that is included in the scope range but that the MADCAP server will not distribute.

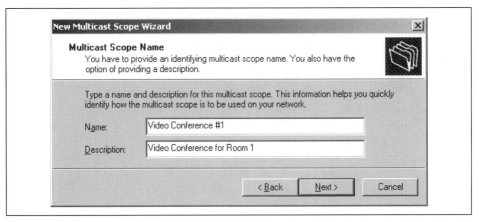

Figure 8-12. Entering a multicast scope name

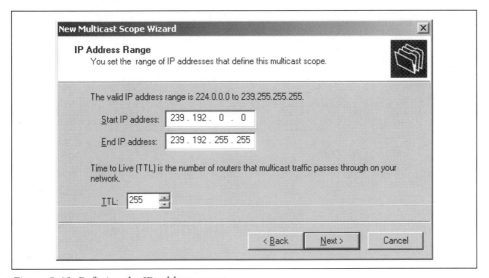

Figure 8-13. Defining the IP address range

6. Next, specify the lease duration to be used for this scope. Lease duration defaults to 30 days.

7. Now you are asked to activate the scope. Select Yes and click Next.

8. Click Finish to create the multicast scope.

In the DHCP console, the multicast scope is now listed below the DHCP scopes.

Summary

In this chapter, I explained the concept of multicasting. Unlike unicast, which is a form of point-to-point communication, and broadcasting, where all computers on a network receive the transmission, multicasting is the process of sending IP packets to a group of systems. Multicasting is typically used in applications that support real-time audio and video conferencing.

In Windows 2000, Microsoft has added a new feature to the DHCP service that creates a MADCAP server. The MADCAP server can be used to dynamically allocate multicast addresses to systems on the network. In this chapter, I walked through the process MADCAP uses to determine which addresses to assign. I then explained how to install and configure the MADCAP server.

9

DHCP Failover: Using Clusters

In this chapter, I will be discussing the use of the Cluster service included in Windows 2000 Advanced Server and Datacenter Server.

The Cluster service allows multiple nodes to be combined to work in unison, either to divide workload or to provide failover capabilities. Combining the Cluster service with the DHCP service provides a degree of DHCP failover.

The installation of a DHCP cluster is a lengthy and detailed process. This chapter explains many of the steps in planning and installing the DHCP cluster.

Windows Clustering

In Windows NT 4.0 Enterprise Edition, Microsoft included a new service known as Windows Clustering. Commonly known as the Cluster service, it is one of two services designed to provide high availability to Windows 2000. The other service is called Network Load Balancing. These services are only available in Windows 2000 Advanced Server and Windows 2000 Datacenter Server.

Applications that may require high availability are typically enterprise applications such as messaging, databases, and yes, DHCP.

Clusters enable a collection of computers to act as one entity. This collection of computers can then share application load or provide failover protection without the user having any knowledge that several servers are involved.

The Cluster Service

The Cluster service makes it possible to connect multiple servers together to form *server clusters*. Server clusters provide increased availability: multiple servers in the server cluster can continue to provide services if one component fails. The administrator can manage the cluster as though she is managing a single server. All devices and resources in the cluster appear as components of a single system.

Cluster configurations

A node is a server or computer that is a member of a cluster. In other words, a node is a computer that contains typical server components, such as system boards, network adapters, and internal disk storage. Two or more nodes work together to form a cluster. In a cluster, the nodes provide fault tolerance for one another because each node contains independent hardware and software. In a Windows 2000 cluster, in addition to the above requirements, a node must be running Windows 2000 Advanced Server or Windows 2000 Datacenter Server with the Cluster service running.

Nodes in a cluster use local and common resources. Local resources are the devices, such as disk drives and network cards, that only the node uses. Common resources are devices to which all nodes in the cluster have access. These devices are typically a data storage array and the private cluster network.

With Windows 2000 Advanced Server, the Cluster service supports up to two nodes in a server cluster (see Figure 9-1).

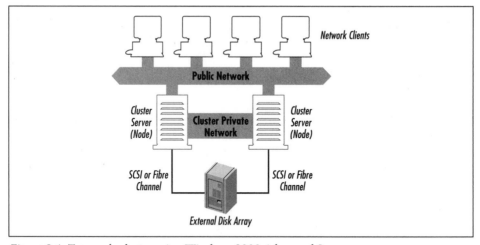

Figure 9-1. Two-node cluster using Windows 2000 Advanced Server

With Windows 2000 Datacenter Server, the Cluster service supports up to four nodes in a server cluster (see Figure 9-2).

Virtual servers

With the Cluster service, applications running with the server cluster can appear to users as *virtual servers* (see Figure 9-3). When client applications connect to an

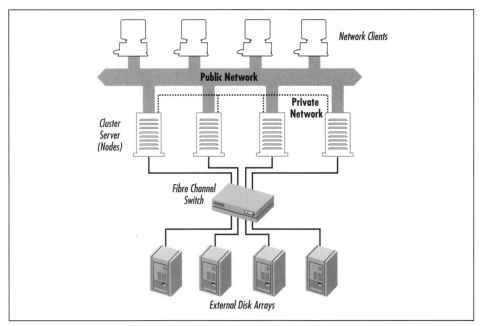

Figure 9-2. Four-node cluster using Windows 2000 Datacenter Server

application on a virtual server, the connection appears as a single server. The client can be connected to any node in the server cluster, but the client will not be aware of which node is hosting it.

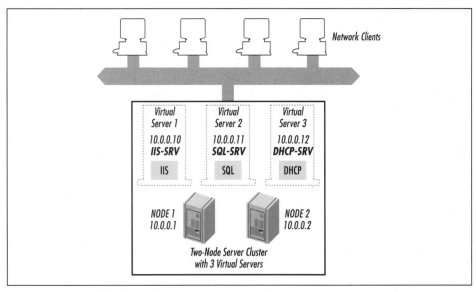

Figure 9-3. Example of virtual servers

Resource groups

A *resource group* is a collection of resources (applications, devices, and data) that the Cluster service treats as a single logical resource. The resource group is managed by the Cluster service. Any operation performed on the resource group affects all individual resources in the group.

Each resource group has a network name and IP address to allow clients to connect to the services it provides.

Application requirements

Before an application can run using the Cluster service, the application must meet certain requirements:

The clients must connect using TCP/IP.
Clients accessing the application on the server cluster must use TCP/IP, DCOM, Named Pipes, or RPC over TCP/IP. Other network protocols, such as NetBEUI and IPX/SPX, cannot take advantage of the failover capabilities that a server cluster provides.

Clients must support automatic reconnect.
When a failover occurs, clients lose network connectivity. If the clients can automatically reconnect, they can continue operating. If not, the client may need to be rebooted.

The application must specify where application data is to be stored.
The application must store data on a disk located on a shared bus, i.e., a bus used by all servers in a cluster. If the application stores data on a disk located on a non-shared bus, the data will not be available if the server containing the disk fails.

Hardware requirements

The Cluster service uses the *shared-nothing* cluster architecture. Shared-nothing architecture means that the cluster nodes share a common bus (data or network), but devices attached to that bus are selectively owned and managed by a single node at a time.

The consideration when planning a Windows 2000 cluster is choosing an external data storage infrastructure.

Since the disk drives or disk array must be common to the entire cluster, an external device must be used. The Cluster service requires the use of one of the following technologies for connecting external data storage devices: a shared SCSI (pronounced "skuzzy") bus or Fibre Channel.

The Small Computer System Interface (SCSI) is an interface that allows computers to communicate with hardware devices such as disk drives, tape drives, CD-ROM drives, and scanners.

There are a number of different SCSI standards (see Table 9-1). As SCSI evolved, the newer standards increased performance and reliability, while maintaining backwards compatibility with older SCSI standards.

Table 9-1. SCSI Standards

SCSI Standard	Maximum Speed (MBps)	Maximum Number of Devices	Maximum Cable Length (meters)
SCSI-1	5	8	6
SCSI-2	5–10	8 or 16	6
Fast SCSI-2	10–20	8	3
Wide SCSI-2	20	16	3
Fast Wide SCSI-2	20	16	3
Ultra SCSI-3, 8-bit	20	8	1.5
Ultra SCSI-3, 16-bit	40	16	1.5
Ultra-2 SCSI	40	8	12
Wide Ultra-2 SCSI	180	16	12
Ultra-3 SCSI	160	16	12

SCSI is a bus technology. SCSI allows multiple devices to be connected to the bus, in a daisy chain fashion. Devices on a SCSI bus can use one of two methods of transmission:

Single-ended

> Single-Ended SCSI refers to the method that devices use to create a signal connection between the host SCSI adapter and the SCSI devices. In the SCSI cable, the signal connection uses one lead for data and one lead for ground. Although single-ended SCSI is less expensive, it is more prone to noise problems. This, in turn, requires the use of shorter cable lengths.

Differential

> With differential SCSI, two signal lines are created. The voltage difference between the two lines is the signal. This, in turn, creates greater noise immunity, and thus greater cable lengths can be used with differential SCSI.

Single-Ended and Differential SCSI devices are not compatible on the same bus.

So, how does SCSI work?

Well, let's start with understanding how a computer talks to its peripherals. In a computer, devices are connected together via the system bus. When the system needs to use a device such as the hard drive, it sends an interrupt signal to the device. Every device has its own interrupt. When the device sees this interrupt, it responds to the request from the system.

The problem with using interrupts is that there are only a limited number of interrupts available. When they are exhausted, no more devices can be attached to the system.

SCSI solves this dilemma by creating another bus. By adding a SCSI host adapter, a second bus is created. SCSI devices attached to this bus use SCSI IDs, a different method of communication, instead of interrupts. When a device is needed, the SCSI host adapter sends a software command (instead of an interrupt) to the SCSI ID. The SCSI device in turn responds to the request. Since only one interrupt is used (by the SCSI host adapter), and the host adapter processes all requests, SCSI is efficient and flexible.

Fibre Channel is a technology that can transmit data up to 1 Gbps between computer devices. These devices can be disk drives, disk arrays, tape devices, or CD-ROM libraries. Hence, with its three-fold increase in performance, Fibre Channel is considered the storage interface that will replace SCSI.

Designed as a channel and network standard, Fibre Channel utilizes network features to provide connectivity, distance, and protocol multiplexing. It also utilizes channel features for simplicity, performance, and guaranteed delivery.

Fibre Channel accomplishes this by creating a Fibre Channel physical layer protocol. This allows upper-layer protocols, e.g., IP or ATM, to function seamlessly and use Fibre Channel just as they would use Ethernet.

Fibre Channel operates by using a fiber hub or a switch. Fiber optic cable (or coaxial and telephone cable) runs between the nodes' Fibre Channel controllers and the fiber hub or switch. The storage device is connected to the fiber hub or switch with a device bus such as SCSI (see Figure 9-4).

Another hardware consideration when using the Cluster service is the network configuration.

The Cluster service uses the network configuration to accomplish two things. The first, obviously, is to communicate with its clients. The other use is to provide node-to-node communication, such as cluster heartbeats, status, and control messages.

The nodes of a cluster must be connected to one or more interconnects. An interconnect is simply a connection to a physical network.

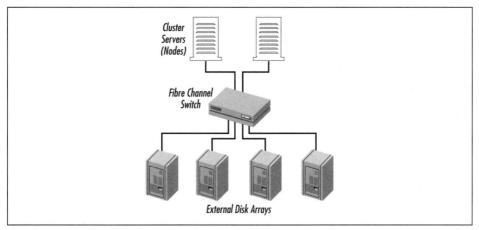

Figure 9-4. A Cluster using Fibre Channel

An interconnect can operate in one of four roles:

Private network interconnect
> Contains only node-to-node communications

Public network interconnect
> Contains only client-to-cluster communications

Public and private interconnect
> Contains both node-to-node and client-to-cluster communications

Neither public nor private network interconnect
> Contains no cluster-related communications

Although a cluster can operate using only a single interconnect with a public and private network interconnect, the use of two interconnects is strongly recommended. Two interconnects eliminate the single point of failure that a single interconnect could cause in disruption of communication between nodes.

The Network Load Balancing Service

The Network Load Balancing service adds even more functionality by scaling the performance of many client/server programs. It accomplishes this by balancing client requests across the multiple servers that make up a server cluster. If any server fails, Network Load Balancing can redistribute the load to the remaining servers in the cluster.

Network Load Balancing accomplishes this by using a virtual IP address, which the client accessing the server cluster uses when making requests. To the client, the server cluster appears as a single computer with a single IP address. Network Load Balancing divides the requests among the servers in the cluster, which then process the request and sends the data back to the client.

Building a Windows 2000 Cluster

For clarification purposes, I will go through the process of building a two-node cluster using Windows 2000 Advanced Server. This cluster will be used to create a DHCP service with failover capability. As you will see, there are many steps that need to be completed before the installation of the Cluster service software.

Assembling the Hardware

Before diving into the installation of the software, I need to first get the hardware together for the cluster. For this example, I used a configuration that is certified by Microsoft and Hewlett-Packard. Although I am utilizing HP equipment, many other manufacturers support the Cluster service as well, such as Compaq and Dell. Refer to the other manufacturers' web sites for their supported Windows 2000 Cluster configurations.

Table 9-2 lists the equipment used to build the cluster.

Table 9-2. Cluster Hardware Equipment List

Hardware	Quantity	Description
Node	2	HP NetServer LC3
Shared storage device	1	HP Rack Storage 12
Disk drives	5	HP 18GB Ultra SCSI
RAID controllers	4	HP NetRAID 3si
Network interface cards	2	3COM 3c905B-TX
Network interface cards	2	HP D5013/B
Ethernet crossover cable	1	Cat 5 Crossover Cable

Before assembling the hardware pieces, double check the following items to verify there are no compatibility issues. These items can be checked by using the manufacturers' and Microsoft's web sites:

- BIOS versions (nodes and SCSI controllers)

- Firmware versions

- Drivers (network adapters and SCSI controllers)

The two nodes are comprised of identical HP NetServer LC3s. This model has dual Pentium II 450 processors and 256 MB RAM. For internal disk storage, I installed three 18 GB hard drives. These drives are controlled by the NetRAID 3si controller using a RAID-1 (mirrored) configuration with a hot spare.

The I/O slots in the LC3 were configured as follows:

Slot 3   NetRAID 3si (for internal storage)

Slot 5   NetRAID 3si (for external cluster storage)

Slot 4   HP D5013/B Network Adapter for Private Cluster Network

Slot 1   3COM 3c905B-TX Network Adapter for Public Network

Internal disk storage is attached to the NetRAID 3si located in Slot 3. This is where Windows 2000 will be installed.

I configured the external storage cabinet, the HP Rack Storage 12, with five 18 GB Ultra SCSI hard drives and a second SCSI connection card. The hard drives are configured as a RAID-5 array with a hot spare. This will be a common storage area for both nodes in the cluster.

The Rack Storage 12 is connected to the NetRAID 3si controllers through the controllers' external connectors.

The private cluster network is created by using the crossover cable and the two Slot 4 Network adapters in the LC3s.

The public network is simply the normal LAN connection from the LC3s to a hub or switch.

Installing the Software

Before installing the Cluster service, several steps must be taken. These steps must be performed on each node before the Cluster service can be installed.

Installing Windows 2000

The first step is to install Windows 2000 Advanced Server. Please see Chapter 5, *The DHCP Server*, for details of installing Windows 2000.

Note that the IP addresses I am using in this example configuration are for demonstration only. You will need to configure your cluster according to your network needs.

When installing Windows 2000 Advanced Server, it is important to remember that both nodes must be either member servers or domain controllers. The nodes cannot be mixed; for example, the cluster cannot include both a member server and a domain controller.

Setting up the private cluster network

The private cluster network is used for node-to-node communication. An example of traffic on this network is cluster status signals (or heartbeats) and cluster management. This traffic is used to monitor the up or down status of the member nodes. If the Cluster service detects that one of the nodes is "down," it initiates a cluster failover. In this case, any designated cluster-aware applications are moved to the "up" node and restarted.

Before continuing, verify that the private network connections are correct. In other words, make sure that the two network adapters to be used for the private network are connected by the crossover cable. To do this, perform the following steps on the first node of the cluster:

1. Right-click My Network Places and select Properties.

2. Right-click on the Local Area Connection icon.

   There should be two icons present. It may be difficult to determine which is the private network. To make it simpler, I used two different makes of network adapters, 3COM and HP. In my configuration, the HP adapter is used for the private network. By placing the mouse over the Local Area Connection icons, the manufacturer and model of the network adapter will be displayed in a tooltip.

3. Select Status from the menu. The Local Area Connection Status dialog box is displayed. If the window shows that the network is disconnected, verify that the crossover cable is connected to the correct ports. Also verify that both nodes are powered on. Click Close to close the dialog box.

4. Right-click on the Local Area Connection icon for the private network. Select Properties.

5. From the Properties dialog box, double-click Internet Protocol (TCP/IP).

6. Click the button for "Use the following IP address:" and enter the following IP address: **10.0.0.1**.

7. In the Subnet Mask field, enter **255.0.0.0**.

8. Click the "Advanced..." button. Select the WINS tab. Select "Disable NetBIOS over TCP/IP."

9. Click OK to close the Advanced TCP/IP Setting dialog box.

10. Click OK to close the Internet Protocol (TCP/IP) dialog box.

11. Repeat these steps again for Node #2, except use IP address 10.0.0.2 instead of 10.0.0.1.

To verify connectivity, type **ping 10.0.0.2** at a command prompt on Node #1. If you get a reply, the nodes are configured correctly. If there is no reply, verify the network settings and cable connection.

Finally, on each node, right-click on the Local Area Connection icon for the private network. Select Rename and rename the icon to Private Cluster Network.

Setting up the public network

The public network is where the cluster communicates with network clients. The Cluster can connect to the network via a switch or hub.

As before, verify that the public network connections are correct before proceeding.

On the first node of the cluster, perform the following steps:

1. Right-click My Network Places and select Properties

2. Right-click on the remaining Local Area Connection icon.

   There should be two icons present. Unlike earlier, there is now only one Local Area Connection. Since the 3COM adapter is used for the public network, display the tooltip to verify that the Local Area Connection is the 3COM adapter.

 To simplify identification of the connections, rename the Local Area Connections accordingly. For example, rename the connection for the production network to Production Network.

---

3. Select Status from the menu. The Local Area Connection Status dialog box is displayed. If the window shows that the network is disconnected, verify that the network cable is connected to the switch or hub. Also, look for a link light on the back of the network adapter to signify a connection. If there is no link light, verify connections and make sure the hub or switch is powered on. Click Close to close the dialog box.

4. Right-click on the Local Area Connection icon for the public network. Select Properties.

5. From the Properties dialog box, double-click Internet Protocol (TCP/IP).

6. Although the IP address for the public network could be obtained by DHCP, this is not possible in this case because the cluster being built will be servicing DHCP. As always, the DHCP server requires a static IP address. Click the button for "Use the following IP address:" and enter **192.168.0.1**.

7. In the Subnet Mask field, enter **255.255.255.0**.

8. Enter the IP addresses to the DNS servers located on the public network.

9. Click OK to close the Internet Protocol (TCP/IP) dialog box.

10. Repeat these steps again for Node #2, but use IP address 192.168.0.2 instead of 192.168.0.1 in step 6.

To verify connectivity, type **ping 192.168.0.2** at a command prompt on Node #1. If you get a reply, the nodes are configured correctly. If there is no reply, verify the network settings and cable connection.

To verify name resolution, try pinging Node #2's computer name.

Finally, on each node, right-click on the Local Area Connection icon for the public network. Select Rename and rename the icon to Public Network.

Joining a domain

Both nodes must be members of the same domain. Therefore they must also be able to access a domain controller and DNS server. In this configuration, I used another system as the domain controller and DNS server.

To join a domain, follow these steps:

1. On Node #1, right-click on My Network Places and select Properties.

2. From the Advanced pulldown menu, select Network Identification. The System Properties dialog box will be displayed.

3. From the Network Identification tab, click Properties.

4. Under "Member of," click Domain. Enter the name of the domain the node is to join.

5. Enter an administrator account and password to join the computer to the domain.

6. Click OK to close the dialog box. Reboot the computer for the changes to take effect.

7. Repeat these steps for Node #2.

Setting up the Cluster Account

The Cluster service uses a special user account known as the Cluster Account. This account is used by the Cluster service when starting any services or devices. The account must be created before installation of the Cluster service.

To create the Cluster Account, follow these steps:

1. Go to Start → Programs → Administrative Tools, and select Active Directory Users and Computers.

2. Double-click on the domain name.

3. Select the Users Organizational Unit (OU).

4. Right-click on the Users OU and select New User from the menu.

5. Enter the following information in the New Object—User dialog box:

First Name	**Cluster**
Last Name	**Service**
Full Name	**Cluster Service**
User Logon Name	**Cluster**

6. Click Next.

7. Check the User Cannot Change Password and Password Never Expires boxes. Click Next.

8. Click Finish to create the Cluster Account.

Since the Cluster Account will be starting services, it must be made a member of the Administrators group:

1. Select the Cluster Account.

2. Right-click on the Cluster Account and select Add Members to a Group.

3. Select the Administrators group and click OK.

Configuring the disk partitions

Before installing the Cluster service, the disk partitions on the external array need to be configured. More importantly, one of the disk partitions that must be configured is known as the quorum disk. The quorum disk is used by the Cluster service to store important information related to the cluster, such as log files and configurations.

To configure the disk partitions, follow these steps:

1. Power off both nodes and the external array. Now power on the external array and the first node.

2. Right-click on My Computer and select Manage from the menu.

3. In the Computer Management MMC, select Disk Management.

   If this is the first time Disk Management has been run, the Write Signature and Upgrade Disk wizard will start. Select any drives displayed to write the signature to, but *do not* upgrade any of the disks. Upgrading changes the disk from basic to dynamic. A basic disk is just that, a disk. However, a dynamic disk can be used to create volume sets or RAID. The Cluster service does not support dynamic disks, therefore they cannot be used. The Cluster service supports only hardware-based RAID.

4. Select the drive on the external array. Right-click on the drive and select Create Partition.

5. The Create Partition Wizard starts. Click Next twice.

6. Enter 500 MB, or the appropriate size according to your data storage needs, for the partition size. Click Next.

7. Select Q as the drive letter. This will be the Quorum Drive. Click Next.

8. The Cluster service requires that the disks be formatted with NTFS. Verify that NTFS is selected. Click Next to format the drive.

At this point, I will create another partition on the external array. This partition will be used for the DHCP database and logs:

1. Select a drive on the external array that has free space available. Right-click on the drive and select Create Partition.

2. The Create Partition Wizard starts. Click Next twice.

3. Enter 500 MB, or the appropriate size according to your data storage needs, for the partition size. Click Next.

4. Select E as the drive letter. Click Next.

5. Click Next to format the drive using NTFS.

After both drives have been created and formatted, close the Computer Management window.

Now, power down Node #1 and power up Node #2. Using Node #2, verify that all partitions on the external array are configured and available. If they are not, follow the previous steps using Node #2 to configure the partitions, making sure that the partitions are exactly the same as the partitions created on Node #1.

Installing the Cluster service

At this point all hardware has been configured, the network configurations are complete, and the disk partitions on the external array are available.

To install the Cluster service, all nodes must be powered down except Node #1. The external disk array must be powered on as well.

To configure the Cluster service, follow these steps:

1. Select Start → Settings → Control Panel.

2. Double-click Add/Remove Programs.

3. Double-click Add/Remove Windows Components.

4. From the Windows Components Wizard, select the Cluster service (see Figure 9-5) and click Next.

5. Select the location of the source files for Windows 2000 Advanced Server. Click Next to continue.

6. The Cluster Service Configuration Wizard will now start (see Figure 9-6). The Hardware Configuration screen is used as a reminder that only hardware configurations listed in the Cluster category of Microsoft's Hardware Compatibility List (HCL) will be supported. Click "I Understand" to agree, then click Next.

7. The next screen to be displayed is Create or Join a Cluster (see Figure 9-7). Since the cluster has not been created yet, select "The first node in the cluster" radio button. Click Next to continue.

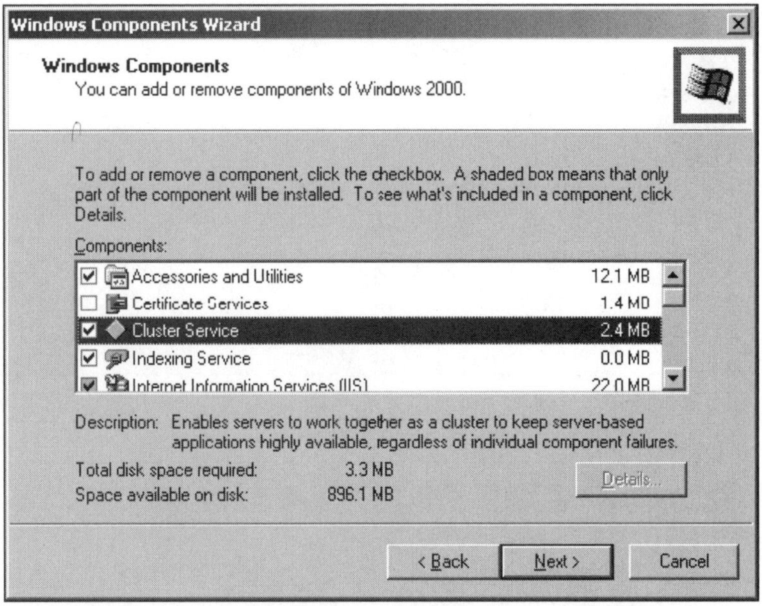

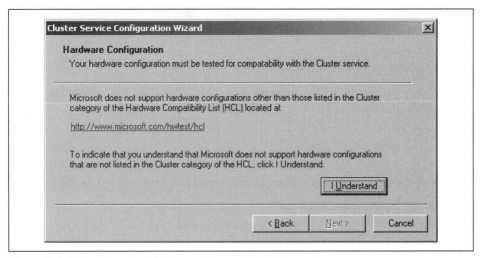

Figure 9-5. Windows Components Wizard

Figure 9-6. Agreeing to the Hardware Compatibility List

If there are any problems with the shared SCSI bus, an error box will be displayed (see Figure 9-8). This error states that the Cluster service has not found any shared disks that meet the clustering criteria. Verify the configuration of the external array as well as the configuration of the partitions (i.e., verify that they are formatted using NTFS).

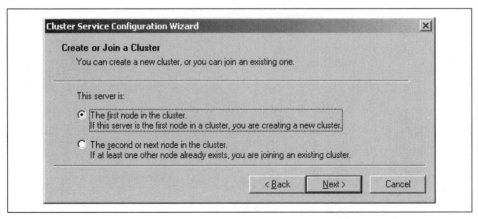

Figure 9-7. Creating a cluster

Figure 9-8. No Disks Found error

8. The next screen is used to name the cluster. Enter DHCP as the cluster name. Click Next to continue.

9. Enter the name of the Cluster Account created earlier (see Figure 9-9). Enter Cluster in the "User name" field, leave the password blank (as it was when the account was created), and, if the user account is a domain account, verify the correct domain is selected. Click Next.

10. The Add or Remove Managed Disks window appears (see Figure 9-10). Now it is time to select the partitions created earlier on the external disk array as managed disks. Managed disks are partitions that will be managed by the Cluster service. Although other disks may appear from other SCSI buses, only disks on the shared SCSI bus can be managed by the Cluster service. If any other disks appear under the Managed Disks windows, select them and click Remove to unmanage them. Click Next.

11. The next screen is used to select the quorum disk (see Figure 9-11). The quorum disk is used for cluster management by storing checkpoint and log files for the cluster. From the dropdown list, select drive Q as the quorum disk. Click Next.

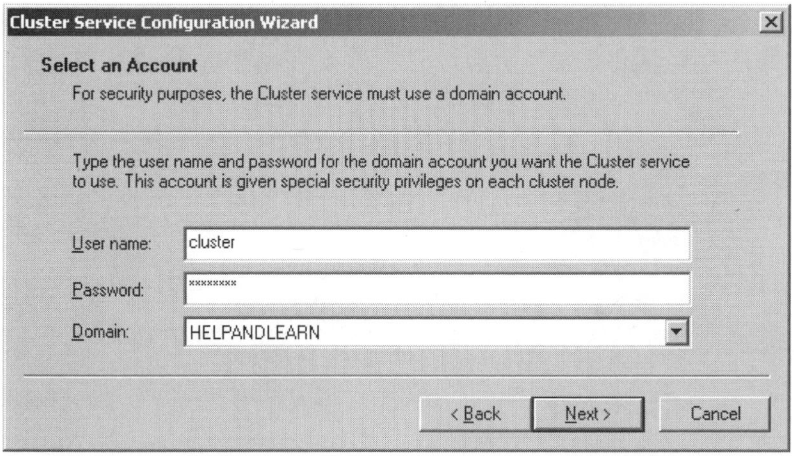

Figure 9-9. Assigning the Cluster Account

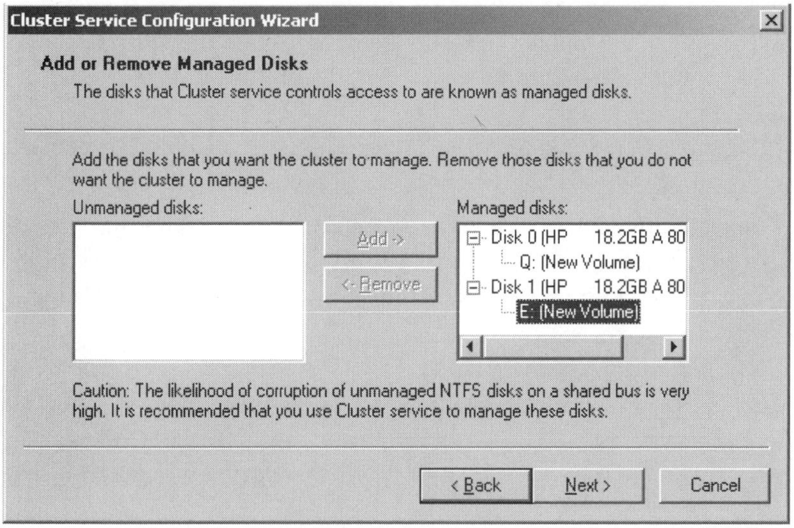

Figure 9-10. Adding and removing managed disks

The next phase of the installation is the network configuration. Although the interfaces have been configured with IP addresses, the Cluster service needs to know which interface is used for the private cluster network and which is used for the public network.

12. Click Next in the Cluster Network Configuration window.

13. The order of the network interfaces may vary. In this case, the private cluster network is displayed first. Select the "Enable this network for cluster use"

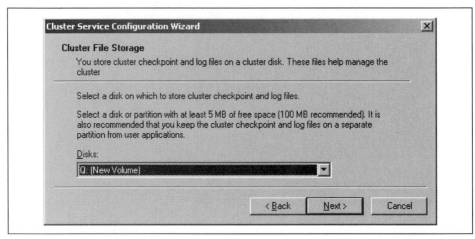

Figure 9-11. Selecting the quorum disk

radio button. Select the "Internal cluster communications only (private net-work)" radio button. Click Next.

14. Now configure the public network interface. Select the "Enable this network for cluster use" radio button. Select the "Client access only (public network)" radio button. Click Next.

15. The next window is used to select the order in which the networks will be used for cluster communication. The reason for selecting the order is that, in the event of a failure on the private cluster network (either the network itself or the interfaces), the Cluster service can move cluster communications to the public network interface. Verify that the private cluster network is the first net-work selected and click Next.

16. The Cluster IP address windows are displayed. This is the IP address that rep-resents the cluster on the network. Enter 192.168.0.50 with the subnet mask of 255.255.255.0. Next, verify that the public network is selected. This associates the cluster IP address with the public network. Click Next to continue.

17. Click Finish to complete the Cluster Configuration Wizard.

    The Cluster service is now configured and running on Node #1. To complete the cluster, Node #2 must now be configured with the Cluster service. Com-pared to Node #1, configuring Node #2 is extremely simple.

18. Power on Node #2. Leave Node #1 and the external array powered on also.

19. On Node #2, go to Start → Settings → Control Panel.

20. Double-click Add/Remove Programs.

21. Double-click Add/Remove Windows Components.

22. From the Windows Components Wizard, select the Cluster Service and click Next.

23. Select the location of the source files for Windows 2000 Advanced Server. Click Next to continue.

24. The Cluster Service Configuration Wizard will now start. The Hardware Configuration screen is displayed. Click I Understand to agree, then click Next.

25. The next screen displayed is Create or Join a Cluster (see Figure 9-12). To add Node #2 to the cluster, select the radio button labelled "The second or next node in the cluster." Click Next to continue.

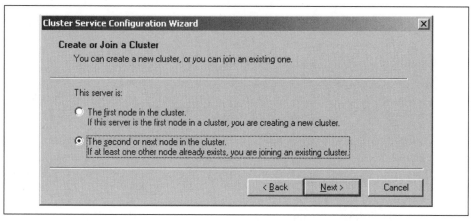

Figure 9-12. Joining a cluster

26. Enter the cluster name, DHCP, for the cluster created earlier. Click Next.

27. The Cluster Configuration Wizard will automatically use the Cluster Account used in the configuration of Node #1. Click Next.

28. Click Finish to complete the Cluster Configuration Wizard.

Well, it took a little while, but you now have a basic functioning Windows 2000 cluster. At this point both nodes should be communicating across the private network. The nodes share a common external disk array, which stores data for any cluster-aware applications. Finally, the cluster itself is represented on the network as a virtual server, with its own IP address. In other words, users see the cluster as a single server, not the individual nodes.

Using Windows Clustering with DHCP

DHCP Server in Windows 2000 is a cluster-aware application. By using the DHCP Server service along with the Cluster service, a type of DHCP failover can be created.

Using a virtual server, the Cluster service allows the DHCP server to run on one node in the cluster. If the node crashes, the Cluster service reconstructs the DHCP server using the virtual IP address and restarts the DHCP Service. Clients continue to use the virtual IP address of the DHCP server for obtaining and renewing leases.

DHCP with clustering requires three resources: a disk resource, an IP address resource, and a network name resource.

The disk resource, stored on a common external drive array, holds the DHCP database. When one node crashes and the second node takes over, the second node has complete knowledge of existing IP address leases and configurations.

The IP address resource is used for the virtual address. This must be a static address, not an address obtained by DHCP. The DHCP Service must bind to this virtual IP address and this address must also be used when authorizing the DHCP server in Active Directory. When configuring DHCP scopes, the virtual IP address must be excluded. DHCP clients will use this virtual IP address to identify the DHCP server.

The network name resource provides a network name that represents the cluster to the network. Combined with the IP address resource, the network name resource creates a virtual server identity for the cluster. Network clients can access the cluster from the single network name, regardless of which node is active.

Finally, the DHCP resource type needs to be configured. The DHCP resource type allows an administrator to configure and manage the DHCP service in the cluster. The resource type points to the location of the DHCP database. The administrator must configure the location of the database and the backups of the database.

The DHCP database path must:

- End with a backslash (\)
- Use a drive letter
- Not use the system variable *%systemroot%*

The following sections explain how to configure the Cluster service to use DHCP.

Creating a resource group

A resource group is a collection of cluster resources. I will create a resource group that will in turn be used when I create the virtual server for DHCP.

1. Select Start → Programs → Administrative Tools. Choose Cluster Administrator.

2. In the Cluster Administrator, right-click on DHCP, the cluster name that we created earlier. Select New → Group to create a new resource group.

3. Once the New Group Wizard starts, enter DHCP Group as the group name and click Next (see Figure 9-13).

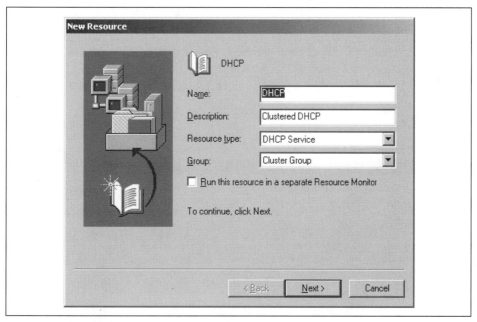

Figure 9-13. Creating a new resource group

4. Under available nodes, select Node #1 to be the preferred owner of the resource group. Click Finish to complete the creation of the resource group.

5. Next, I need to move a disk resource (drive E) into the DHCP Group. This disk will be used to store the DHCP database. In the Cluster Administrator, select the Cluster Group. In the righthand pane, select drive E. Right-click on drive E and select Change Group, then DHCP Group (see Figure 9-14). Confirm the move by answering Yes to the following two questions.

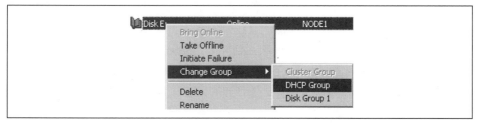

Figure 9-14. Moving resources into a resource group

Creating a virtual server

In this section I will create a virtual server. A virtual server contains a network name resource, an IP address, and the resource type for the application running on the virtual server.

1. In Cluster Administrator, right-click on the cluster, DHCP, and select Configure Application to create a virtual server.

2. The Cluster Application Wizard starts. Click Next to continue. On the Select or Create a Virtual Server screen, select the "Create a new virtual server" radio button (see Figure 9-15). Click Next.

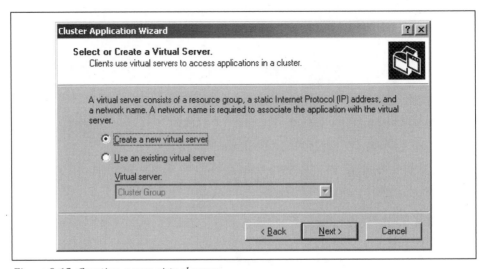

Figure 9-15. Creating a new virtual server

3. In the next window, select "Use an existing resource group" and select DHCP Group from the pull-down list (see Figure 9-16).

4. Next, name the virtual server. Enter **DHCP Virtual Server** in the dialog box and click Next.

5. The Virtual Server Access Information screen is displayed (see Figure 9-17). This screen is used to enter the IP address and network name to be used by the virtual server. Enter the network name **DHCPGROUP** and the IP address **192.168.0.49**. Click Next to continue.

6. The Advanced Properties screen is displayed (see Figure 9-18). This screen is used to set advanced properties like node ownership and failover response. Click Next.

7. On the next screen, answer Yes to create an application resource now.

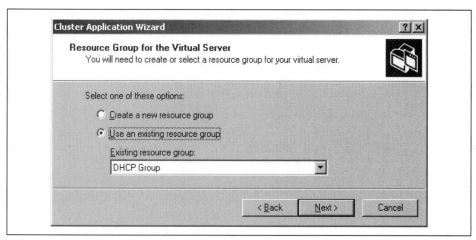

Figure 9-16. Selecting a resource group

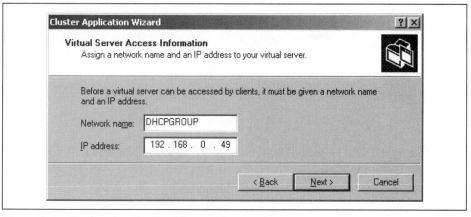

Figure 9-17. Configuring the IP address and network name

8. On the Application Resource Type screen, select the DHCP Service resource type from the pull-down list (see Figure 9-19). Click Next to continue.

9. In the Application Resource Name and Description screen, enter **DHCP Service for Virtual Server** as the name of the application. Click the Advanced Properties button.

10. From the Resource Type Advanced Properties screen, select the Dependencies tab, then click Modify.

11. In the Available Resources Pane, hold the Ctrl key down and select Disk E:, DHCP Group IP Address, and DHCP Group Name. Click the left arrow to move the resources to the Dependencies pane (see Figure 9-20). Click OK. Click Next.

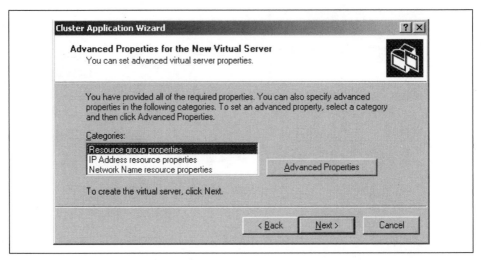

Figure 9-18. Virtual server advanced properties

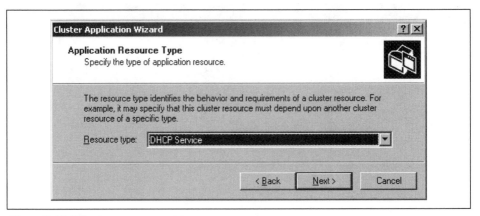

Figure 9-19. Selecting a resource type

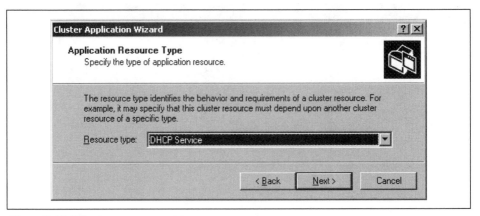

Figure 9-20. Modifying resource dependencies

12. The DHCP Service Parameters screen is used to modify the database, audit file, and backup paths. Verify that the paths are pointing to Disk E: (see Figure 9-21). Click Next to complete the creation of the DHCP virtual server.

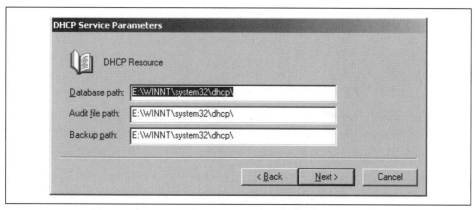

Figure 9-21. Modifying DHCP service parameters

13. Once the virtual server is created, it must be brought online. This can be accomplished using the Cluster Administrator. Right-click on the DHCP virtual server and select Bring Online (see Figure 9-22). After a couple of moments, all resources belonging to the DHCP virtual server are brought online.

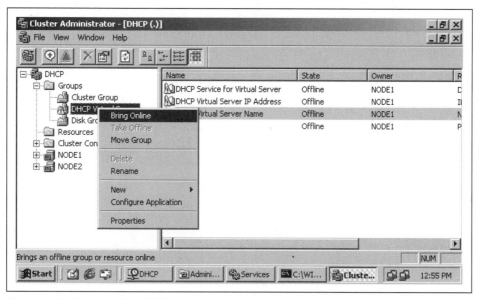

Figure 9-22. Bringing the DHCP virtual server online

At this point the DHCP virtual server is online. Any scopes created on the DHCP server will now be servicing clients. Using a DHCP client on a workstation, verify that the DHCP service is available and functioning properly.

Summary

This chapter discussed using a DHCP cluster to provide a level of fault tolerance for DHCP in Windows 2000. Since DHCP is a mission-critical network application for most organizations, having a degree of failover protection is a requirement.

The DHCP Service in Windows 2000 is a cluster-aware application. This means that the service can be installed on a cluster and in the event that a node in the cluster fails, the Cluster service will start the DHCP Service on another node.

Installing a Windows 2000 Cluster can be a lengthy process, and it is important to do planning and research before attempting the installation. This chapter covered this entire planning and build process.

10

Integrating DHCP and DNS

Before Windows 2000, networks using Microsoft operating systems relied on NetBIOS for network clients to locate servers and resources. One problem with NetBIOS is that it doesn't work with TCP/IP, and hence, the Internet. The Internet and TCP/IP rely on the use of either host files or DNS for name resolution. Microsoft operating systems did not support these systems for name resolution. With Microsoft starting late in the Internet game, WINS was developed to provide NetBIOS name to IP address name resolution.

In Windows 2000, the Domain Name System (DNS) has replaced the Windows Internet Naming System (WINS) as the primary method of name registration and resolution. As such, DNS needed to include much of the functionality in WINS. This chapter provides an overview of some of these new features before delving into the piece of DNS that is tightly integrated with DHCP: Dynamic Update. One of the benefits of using WINS was that WINS clients could automatically and dynamically register their NetBIOS names in the WINS database. Dynamic Update adds this support to DNS using hostnames, the DNS database, and DHCP.

Domain Name System

During the early days of the Internet, the hostnames of computers were stored in a *HOSTS* file, a static text file listing hostnames and their corresponding IP addresses. Since it was a static text file, it needed to be administered by hand. Typically, the *HOSTS* file was stored in a central location, which in turn was downloaded to all computers on the network. As the network grew, this method of updating the *HOSTS* file created more network traffic and took longer as the *HOSTS* file grew larger. DNS was introduced in 1984 to help alleviate these problems.

DNS is designed as a hierarchical distributed database which holds all hostnames. The database is then distributed among several other DNS servers. The distribution of the database decreases the load on any one DNS server.

Distributing the DNS database also allows it to be divided into separate administrative zones. Dividing the database into zones makes the database's size virtually unlimited while keeping it manageable. Please refer to Chapter 1, *TCP/IP Overview*, to review the structure of DNS.

DNS is defined in RFC1034, "Domain Names—Concepts and Facilities" (*http://www.ietf.org/rfc/rfc1034.txt*) and RFC1035, "Domain Names—Implementation and Specification" (*http://www.ietf.org/rfc/rfc1035.txt*).

Windows 2000 DNS Server

The DNS Server that ships with Windows 2000 is compliant with RFCs 1034 and 1035. It also supports the following RFCs:

- RFC1122, "Requirements for Internet Hosts—Communication Layers"
  http://www.ietf.org/rfc/rfc1122.txt

  This RFC outlines how software vendors should develop and configure Internet host software at the lower layers of the OSI Model (Transport, Network, and Data Link). This covers protocols such as ARP, IP, ICMP, IGMP, TCP, and UDP.

- RFC1123, "Requirements for Internet Hosts—Application and Support"
  http://www.ietf.org/rfc/rfc1123.txt

  A companion to RFC1122, this RFC outlines how software vendors should develop and configure Internet host software at the upper layers of the OSI Model (Application, Presentation, and Session). This covers protocols such as Telnet, SMTP, FTP, TFTP, and DNS.

- RFC1886, "DNS Extensions to Support IPv6"
  http://www.ietf.org/rfc/rfc1886.txt

  This RFC specifies the changes needed in DNS to support IPv6. It defines a new resource record (aaaa) which is used to map a domain name to an IPv6 address, as well as defining name queries using IPv6.

- RFC1995, "Incremental Zone Transfer in DNS"
  http://www.ietf.org/rfc/rfc1995.txt

  This RFC defines the inclusion of an incremental zone transfer capability to DNS. Incremental zone transfer is a more efficient way of updating the zone files on name servers. This is accomplished by only sending records that have changed since the last zone transfer. Without incremental zone transfer, the entire zone needs to be transmitted to the name servers.

- RFC1996, "A Mechanism for Prompt DNS Notification of Zone Changes"
  http://www.ietf.org/rfc/rfc1996.txt

  This RFC, directly related to RFC1995, provides a method for a master server to notify slave servers that a change has occurred to the zone.

- RFC2136, "Dynamic Updates in DNS (DNS UPDATE)"
  http://www.ietf.org/rfc/rfc2136.txt

  This RFC adds the capability to DNS to do dynamic updates. Standard DNS is a static database that must be maintained by an administrator. Dynamic updates allow DNS to receive updates to resource records in a zone via a DHCP server or DHCP client.

- RFC2181, "Clarifications to the DNS Specification"
  http://www.ietf.org/rfc/rfc2181.txt

  This RFC was published to better explain some topics in DNS, such as Time to Lives (TTL) and Start of Authority (SOA).

- RFC2308, "Negative Caching of DNS Queries"
  http://www.ietf.org/rfc/rfc2308.txt

  This RFC clarifies the negative caching capability in DNS. Negative caching is the capability of storing negative responses (i.e., hostnames that were not resolved to IP addresses) and replicating the cache to other name servers. In turn, negative caching helps reduce network traffic.

- RFC2845, "Secret Key Transaction Authentication for DNS (TSIG)"
  http://www.ietf.org/rfc/rfc2845.txt

  This RFC defines the TSIG protocol, which provides a secret key method of authentication between DNS clients or servers.

- RFC2782, "A DNS RR for specifying the location of services (DNS SRV)"
  http://www.ietf.org/rfc/rfc2782.txt

  This RFC defines the SRV resource record, which is used to locate network services, such as domain controllers.

An Internet Draft is the working document that the Internet Engineering Task Force (IETF) uses when developing and refining new Internet standards. Please note that Internet Drafts are subject to change. There are several Internet Drafts that are supported:

- "Interaction between DHCP and DNS"
  http://search.ietf.org/internet-drafts/draft-ietf-dhc-dhcp-dns-12.txt)

  This draft describes the process that DHCP clients and servers use when updating DNS via dynamic update.

- "Secret Key Establishment for DNS (TKEY RR)"
  http://search.ietf.org/internet-drafts/draft-ietf-dnsext-tkey-04.txt

  This draft outlines the use of shared secret keys for DNS queries and responses. It defines a new resource record called a TKEY.

- "Using the UTF-8 Character Set in the Domain Name System"
  http://search.ietf.org/internet-drafts/draft-skwan-utf8-dns-04.txt

  This draft specifies that DNS names are represented using the ASCII character encoding known as UTF-8. Standard DNS specifies the use of ASCII character encoding only.

- "GSS Algorithm for TSIG (GSS-TSIG)"
  http://www.ietf.org/internet-drafts/draft-skwan-gss-tsig-04.txt

  This draft specifies the use of Generic Security Service (GSS) for TSIG. TSIG is used for transaction level authentication in DNS.

As you can see, Microsoft was determined to make the Windows 2000 DNS Server fully RFC compliant. By also taking into account the Internet Drafts, which will likely become RFCs, Microsoft took a proactive step in integrating many future enhancements in the Windows 2000 DNS Server.

Resource Records

The DNS database contains resource records (RR) that identify distinct resources in the database. A resource record contains the following items:

Owner
  Specifies the name of the domain where the resource record is located.

Type
  Specifies the type of resource for the resource record (i.e., a host, name server, mail exchanger, etc.).

Class
  Identifies the protocol family (usually the Internet class).

TTL
  Specifies the Time to Live for the resource record, in seconds.

Rdata
  Specifies the actual data for the resource record. This can change depending on the type of resource (i.e., a hostname for NS, an IP address for A).

Table 10-1 lists some of the common resource records found in DNS.

Table 10-1. Common Resource Records

Description	Type	Class
Start of Authority	SOA	IN (Internet)
Host	A	IN (Internet)
Pointer	PTR	IN (Internet)
Name Server	NS	IN (Internet)
Mail Exchanger	MX	IN (Internet)
Canonical Name	CNAME	IN (Internet)

DNS Database Distribution

As noted in Chapter 1, a DNS database is broken up into multiple zones. A zone is a portion of the database containing RRs of hosts. These hosts are located in that contiguous portion of the DNS namespace represented by the zone.

A DNS name server is the repository of the zone or zones' files. A zone file is an ASCII text file that contains the configuration data for a given zone, or in other words, the resource records for the zone. The first record in a zone file is the Start of Authority (SOA) record. This record identifies the primary DNS server for the zone. A *primary server* is responsible for updating the files in the zone. Another type of DNS server called a *secondary server* holds a read-only copy of the zone file. A secondary server provides fault tolerance in the event of a communication failure.

 A DNS server can be the primary server for one zone and a secondary server for another zone. Therefore the function of the DNS server is dependent on the zone in question, not the server itself.

All changes made to a zone are first made at the primary server and then replicated to the secondary server. This replication is known as a *zone transfer*. The replication is accomplished by simply copying the zone file from the primary to the secondary.

Zone transfers are handled automatically by the DNS protocol. There are two types of zone transfers: *full zone transfer* (AXFR) and *incremental zone transfer* (IXFR). A full zone transfer copies the entire zone file. An incremental zone transfer only copies resource records that have changed in the zone. The Windows 2000 DNS Server supports both types of zone transfers.

DNS Replication Using Active Directory

Besides using the traditional method of replicating the DNS database through zone transfers, Windows 2000 DNS Server also supports the use of Active Directory for database storage and replication.

Active Directory storage

Active Directory is an X.500-compliant database that uses a hierarchical tree structure to store objects. These objects represent resources that are available on the Windows 2000–based network. There are two types of objects found in Active Directory:

Container objects

    These objects are used for organizational reasons. They can contain other container objects or leaf objects.

Leaf objects

    These objects represent specific resources in the Active Directory.

Each object in Active Directory has attributes that define its characteristics. For Active Directory–integrated DNS, the following objects are defined:

DnsZone

    This object is a container object. It does just what its name implies: it represents a DNS Zone. This container object contains leaf objects called DnsNodes.

DnsNode

    This object is a leaf object. It represents a host in a zone and its associated resource records (DnsRecord).

DnsRecord

    This is an attribute of the DnsNode object. It is a multi-valued attribute containing the type of resource record, its class, etc.

DNS replication in Active Directory

With the zone information stored in Active Directory, all updates are sent to a DNS server, which in turn writes the data to Active Directory. Active Directory then replicates that data to the other domain controllers. DNS servers running on these domain controllers then access the updated database.

Since it uses a multi-master replication model, an update made to one DNS server is automatically replicated to the rest of the DNS servers. One potential problem with using the multi-master replication model occurs if changes are made to the same object on two or more separate DNS servers. In this case, Active Directory uses the timestamps of the updates. The latest update is preferred and kept.

Converting zones

Windows 2000 includes the capability to convert zones from standard primary, standard secondary, or Active Directory–integrated. There are a couple of reasons why you may want to convert a zone from one zone type to another.

First, it allows you to reconfigure the DNS topology. Take, for example, a situation where a standard primary zone is configured on a server that is also a domain controller, DHCP server, and WINS server. The standard secondary zones are located on other domain controllers. Due to the amount of network traffic and multiple dependencies on this server, you can install a new DNS server and configure it with a standard secondary zone. Next, convert the standard secondary zone on this server to the standard primary zone for the domain. You have now removed a dependency on the original server. You also have the option to remove the standard secondary zone on the original server to help reduce the load.

Secondly, you can convert a standard primary or standard secondary zone to be Active Directory–integrated. With an Active Directory–integrated zone, all zone information is stored within Active Directory and is replicated between all domain controllers during regular domain replication.

Zones can be converted from any type of DNS zone to any other type. To convert a DNS zone, follow these steps:

1. In the DNS console, right-click on the zone to be converted. Select Properties.

2. Click the Change button.

3. The Change Zone Type dialog box is displayed. Select a zone type to convert to (see Figure 10-1). Choose from the following options:

   Active Directory–integrated
   > This option is available only if the DNS server is located on a domain controller. Zone data is stored and replicated as a part of Active Directory.

   Standard primary
   > This option converts the zone to a standard primary zone. If changing from an Active Directory–integrated zone to a standard primary zone, the DNS server loading the primary zone must be the single primary for this zone. Accordingly, the zone must be deleted from Active Directory when the conversion is complete.

   Standard secondary
   > This option converts the zone to a standard secondary zone. An IP address of a DNS server that contains the source data for the zone must be entered.

4. Click OK to close the Change Zone Type dialog box.

5. Click OK to close the DNS Server Properties dialog box.

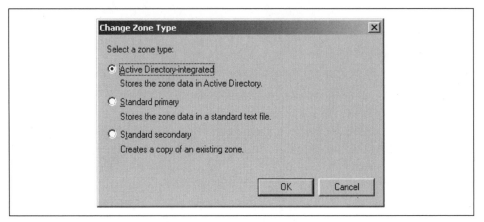

Figure 10-1. Converting zone type

Incremental Zone Transfer

Incremental zone transfer (IXFR) allows changes in the DNS database to be propagated more quickly than the normal full zone transfer (AXFR). Since an AXFR transfers the entire zone file from the master server to the slave DNS server, a more efficient method of sending changes was designed. IXFR is much more efficient since it only sends the changes that are required to make the slave's zone file current.

The incremental zone transfer process

A slave name server sends an IXFR message to the master name server. The IXFR message contains the SOA serial number from the slave's copy of the zone file.

The master name server keeps the latest SOA serial number from its copy of the zone file. When it receives the IXFR request from the slave, it compares the two numbers. The master then sends only the changes required to make the slave's copy current.

Nonetheless, a full zone transfer may be required if the number of changes is larger than the entire zone file.

Domain Locator Service

The Domain Locator Service in Windows 2000 is implemented as part of the Netlogon Service. It is a service that allows a client to locate a domain controller.

Before Windows 2000, Windows clients used NetBIOS to determine what domain controllers were available on the network. In Windows 2000, DNS is used for name resolution.

When a domain controller boots up, the Netlogon Service registers the server's SRV resource records in DNS. The SRV resource record is used to define a service location (e.g., which server or servers are domain controllers) for a domain. The domain controller's Netlogon Service also registers the server's A and CNAME resource records.

To locate a domain controller, the client's Domain Locator Service submits a DNS query to the DNS server for the domain controller. The DNS server responds with a list of domain controllers. After the query is resolved, an LDAP request is then sent to the domain controllers listed to determine their availability. The first domain controller to respond is then used by the client.

Dynamic Update

It is important to remember that the entire basis of DNS was rooted in the *HOSTS* file—a static text file. As such, DNS has traditionally been maintained manually by a network administrator. The administrator made edits to the zone file by hand.

However, with the advent of DHCP and dynamic IP addressing, the operation of manually updating the DNS database quickly became inefficient and unmanageable. Since an administrator could not possibly process the number of updates required, many organizations became very selective towards DNS updates. Only important devices, such as servers, network printers, routers, etc. would be assigned hostnames and added to the DNS database.

To handle the overburdening load of DNS updates, the IETF released RFC2136, "Dynamic Updates in DNS (DNS UPDATE)." This RFC defined a new DNS message type called UPDATE. The UPDATE message is used to define and remove resource records from a designated zone. It also has the ability to perform tests to determine if a particular resource record currently exists in the DNS database.

Since changes can only occur on the primary name server for a zone, the RFC also specified that if a secondary server receives an UPDATE message, it must forward the UPDATE request to the primary name server. Of course, with an Active Directory–integrated DNS database, all updates are processed by a domain controller.

Another concern is zone transfers. During zone transfers, the zone file is locked while the secondary server receives the updated file. This is done so that the secondary server receives an accurate picture of the zone.

What happens if the DNS server receives UPDATE messages while a zone transfer is occurring? The Windows 2000 DNS Server queues the UPDATE messages during the transfer and processes them once the zone file is unlocked.

By using dynamic update along with DHCP, the A and PTR resource records in the DNS database can be made consistent with the IP address assignments located in the DHCP database.

When a DHCP client receives an IP address from a DHCP server, its A resource record is updated with the FQDN of the client. The client's PTR resource record is updated as well with the newly assigned IP addresses. These updates are performed using UPDATE messages.

The Dynamic Update Procedure

During boot up, the Windows 2000 DHCP client attempts to negotiate the dynamic update procedure with the DHCP server.

There are three different dynamic update procedures possible:

- DHCP client updates the A resource record, DHCP server updates the PTR resource record.
- DHCP server updates both the A and PTR resource records.
- DHCP server is configured to not perform dynamic updates. In this case, the DHCP client attempts to update both the A and PTR resource records.

Dynamic update operates by using an additional DHCP client option known as the Client FQDN Option (81). This allows the client to provide its fully qualified domain name to the DHCP server and notify the DHCP server how to perform any dynamic updates on the client's behalf.

Note that only Windows 2000 DHCP clients support dynamic update. Clients that do not support it, i.e., pre-Windows 2000 DHCP clients, must rely on the DHCP server to perform updates on their behalf.

Windows 2000 DHCP clients

Windows 2000 DHCP clients support and perform their own dynamic updates (see Figure 10-2). The following list steps through the dynamic update process found in Windows 2000 DHCP clients:

1. The client sends a DHCPREQUEST message to the DHCP server.
2. The DHCP server responds to the client's request with an IP address using a DHCPACK message.
3. Depending on the configuration of the DHCP server and client, one of the following occurs:
   - The DHCP client sends a DNS UPDATE message to the DNS server to update or add an A (hostname to IP address) resource record using the client's hostname.

— The DHCP server sends a DNS UPDATE message to the DNS server to update or add the A resource record.

4. The DHCP server sends a DNS UPDATE message to the DNS server to update or add a PTR (reverse lookup, IP address to hostname) resource record for the DHCP client.

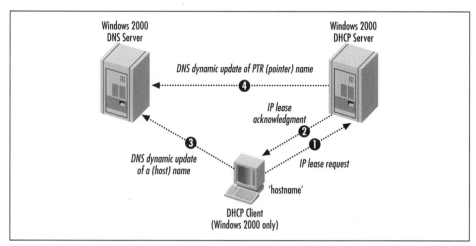

Figure 10-2. Dynamic update with Windows 2000 DHCP clients

Pre-Windows 2000 DHCP clients

Since DHCP clients from earlier versions of Windows do not support DDNS, the dynamic update process is carried out by the Windows 2000 DHCP server (see Figure 10-3):

1. The client sends a DHCPREQUEST message to the DHCP server.

2. The DHCP server responds to the client's request with an IP address using a DHCPACK message.

3. The DHCP server sends a DNS UPDATE message to the DNS server to update or add the A resource record for the client.

4. The DHCP server sends a DNS UPDATE message to the DNS server to update or add a PTR resource record for the client.

Configuring the DNS Server for Dynamic Updates

For the DNS server to receive and process dynamic updates, you need to enable dynamic updates:

1. Open the DNS Manager and right-click on the primary DNS server. Go to Properties.

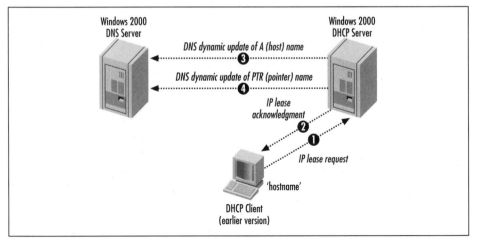

Figure 10-3. Dynamic update with pre-Windows 2000 DHCP clients

2. On the General tab, select the "Allow dynamic updates?" list box (see Figure 10-4).

   This option determines how this zone will handle dynamic DNS updates. For standard zones, you can enable or disable dynamic updates. With zones integrated into Active Directory, you can choose to allow only secure updates. The following choices are available:

   No
   > Do not perform dynamic updates.

   Yes
   > Always perform dynamic updates.

   Only secure updates
   > Only perform dynamic updates if the access control list (ACL) allows it.

3. Select Yes.

4. Click OK to close the DNS Zone properties dialog box.

Configuring the DHCP Server for Dynamic Updates

The DHCP Server needs to be configured to perform dynamic updates of A and PTR resource records for DHCP clients. As noted earlier in this chapter, the process makes use of a DHCP option, the Client FQDN Option (81). The DHCP client sends this option along with instructions on how the DHCP server should handle any updates on behalf of the client.

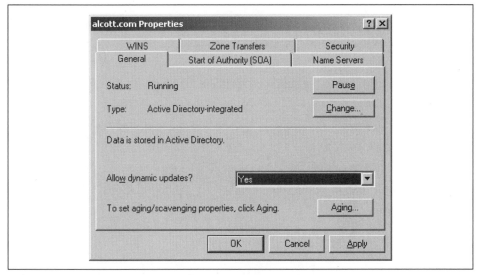

Figure 10-4. Enabling dynamic updates on the DNS server

The DHCP server can be configured in the following ways:

- The DHCP server updates the client's resource records given the instructions from the client.

- The DHCP server always updates the client's resource records.

- The DHCP server never updates the client's resource records.

To configure the DHCP server for dynamic updates, follow these steps:

1. Open the DHCP console. Right-click on the desired DHCP server and select Properties.

2. The DHCP Server Properties dialog box is displayed. Click on the DNS tab (see Figure 10-5).

3. Configure how the DHCP server will process dynamic updates.

   By default, the DHCP server is set to perform dynamic updates only if the DHCP client requests it. This is designated by selecting "Update DNS only if DHCP client requests."

   Select "Always update DNS" to have the DHCP server always update the client's resource records.

   To disable dynamic updates, uncheck "Automatically update the DHCP client information in DNS."

4. To have the DHCP server automatically delete a client's A resource record when its lease expires, check the "Discard forward (name-to-address) lookups when lease expires" option.

5. To have the DHCP server process dynamic updates on behalf of clients that are not capable of doing it themselves (pre-Windows 2000 DHCP clients), check the "Enable updates for DNS clients that do not support dynamic update" option.

6. Click OK to close the DHCP Server Properties dialog box.

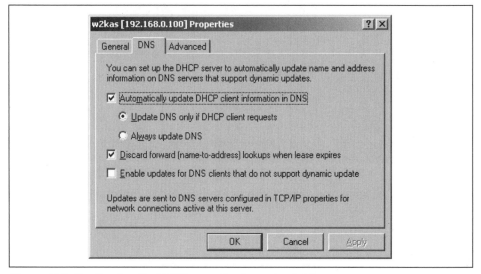

Figure 10-5. Configuring the DHCP server for dynamic updates

Secure Dynamic Update

The Windows 2000 DNS Server provides a secure way to perform dynamic updates in Active Directory–integrated zones. By default, any authenticated user can create the A or PTR resource records in any zone. If an update was performed that was incorrect, either by simple error or hostile intent, name resolution problems could take place in the DNS database.

Secure dynamic updates are accomplished by defining an access control list (ACL) for a zone. An ACL is a list of users or groups that are permitted to change or update resource records for that zone. With secure dynamic updates, only objects (e.g., users, owners, DHCP servers) specified in the ACL are permitted to update the A and PTR resource records

A secure dynamic update follows this procedure (see Figure 10-6):

1. The DHCP client queries the local name server to find out which server is authoritative for the hostname it is trying to update. The local name server then responds with the IP address of the authoritative name server.

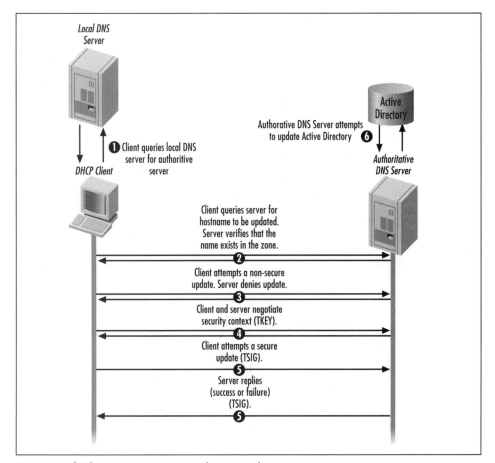

Figure 10-6. The Secure Dynamic Update procedure

2. The client queries the authoritative name server for the hostname it wants to update. This is for verification purposes. If the name exists in the zone, the authoritative server confirms it.

3. The client attempts a non-secure update. If the server is configured to perform non-secure updates, the server simply processes the update request. If the server is configured to accept only secure dynamic updates, the server refuses to process the request.

4. At this point, the client and the server begin to negotiate a security context. This negotiation takes place using the DNS protocol using a resource record known as TKEY. The TKEY resource record holds the transaction key.

   For Windows 2000, clients and servers propose to use Kerberos to provide the security context. Using Kerberos, they verify each other's identity.

The security context is then used to produce and authenticate transaction signatures. These transaction signatures are used for all messages between the client and the server.

5. The client sends a secure dynamic update to the authoritative server. Again, the conversation uses the DNS protocol, using another resource record known as TSIG. TSIG is used to handle the transaction signatures.

6. The server tries to update Active Directory. Depending on the ACL for the zone, the server will or will not be able to perform the update.

7. The server sends a reply to the client stating that the update took place or that the update was denied.

Configuring the DNS server for secure dynamic updates

To use secure dynamic updates, the DNS database must be integrated with Active Directory. Next, the DNS server needs to be configured. Follow these steps:

1. Open the DNS Manager and right-click on the primary DNS server. Go to Properties.

2. On the General tab, select the "Allow dynamic updates?" list box.

   This option determines how this zone will handle dynamic DNS updates. For standard zones, you can enable or disable dynamic updates. With zones integrated into Active Directory, you can choose to allow only secure updates. The following choices are available:

   No
   > Do not perform dynamic updates.

   Yes
   > Always perform dynamic updates.

   Only secure updates
   > Only perform dynamic updates if the ACL allows it.

3. Select "Only secure updates."

4. Click OK to close the DNS Zone properties dialog box.

Now the DNS server is configured to perform update requests only from objects that have permission to do so.

The DnsUpdateProxy group

As described earlier in the chapter, the DHCP server can be configured to perform dynamic updates on behalf of pre-Windows 2000 DHCP clients. Using Secure Dynamic Update in this situation has the potential to cause stale resource records.

If the DHCP server performs an update of a resource record, the DHCP server becomes the owner of that record. In this case, only the DHCP server can update the record.

Now, what happens if that DHCP server goes down? If another DHCP server tries to update the record on behalf of the pre-Windows 2000 DHCP client, the update fails because the second DHCP server is not the owner of the record.

To solve this problem, there is a group called DnsUpdateProxy. By adding all DHCP servers that will be servicing DHCP requests from pre-Windows 2000 DHCP clients to this group, the problem is fixed. No object created by a member of the DnsUpdateProxy group has security set.

To configure the DnsUpdateProxy group, follow these steps:

1. Select Start → Programs → Administrative Tools, and choose Active Directory Users and Computers.

2. In the tree pane, expand the desired domain.

3. Select the Users organizational unit.

4. From the list in the contents pane, double-click the DnsUpdateProxy group.

5. Click on the Members tab.

6. Click the Add button and select the DHCP servers that will be servicing requests from pre-Windows 2000 DHCP clients. Click Add to add them to the list. Click OK to close the dialog box.

7. Click OK to close the DnsUpdateProxy Properties dialog box.

 If a DHCP server is installed on a domain controller and is also a member of the DnsUpdateProxy group, any DNS entries owned by that server are unsecure. These DNS entries include all the SRV, A, and CNAME entries that are automatically registered by the Netlogon service. For this reason, it is recommended that the DHCP server be installed on a member server.

Configuring the DNS Server for Scavenging

Scavenging allows old resource records that are no longer in use to be purged from the DNS database. Old, unused resource records can cause problems with the database. Some of these problems include the following:

Degrading DNS server performance

When answering client queries for name resolutions, the DNS server needs to review the entire zone file. As stale resource records accumulate, the DNS server has to spend more time reviewing these records.

Possible incorrect name resolutions

Old, unused resource records may be used by the DNS server when answering client queries. If so, the client, in turn, uses outdated information, causing name resolution problems.

Disk space and zone transfer problems

As stale records accumulate, the DNS database continues to grow, using up disk space and increasing zone transfer time.

To correct these problems, the DNS server in Windows 2000 uses the following features:

Time stamping

Resource records added dynamically to the DNS database are marked with a timestamp. The timestamp is the current date and time of the DNS server. Resource records added manually have a timestamp of zero. This tells the DNS server that these resource records should not be subjected to the scavenging process.

Aging of resource records

This process determines when a resource record was last refreshed and when the resource record can be scavenged.

Scavenging of resource records

This process scavenges and removes any resource records that persist beyond the specified refresh period.

While using dynamic updates, it is very important to enable and configure this option correctly since DHCP clients and servers will be adding A and PRT resource records to the DNS database. Over time, the DNS database can quickly become cluttered and inefficient. To configure the DNS server for scavenging, follow these steps:

1. Open the DNS Manager and right-click on the primary DNS server. Go to Properties.

2. On the General tab, click on the "Aging . . . " button.

3. The Zone Aging/Scavenging Properties dialog box will be displayed (see Figure 10-7). Select "Scavenge stale resource records" to enable scavenging.

4. Specify the no-refresh interval. This setting determines the amount of time between timestamp refreshes. In other words, any attempt by a DHCP client

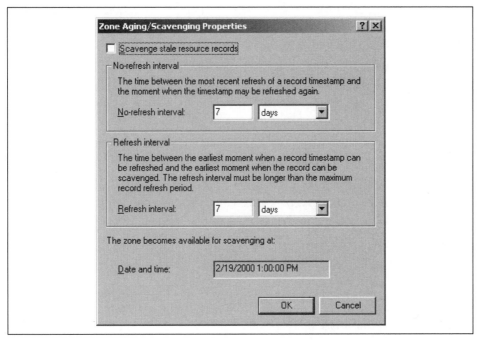

Figure 10-7. Configuring scavenging properties on the DNS server

or server to refresh a given resource record is suppressed by the DNS server during this time period. The default interval is 7 days.

 Do not set the no-refresh interval setting too short. Doing so causes more updates to occur in the DNS database, and thus more replication traffic for Active Directory. This degrades server performance.

5. Specify the refresh interval. This setting determines the amount of time that the DNS server accepts timestamp refreshes for a resource record. This interval must be greater than the maximum refresh period for resource records in the zone (see Table 10-2). The default interval is 7 days.

Table 10-2. Maximum Refresh Periods

Service	Maximum Refresh Period
Netlogon	60 minutes
Clustering	15 minutes
DHCP Client	24 hours
DHCP Server	4 days (or 50% of lease duration)

The Windows 2000 DHCP Client sends attempts to refresh its A and PTR records once every 24 hours. Note that this occurs for both dynamically and statically assigned IP addresses.

The Windows 2000 DHCP Server sends refresh attempts when it is serving as a DNS update proxy for it clients. This occurs when 50% of the lease duration has expired. Since the default lease duration in Windows 2000 is 8 days, the maximum refresh period is typically 4 days.

6. Click OK to close the Zone Aging/Scavenging Properties dialog box. Click OK again to close the DNS Zone properties dialog box.

Remember that scavenging helps keep the DNS database clean and efficient. Stale resource records can degrade performance of the DNS server and need to be purged to obtain the best performance.

Summary

In this chapter, I covered some of the new features found in the Windows 2000 DNS Server. Some of these features are designed to replace the functionality found in the previous method of name resolution, WINS.

The new Dynamic Update feature is the most important of these. Dynamic Update provides a way to update the DNS database automatically when a client obtains an IP address via DHCP. Previously these updates had to be manually entered by an administrator.

11

Monitoring and Troubleshooting DHCP

Now the DHCP server is up and running, DHCP clients are requesting and receiving DHCP offers, and everyone is happy. One way to keep everyone happy is to monitor the health of the DHCP service and to quickly troubleshoot and resolve any potential DHCP problems.

Monitoring DHCP in Windows 2000 is a vast improvement over previous versions of Windows NT. By monitoring, an administrator can be notified if a DHCP server is being overloaded or if it is experiencing other difficulties.

When DHCP is up and running, it is pretty much transparent. An administrator could go months without having any problems. However, when problems do crop up, an administrator must turn to his toolbox to troubleshoot the situation.

Monitoring DHCP

One of the new features found in Windows 2000 is the ability to monitor DHCP servers. The DHCP service is a critical component in a network environment and as such needs to be monitored to ensure it is operating at peak performance.

Windows 2000 also includes the ability to enable audit logging for the DHCP server.

Using System Monitor

Windows 2000 supplies a set of counters that are used to monitor different aspects of the DHCP server. These counters track items such as the following:

- The average time it takes the DHCP server to process a DHCP request
- The number of messages (divided by the type of DHCP message) per second the DHCP server receives

- The number of packets dropped because the DHCP server was too busy to handle the packets

To access these counters, an administrator must use System Monitor. To start System Monitor, follow these steps:

1. Select Start → Programs → Administrative Tools, then choose Performance.

2. The Performance console starts (see Figure 11-1). Select System Monitor.

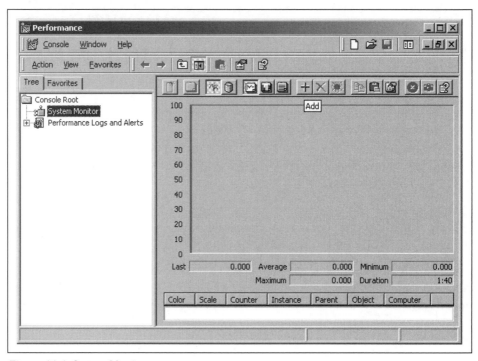

Figure 11-1. System Monitor

3. To add counters to the System Monitor, click on the + button along the top of the System Monitor.

   The Add Counters dialog box is now displayed (see Figure 11-2). This dialog box can be used to add counters for the current computer or for remote computers.

4. Select the desired counter and click the Add button. Click Close when finished selecting counters.

The following list describes the System Monitor counters that are associated with the DHCP server. To add these counters from the Add Counter dialog box, select DHCP Server from the Performance object pull-down list.

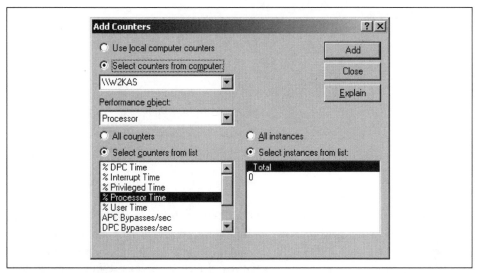

Figure 11-2. Adding counters to the System Monitor

Acks/sec

Rate of DHCP ACK messages sent by the DHCP server

Active Queue Length

The number of packets in the processing queue of the DHCP server

Conflict Check Queue Length

The number of packets in the DHCP server's processing queue awaiting conflict detection

Declines/sec

Rate of DHCP DECLINE messages received by the DHCP server

Discovers/sec

Rate of DHCP DISCOVER messages received by the DHCP server

Duplicates Dropped/sec

The rate at which the DHCP server received duplicate packets

Informs/sec

Rate of DHCP INFORM messages received by the DHCP server

Milliseconds per packet (Avg)

The average time per packet taken by the DHCP server to send a response

Nacks/sec

Rate of DHCP NACK messages sent by the DHCP server

Offers/sec

Rate of DHCP OFFER messages sent by the DHCP server

Packets Expired/sec
> The rate at which packets are expired in the DHCP server's message queue

Packets Received/sec
> The rate at which packets are received by the DHCP server

Releases/sec
> Rate of DHCP RELEASE messages received by the DHCP server

Requests/sec
> Rate of DHCP REQUEST messages received by the DHCP server

DHCP Audit Logging

In previous versions of Windows NT, DHCP Server did not provide adequate audit logging capability. This capability is important in network security, where an administrator may want to know the owner of a particular IP address during a particular time period. Although earlier versions of DHCP Server provided limited logging capabilities, the ability to get address lease information is new.

The audit log that DHCP Server produces is simply a comma delimited text file that can be viewed with Notepad. Table 11-1 lists the various event IDs that can be found in the log file.

Table 11-1. DHCP Audit Log Event IDs

Event ID	Meaning
00	The log was started.
01	The log was stopped.
02	The log was temporarily paused due to low disk space.
10	A new IP address was leased to a client.
11	A lease was renewed by a client.
12	A lease was released by a client.
13	An IP address was found to be in use on the network.
14	A lease request could not be satisfied because the scope's address pool was exhausted.
15	A lease was denied.
16	A lease was deleted.
17	A lease was expired.
20	A BOOTP address was leased to a client.
21	A dynamic BOOTP address was leased to a client.
22	A BOOTP request could not be satisfied because the scope's address pool for BOOTP was exhausted.
23	A BOOTP IP address was deleted after checking to see it was not in use.
50+	Codes above 50 are used for Rogue Server Detection information.

The audit log is saved with a filename consisting of the current day of the week. For example, if the DHCP Server service starts on a Wednesday, the file name is *DhcpSrvLog.Wed.*

Whenever the DHCP Server service starts, or when the server's clock turns past midnight, the server closes the previous day's log file and opens the next day's log file. In other words, at 12:00 A.M. on Wednesday, the service closes *DhcpSrvLog.Wed* and opens *DhcpSrvLog.Thu.* The DHCP Server service then writes header information to the log file. If the log file being written to was not modified in the previous 24 hours, the log file is overwritten. If the log file was modified in the previous 24 hours, the log file is appended.

One problem with the auditing feature found in earlier versions of Windows NT is that the audit log is a single file and is permitted to grow until disk space runs out. In Windows 2000, the DHCP Server service periodically performs disk checks to verify that disk space is available. The DHCP server performs disk checks when either a certain number of events are logged or when the date changes on the server. If the disk is full, the DHCP Server service closes the current log file and ignores requests to log any additional events until the situation is rectified.

To modify the disk check settings, described in the following list, use Regedit to add or modify these values in the following location:

HKLM\SYSTEM\CurrentControlSet\Services\DHCPServer\Parameters

DhcpLogDiskSpaceCheckInterval
Specifies the the amount of time before the DHCP server performs a disk check. The setting is 50 minutes by default.

DhcpLogMinSpaceOnDisk
Specifies the minimum space that must be available on the hard disk. The setting is 20 MB by default.

DhcpLogFilesMaxSize
Specifies the maximum allocated size of the audit log. The setting is 7 MB by default. Notice that the registry setting is for DHCP log files, not file. In other words, with a value of 7 MB, the DHCP server creates seven 1 MB log files, or one for each day of the week.

To enable the DHCP audit log, follow these steps:

1. Open the DHCP console. Right-click on the desired DHCP server and select Properties.

2. From the General tab, check the "Enable DHCP audit logging" box (see Figure 11-3).

3. Click OK to close the DHCP Server Properties dialog box.

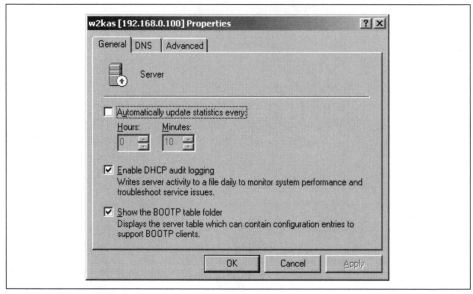

Figure 11-3. Enabling DHCP audit logging

To specify the location of where the DHCP audit logs will be written to, follow these steps:

1. Open the DHCP console. Right-click on the desired DHCP server and select Properties.

2. From the Advanced tab, edit the "Audit log file path" value (see Figure 11-4).

3. Click OK to close the DHCP Server Properties dialog box.

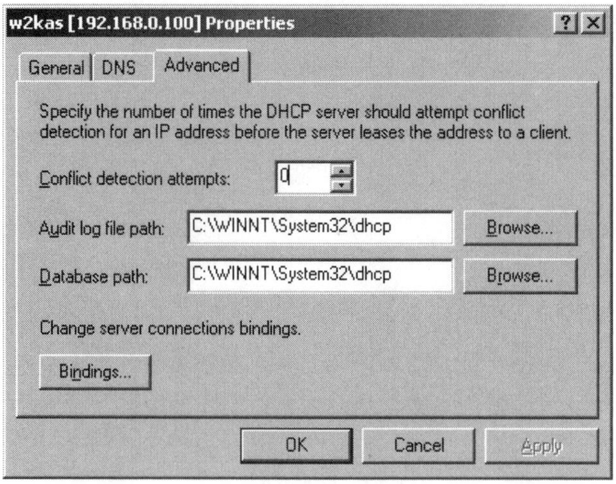

Figure 11-4. Specifying the audit log file path

Troubleshooting DHCP

In most network environments, DHCP is completely transparent. A DHCP client boots up, gets an IP address, and begins to utilize network resources. However, occasionally things go wrong and need troubleshooting to be resolved.

The following sections cover some of the problems faced when troubleshooting DHCP.

DHCP Servers

DHCP servers typically run flawlessly. Usually the only problem a DHCP server may have is the failure to start the DHCP Server service, or that a group of DHCP clients cannot obtain an IP address lease from the server.

If either of these situations occur, verify that the DHCP service is started:

1. Right-click on My Computer and select Manage.
2. From the Computer Management console, select Services and Applications.
3. Double-click on Services in the right-hand pane.
4. From the list of services, locate the DHCP Server service (see Figure 11-5). Verify that it is started.
5. If the service is not started, right-click on the DHCP Server service and select Start. If the service fails to start, use the Event Viewer in the Computer Management console to locate the reason.

Problem: The DHCP server fails to lease addresses for a new scope.

If an existing scope has been removed from a DHCP server and replaced with a new scope, DHCP clients may fail to obtain leases from the new scope. Typically this situation happens if an administrator is renumbering an existing network.

When multiple scopes are created and activated on a DHCP server, the server decides which scope will be used by determining which scope contains the server's first bound IP address. Adding secondary IP addresses to the DHCP server's interface does not fix the problem. Since only one scope for a given network can be active at one time, only that scope can be used to lease addresses to the DHCP clients.

To solve this problem, simply change the DHCP server's primary IP address to an IP address in the new numbering range. However, for connectivity reasons (i.e., the server provides other services besides DHCP) it might not be possible for the primary IP address to be changed.

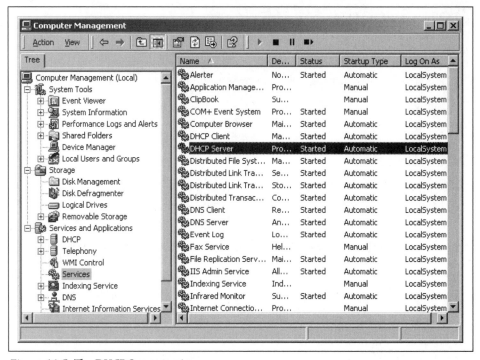

Figure 11-5. The DHCP Server service

In that case, another way to solve this problem is to configure the DHCP server with a superscope that includes both the old scope and new scope:

1. Create the new scope.

2. Configure any DHCP options required for the new scope.

3. Create a superscope that includes the new scope and the old scope.

4. Activate the superscope.

5. Exclude all addresses in the old scope and leave it active.

DHCP Clients

When troubleshooting DHCP clients, an administrator's best friends are the IPCONFIG and WINIPCFG utilities. These two utilities are essentially the same, except that IPCONFIG is used with Windows NT and 2000 systems and is command-line based, while WINIPCFG is used with Windows 95 and 98 and is GUI-based. In this section I will be referring to IPCONFIG, but the same concepts can be achieved using WINIPCFG. I will point out any differences in behavior between the two utilities.

Problem: The DHCP client does not have an IP address.

This is the most common problem that a DHCP client faces, because this is what DHCP is used for. In this situation, the following items should be checked.

Is the DHCP server down? As always, observe the current state of the network environment. If the DHCP server is down, the DHCP client cannot receive an IP address. To check if the server is up, try pinging the DHCP server's IP address from another workstation. If the server is up, proceed to the next step.

Verify network cable connection. If a desktop computer is being used, verify that the network cable is fully plugged in. When plugging in an RJ45 cable, the cable's male connector clicks when fully inserted in the female RJ45 connector in the network adapter.

If a laptop is being used, verifying the connection depends on the type of connector the laptop is using. An XJACK connector slides out from the PCCARD network adapter and operates much like a typical RJ45 connector on a desktop. Another type of connector used by laptops is the dongle (see Figure 11-6). A dongle has a thin connector at one end that plugs into the PCCARD. The other end supports a female RJ45 connector. The PCCARD end of the dongle can work its way loose, so verify that it is fully inserted. Also verify the RJ45 end by inserting the cable until it clicks.

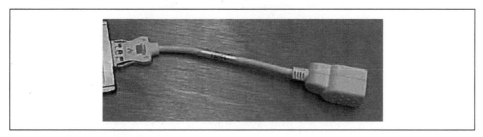

Figure 11-6. Laptop dongle

Once the cable has been connected, check for a link light. A link light is typically found on the network card either above or below the RJ45 connector. On a laptop, the link light is found on the dongle. If the link light is on, run **ipconfig /renew** to receive an IP address.

If the link light is not on, there may be a couple of problems.

First, the patch cable going from the network adapter to the data port may be bad. Replace the patch cable and check for the link light again. If there is now a link light, run **ipconfig /renew** to receive an IP address.

If the link light is still not present, get a cable tester and test the data port. Follow the instructions provided by the manufacturer of the tester. If the tester determines the data port is OK, verify that the software configuration, such as the network adapter driver, is correctly installed. If you have a spare network adapter, try replacing the network adapter.

If the tester determines the data port is bad, contact the network administrator to get the network connections checked. This would include any patches in wiring closets and switch or hub configurations.

Besides physically checking the cable, there are other ways to verify connectivity. In Windows 2000, running `ipconfig /release` or `ipconfig /renew` with a disconnected cable produces this message:

```
C:\>ipconfig /release
Windows 2000 IP Configuration
No operation can be performed on adapter Local Area Connection as this connection
has its media/cable disconnected.
```

In Windows 95 or 98, while running WINIPCFG, a dialog box is displayed (see Figure 11-7).

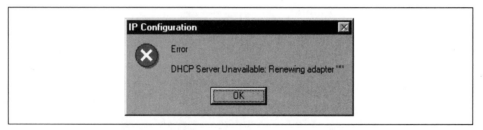

Figure 11-7. WINIPCFG error message

Ping the local loopback address. If the network adapter and cabling checks out OK, start focusing on the software configuration. One quick way to check the IP protocol stack is to ping the local loopback address, 127.0.0.1.

The local loopback address is a special IP address used by hosts to send messages to themselves. As such, it can be used to test the clients IP stack. By typing **ping 127.0.0.1**, the following output should be displayed:

```
C:\>ping 127.0.0.1
Pinging 127.0.0.1 with 32 bytes of data:
Reply from 127.0.0.1: bytes=32 time<10ms TTL=128
Reply from 127.0.0.1: bytes=32 time<10ms TTL=128
Reply from 127.0.0.1: bytes=32 time<10ms TTL=128
Reply from 127.0.0.1: bytes=32 time<10ms TTL=128
Ping statistics for 127.0.0.1:
    Packets: Sent = 4, Received = 4, Lost = 0 (0% loss),
Approximate round trip times in milli-seconds:
    Minimum = 0ms, Maximum = 0ms, Average = 0ms
```

If this output is displayed, proceed to the next step, running `ipconfig /renew`.

You should also attempt to ping other computers on your subnet, as well as the router on your network. This will help you eliminate connectivity problems associated with conditions on the network itself.

If this output is not displayed, there may be other problems. Some TCP/IP configuration files may not be installed or they may be corrupted. To fix this, remove and reinstall TCP/IP.

In Windows 2000, follow these steps to remove and reinstall TCP/IP:

1. Log on as a user with Administrator rights. Right-click on My Network Places and select Properties.

2. From the Network and Dial-up Connections windows, right-click on Local Area Connection and select Properties.

3. From the Local Area Connection Properties dialog box, select Internet Protocol (TCP/IP) and click on the Uninstall button. Click Yes to confirm the uninstallation. Click OK to reboot the computer.

4. Once the computer restarts, log on as a user with Administrator rights. Right-click on My Network Places and select Properties.

5. In the Network and Dial-up Connections window, right-click on Local Area Connection and select Properties.

6. From the Local Area Connection Properties dialog box, click Install.

7. From the Select Network Component dialog box, select Protocol and click "Add..."

8. From the Select Network Protocol dialog box, select Internet Protocol (TCP/IP) and click OK.

9. Click Close to close the Local Area Connection Properties dialog box.

In Windows NT 4.0, follow these steps to remove and reinstall TCP/IP:

1. Log on as a user with Administrator rights. Select Start → Settings → Control Panel.

2. In Control Panel, double-click Network and select the Protocols tab. From the Protocols page, select TCP/IP Protocol, click Remove, and then click Yes.

3. Click Close to close the Network applet, and then click Yes to restart the computer.

4. Log on as a user with Administrator rights.

5. In Control Panel, double-click Network, and then select the Protocols tab. Click Add, select TCP/IP Protocol, and then click OK.

6. To use DHCP, click Yes when prompted. If prompted, type the path for the Windows NT source files. Click Continue.

7. When copying is finished, click Close. Restart your computer.

In Windows 95/98, follow these steps to remove and reinstall TCP/IP:

1. Select Start → Settings → Control Panel.

2. In Control Panel, double-click Network.

3. Remove all TCP/IP-related network components. To accomplish this, click a component on the Configuration tab and then click Remove. Repeat this process until all of the TCP/IP-related network components are removed from network properties.

4. Click OK, and then click Yes to restart your computer.

5. After the computer restarts, Select Start → Settings → Control Panel.

6. In Control Panel, double-click Network, and then select the Protocols tab.

7. On the Configuration tab, click Add, then click Protocol, and then click Add. In the Manufacturers pane, select Microsoft; in the Network Protocols pane, click TCP/IP. Then click OK.

8. Click OK, and then click Yes to restart your computer.

At this point, type **ipconfig /all** to verify that the client now has an IP address. If the client does not have an IP address, proceed to the next step, running ipconfig /renew.

Running ipconfig /renew. In most cases, simply running ipconfig /renew from a command prompt will correct any DHCP-related problems with the client. Of course, this assumes that there are no problems relating to connectivity or the protocol stack, as discussed earlier in this chapter.

Typing ipconfig /renew causes the DHCP client to begin the DHCP conversation to request an IP address.

Once the conversation is complete and the DHCP client has received an IP address, IPCONFIG will output information much like the following:

```
C:\>ipconfig /renew
Windows 2000 IP Configuration
Ethernet adapter Local Area Connection:
   Connection-specific DNS Suffix . : helpandlearn.com
   IP Address. . . . . . . . . . . : 192.168.0.50
   Subnet Mask . . . . . . . . . . : 255.255.255.0
   Default Gateway . . . . . . . . : 192.168.0.1
```

Running ipconfig /release. If, when running ipconfig /renew, an error message is displayed stating that the DHCP client was unable to receive an IP address, try running `ipconfig /release` first. Running `ipconfig /release` causes the DHCP client to release its currently configured IP address:

```
C:\>ipconfig /release
Windows 2000 IP Configuration
IP address successfully released for adapter "Local Area Connection"
```

Problem: The DHCP client has an auto-configured IP address.

In Windows 98 and Windows 2000, Microsoft added a new feature known as Automatic Private IP Addressing (APIPA). These operating systems will use this feature when the DHCP client cannot locate a DHCP server. Please see Chapter 6, *DHCP Clients*, for more information about APIPA.

If a DHCP client is using APIPA, it will have an IP address in the range 169.254.0.1 through 169.254.255.254. The subnet mask is set to 255.255.0.0.

Troubleshooting a DHCP client that is using APIPA can be tricky because when the user or administrator investigates the problem, she is able to see and connect to other systems in the 169.254 subnet so it won't appear to be a connectivity problem. Therefore, an administrator must be aware of the characteristics of APIPA.

Before attempting to fix the client, determine why the client is using APIPA:

- Is the DHCP server running, and is it configured with a scope for this subnet?

- Is the DHCP server on a different subnet, and is the relay agent operating correctly?

These questions need to be answered before fixing the DHCP client.

After verifying that DHCP is available on the subnet, run `ipconfig /release` followed by `ipconfig /renew` at a command prompt to get a DHCP client to use a DHCP address instead of an APIPA address.

Problem: The DHCP client is missing some DHCP options.

If a DHCP client is not using some DHCP options that it should be, verify the following:

- The DHCP server is configured to distribute options via either server or scope options. Use the DHCP console on the DHCP server to view the current configuration.

- The DHCP client supports the options being distributed. Microsoft DHCP clients only support certain options. See Chapter 6, for a complete list of Microsoft-supported DHCP options.

DHCP Relay Agents

DHCP Relay Agent is a very simple application, and as such it does not usually experience many problems. If the DHCP relay agent is not forwarding DHCP requests and offers, verify the following:

- The interface on the system running the Windows 2000 DHCP relay agent is:

    — Connected to the network that contains the DHCP clients.

    — Added to the DHCP relay agent in the RRAS console (see Chapter 7, *Advanced DHCP*).

- The "Relay DHCP packets" check box is selected in the DHCP Relay Agent Properties for the selected interface.

- In the DHCP Relay Agent global properties, the IP address of the DHCP server is listed and correct.

- From the DHCP relay agent, ping the DHCP servers. If the server cannot be pinged, troubleshoot the connectivity problem. If the DHCP server can be pinged from the DHCP relay agent, try pinging the DHCP server from a working workstation.

- Make sure that there are no access lists that are denying access to UDP ports 67 and 68.

Summary

This chapter covered monitoring and troubleshooting DHCP.

DHCP monitoring in Windows 2000 offers many different counters that an administrator can use to help evaluate the state of the DHCP environment. Windows 2000 also includes enhanced audit logging, allowing an administrator to determine many things, including who owned an IP address and when.

DHCP is a very elegant protocol that operates transparently on the network. But when it does break, an administrator needs to jump into action before the network comes to a screeching halt. By using IPCONFIG and WINIPCFG, most DHCP problems can be solved, but there are times when more intuition and skills are required to hunt down and alleviate the problem.

12

What Lies Ahead: IPv6 and DHCPv6

This chapter takes a peek at an upcoming change that will affect the Internet and possibly any organization using TCP/IP and DHCP. Although Windows 2000 does not ship with IPv6 support, it will be added in future releases.

IPv6

Currently the Internet uses Internet Protocol version 4, which was designed over 20 years ago. A very versatile protocol, IPv4 has evolved as the Internet has grown. However, over the years IPv4's limitations have become more obvious. The biggest problem is its limiting 16-bit address space, with a maximum of 4,294,967,296 possible addresses. Other problems include poor scalability and lack of encryption and authentication measures.

With these limitations in mind, the IETF set out to create the next version of IP, Internet Protocol version 6 (IPv6), also known as IPng (Internet Protocol Next Generation). The IETF created a comprehensive set of specifications that define IPv6. Table 12-1 lists of some of the IPv6 RFCs.

Table 12-1. IPv6 RFCs

RFC #	RFC Title	URL
RFC2460	Internet Protocol, Version 6 (IPv6) Specification	*http://www.ietf.org/rfc/rfc2460.txt*
RFC2463	Internet Control Message Protocol (ICMPv6) for the Internet Protocol Version 6 (IPv6) Specification	*http://www.ietf.org/rfc/rfc2463.txt*
RFC2373	IP Version 6 Addressing Architecture	*http://www.ietf.org/rfc/rfc2373.txt*
RFC1886	DNS Extensions to Support IP Version 6	*http://www.ietf.org/rfc/rfc1886.txt*

Table 12-1. IPv6 RFCs (continued)

RFC #	RFC Title	URL
RFC1971	IPv6 Stateless Address Autoconfiguration	*http://www.ietf.org/rfc/rfc1971.txt*

These and other RFCs developed by the IETF provide the following enhancements found in IPv6:

Expanded addressing capabilities
> Since the biggest problem with IPv4 is the limited address space, IPv6 increases the size of the IP address from 32 to 128 bits. With this increased address space, every network device can have a unique IP address, from your cell phone to your coffee machine.

Hierarchical address space
> In IPv4, the address space is divided into two areas: network and host. In IPv6, the address space takes up a more hierarchical nature, allowing geographic areas to be represented. This is much like how an area code represents the geographic portion of a telephone number.

A streamlined 40-byte header
> To allow for faster processing of the IP packet, a number of IPv4 fields have been dropped or made optional. This results in a 40-byte fixed-length header, whereas IPv4 headers have a variable length. See Figure 12-1 for a comparison of the two headers.

Flow labeling and priority
> IPv6 provides the capability to label and prioritize "flows." A flow may be an audio or video transmission that is time sensitive.

IPv6 Address Architecture

One of the top priorities for the IETF was to use a larger address space for IPv6. With the ever-growing need for IP addresses for multimedia applications, personal digital assistants (PDAs), mobile users, and network-based appliances, the IETF decided to increase the address space to 128 bits. This provides an enormous number of addresses, totaling 340,282,366,920,938,463,463,374,607,431,768,211,456. Thus there should be plenty of unique IP addresses for decades to come.

With 128 bits, an IPv6 address is noted differently than an IPv4 address. Addresses in IPv4 use dotted decimal notation, where four decimal octets represent the 32-bit binary address. IP addresses in IPv6 use a hexidecimal text string to represent the 128-bit number. The IPv6 address is displayed as follows:

```
xxxx:xxxx:xxxx:xxxx:xxxx:xxxx:xxxx:xxxx
```

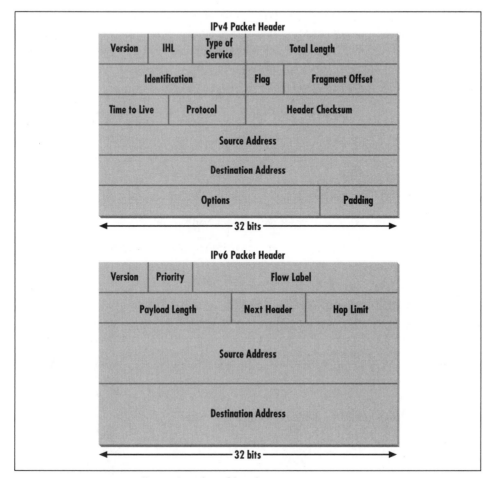

Figure 12-1. Comparing the IPv4 and IPv6 headers

The colons separate the eight 16-bit pieces of the address. The x's represent the four hexidecimal numbers that represent a 16-bit piece. For example, 1234:5678:9ABC:DEF0:1234:5678:9ABC:DEF0 represents an IPv6 IP address.

Memorizing an IPv6 IP address is not easy, so the IETF created a shorthand way to represent it. This shorthand method states that any leading zeros in a 16-bit section can be dropped and that multiple contiguous sections of zeros can be represented by a double colon (::). For example, the IPv6 address 1080:0000:0000:0000:0008:0800:0004:417A can be written as 1080::8:800:4:417A. Note that only one double colon can be used. If more than one were used, IPv6 would not be able to calculate the number of 16-bit sections that contain zeros.

Besides providing a vast number of IP addresses, the IPv6 address architecture provides the ability to create advanced hierarchical address spaces. This results in more efficient routing architectures.

IPv4 was designed using a class-based address architecture. In the IPv4 IP address, the bits were divided between network and host addresses (see Figure 12-2). With the Internet growing at an incredible pace, the limits of the non-hierarchical class-based address architecture are increasingly known. These limitations occur at both the local and global levels of networking.

At the local level, subnetting was developed to divide the address space more efficiently. For example, a single Class C network address can be divided (or subnetted) into smaller logical networks. These smaller networks can then represent several physical networks.

At the global level, supernetting was developed to combine a number of subnetted networks into a single network number. As a result, routing tables are reduced in size, resulting in better performance for backbone routers.

The IPv6 address hierarchy is divided into several layers. This results in a highly scalable address space.

The first level of the hierarchy is assigned to the top level aggregators (TLA). The TLAs are the public exchanges where large providers and telephone companies establish interconnections. An example of a public exchange is the five access points in the United States where the major ISPs link together (see Figure 12-2).

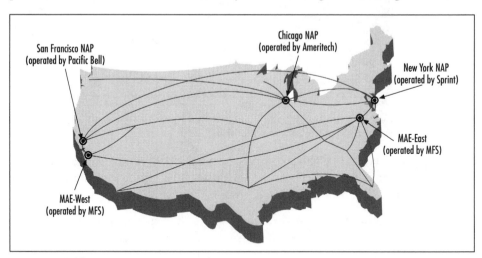

Figure 12-2. The major U.S. Internet access points

With IPv6, the TLAs will be assigned blocks of addresses. The TLAs will then allocate blocks of addresses to next level aggregators (NLA). NLAs are large ISPs and large global corporations. If the NLA is an ISP, it further allocates its assigned addresses to its subscribers or site level aggregators (SLA).

So how does this addressing hierarchy make things more efficient? By assigning numbers from the top (regional) levels down, NLAs that reside within the same TLA will have addresses that share the same TLA prefix. Subscribers (SLAs) of the same NLA will have addresses that share the same NLA prefix (see Figure 12-3).

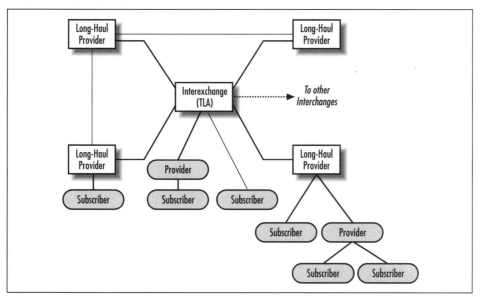

Figure 12-3. The IPv6 addressing hierarchy

The format of IPv6 addresses is as follows (see Figure 12-4):

- The first field is 3 bits long and designates the type of address (unicast, multi-cast, etc.).

- The next field is 13 bits and designates one of the TLAs throughout the globe.

- The following 32-bit field represents the NLA. These 32 bits can be further sub-divided by the NLA as shown in Figure 12-5. For example, if an NLA was a large ISP whose subscribers were smaller ISPs, the NLA field could be subdivided.

- The next field is 16 bits long and represents the SLA. A single SLA field can represent up to 65,534 subnets.

- The remaining field is 64 bits long and represents the interface or host ID.

The interface ID is autoconfigured in IPv6 unless configured otherwise (i.e., using DHCP). This type of configuration is known as *stateless autoconfiguration*. The host determines whether it should use stateless or stateful autoconfiguration by reading router advertisements.

An autoconfigured interface ID is a combination of the host's MAC address and the local network address.

3	13	32 bits	16 bits	64 bits
001	TLA	NLA	SLA	Interface ID
		Public Topology	Site Topology	Local Interface

Figure 12-4. The IPv6 address format

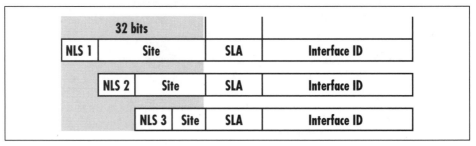

Figure 12-5. Subdividing the NLA field

DHCP for IPv6

DHCP for IPv6, also known as DHCPv6, enables DHCP servers to deliver configuration parameters to IPv6 hosts. As stated earlier, IPv6 hosts by default use stateless autoconfiguration unless configured otherwise. DHCPv6 represents the stateful autoconfiguration option.

Much like DHCP in IPv4, DHCPv6 uses a client/server model. The DHCP server and the DHCP client converse with a series of messages to request, offer, and lease an IP address. Unlike DHCP in IPv4, DHCPv6 uses a combination of unicast and multicast messages for the bulk of the conversation instead of broadcast messages.

Table 12-2 shows the well-known multicast addresses that are used when DHCPv6 transmits multicast messages.

Table 12-2. Well-Known Multicast Addresses and Multicast Groups

Multicast Group Name	Multicast Address	Members
All-DHCP-Agents	FF02:0:0:0:0:0:1:2	All DHCP servers and relay agents
All-DHCP-Servers	FF05:0:0:0:0:0:1:3	All DHCP servers
All-DHCP-Relays	FF05:0:0:0:0:0:1:4	All DHCP relay agents

All DHCP messages being transmitted to a DHCP server are transmitted using UDP port 547. All DHCP messages being transmitted to a DHCP client are transmitted using UDP port 546.

The DHCPv6 Conversation

The following message types can be found in a DHCPv6 conversation. Notice the many similarities to the original DHCP message types.

01 DHCP Solicit

>This message is an IP multicast message sent by a DHCP client to a DHCP server or relay agent.

02 DHCP Advertise

>This message is an IP unicast message sent by a DHCP server or relay agent in response to a DHCP Solicit message.

03 DHCP Request

>This message is an IP unicast message sent by a DHCP client to request configuration information from a DHCP server.

04 DHCP Reply

>This message is an IP unicast message sent by a DHCP server in response to a client's DHCP Request.

05 DHCP Release

>This message is an IP unicast message sent by the client to notify the DHCP server that the DHCP client is releasing its IP address.

06 DHCP Reconfigure

>This message is an IP unicast or multicast message used by the DHCP server to notify a DHCP client that it has new configuration information. The client is expected to send a DHCP Request message to reconfigure.

The DHCP Solicit message

To begin the DHCPv6 conversation, the DHCP client sends a DHCP Solicit message from the interface to be configured. This message is sent to the All-DHCP-Agents multicast group. Any relay agent receiving the Solicit message must forward the message to the All-DHCP-Servers multicast group.

The DHCP Solicit message follows the format shown in Figure 12-6.

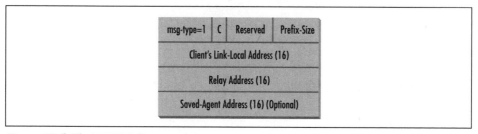

Figure 12-6. The DHCP Solicit message

The fields are described in Table 12-3.

Table 12-3. DHCP Solicit Message Fields

Field	Description
msg-type	Specifies the DHCP message type.
C	If this bit is set, all DHCP servers receiving the Solicit message must deallocate resources associated with the DHCP client. The DHCP client should also provide a saved-agent address to locate the client's address binding.
Prefix-Size	The number of leftmost bits of the agent's IP address that designate the routing prefix.
Reserved	Not used, set to zero.
Client's Link-Local Address	The IP link-local address of the interface that the DHCP client used to issue the DHCP Solicit message.
Relay Address	If the Solicit message was received by a DHCP relay agent, the relay agent places its IP address in this field. If not, the client places zeros in this field.
Saved Agent Address	If used, this field contains the IP address of the client's DHCP server.

The DHCP Advertise message

After receiving a DHCP Solicit message from a DHCP client, a DHCP server responds with a unicast DHCP Advertise message. If the message arrived via a relay agent, the DHCP server sends the Advertise message back through the relay agent.

The DHCP Advertise message follows the format shown in Figure 12-7. All fields are filled in by the DHCP server and are not modified by any relay agents.

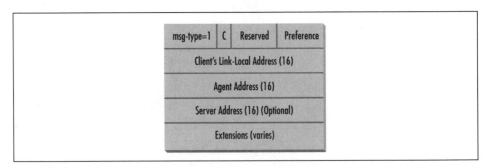

Figure 12-7. The DHCP Advertise message

The fields are described in Table 12-4.

Table 12-4. DHCP Advertise Message Fields

Field	Description
msg-type	Specifies the DHCP message type.
S	If this bit is set, the DHCP server address is included.
Preference	Indicates the preference level of the DHCP server (1 to 255). Once a client receives all Advertise messages, the client chooses the server with the highest preference.
Client's Link-Local Address	The IP link-local address of the interface that the DHCP client used to issue the DHCP Solicit message.
Agent Address	The IP address of a DHCP agent on the same link as the client.
Server Address	The IP address of the DHCP server (if used).
Extensions	Specifies any DHCPv6 extensions.

The DHCP Request message

To receive any configuration parameters from the DHCP server, the DHCP client must issue a DHCP Request message. This unicast message is used to request configuration parameters as well as any DHCP extensions the client may require. The DHCP client sets the destination address to that of the DHCP server selected during the DHCP advertise message process.

The DHCP Advertise message follows the format shown in Figure 12-8. All fields are filled in by the DHCP client.

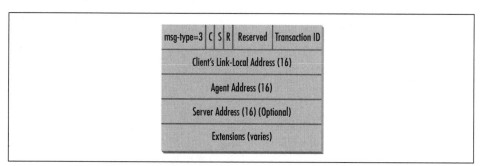

Figure 12-8. The DHCP Request message

The fields are described in Table 12-5.

Table 12-5. DHCP Request Message Fields

Field	Description
msg-type	Specifies the DHCP message type.
C	If this bit is set, the client requests the server remove all resources associated with the client.

Table 12-5. DHCP Request Message Fields (continued)

Field	Description
S	If this bit is set, the DHCP server address is included.
R	If this bit is set, the client has rebooted.
Rsvd	Not used, set to zero.
Transaction ID	A transaction identifier used to identify the particular request message.
Client's Link-Local Address	The IP link-local address of the interface that the DHCP client used to issue the DHCP Solicit message.
Agent Address	The IP address of a DHCP agent on the same link as the client.
Server Address	The IP address of the DHCP server (if used).
Extensions	Specifies any DHCPv6 extensions.

The DHCP Reply message

Upon receiving a DHCP Request message, the DHCP server responds with a DHCP Reply message. This unicast message is sent to the DHCP client, unless the client set the S bit. In that case, the client has to send the request through a relay agent. When responding, the DHCP server sets the L bit in the DHCP Reply message and addresses the message to the relay agent specified in the agent address field of the DHCP Request message.

The DHCP Reply message follows the format shown in Figure 12-9. All fields are filled in by the DHCP server.

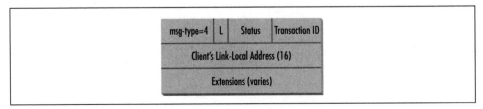

Figure 12-9. The DHCP Reply message

The fields are described in Table 12-6.

Table 12-6. DHCP Reply Message Fields

Field	Description
msg-type	Specifies the DHCP message type.
L	If this bit is set, the client's link-local address is present.

Table 12-6. DHCP Reply Message Fields (continued)

Field	Description
Status	Specifies the status of the request: 0: success 16: failure, reason unspecified 17: authentication failed or nonexistent 18: poorly formed request or release 19: resources unavailable 20: client record not available 21: invalid client IP address in release 23: relay cannot find server address 64: server unreachable
Transaction ID	A transaction identifier used to identify the particular request message.
Client's Link-Local Address	The IP link-local address of the interface that the DHCP client used to issue the DHCP Solicit message.
Extensions	Specifies any DHCPv6 extensions.

The DHCP Release message

A DHCP Release message is used to release IP address configurations. A DHCP client sends a DHCP Release message directly to the DHCP server because it already has a valid IP address configuration.

The DHCP Release message follows the format shown in Figure 12-10. All fields are filled in by the DHCP client.

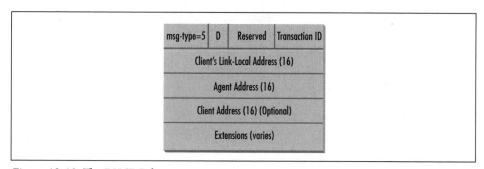

Figure 12-10. The DHCP Release message

The fields are described in Table 12-7.

Table 12-7. DHCP Release Message Fields

Field	Description
msg-type	Specifies the DHCP message type.
D	If this bit is set, the DHCP server is to send the DHCP Reply message directly to the client.

Table 12-7. DHCP Release Message Fields (continued)

Field	Description
Reserved	Not used, set to zero.
Transaction ID	A transaction identifier used to identify the particular request message.
Client's Link-Local Address	The IP link-local address of the interface that the DHCP client used to issue the DHCP Solicit message.
Agent Address	The IP address of a DHCP agent on the same link as the client.
Client Address	The IP address of the DHCP client.
Extensions	Specifies any DHCPv6 extensions.

The DHCP Reconfigure message

A DHCP Reconfigure message is used to notify DHCP clients of important changes to their IP address configurations. A DHCP server sends a DHCP Reconfigure message directly to the DHCP client because it already has a valid IP address configuration.

The DHCP Release message follows the format shown in Figure 12-11. All fields are filled in by the DHCP server.

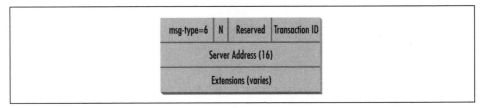

Figure 12-11. The DHCP Reconfigure message

The fields are described in Table 12-8.

Table 12-8. DHCP Reconfigure Message Fields

Field	Description
msg-type	Specifies the DHCP message type.
N	If this bit is set, the DHCP client should not expect a DHCP Reply message in response to any DHCP Requests.
Reserved	Not used, set to zero.
Transaction ID	A transaction identifier used to identify the particular request message.
Server Address	The IP address of the DHCP server.
Extensions	Specifies any DHCPv6 extensions.

DHCP Extensions for IPv6

DHCPv6 uses the `extensions` field in the DHCP messages to carry configuration information to the DHCP clients. The extensions follow a standardized format that is described in the Internet Draft, "Extensions for the Dynamic Host Configuration Protocol for IPv6."

The `extensions` field operates much like the `options` field found in the original DHCP.

The size of the `extensions` field can be a fixed length or variable length. The first field in an extension is the `type` field; it identifies the extension type. The `type` field is 2 octets long. Extension types are discussed later in this section. The next field is the `length` field, and it is also 2 octets long. The `length` field specifies the length of the extension, not including the `type` and `length` field.

The following section describes some of the DHCPv6 extensions. For a complete listing, refer to the Internet Draft.

IP Address Extension

The IP Address Extension is the most important extension included in a DHCPv6 message. The DHCP client uses the IP Address Extension to request an IP address from the DHCP server.

Unlike DHCP in IPv4, the IP Address Extension can be used to request multiple IP addresses for a DHCP client. Since an IP Address Extension can only hold one IP address, this is accomplished by using multiple IP Address Extensions. See Figure 12-12 for the format of the IP Address Extension field.

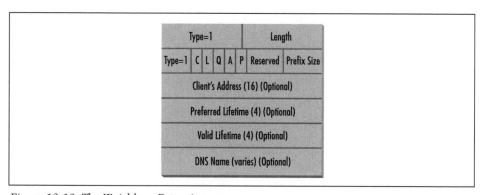

Figure 12-12. The IP Address Extension

The fields in the IP Address Extension are described in Table 12-9.

Table 12-9. IP Address Extension Fields

Field	Description
Type	1 (i.e., an IP Address Extension).
Length	The length of the extension in octets.
Status	This field is used to notify the client that the server was not able to process the client's request.
C	If this bit is set, the client address field is present.
L	If this bit is set, the preferred and valid lifetimes fields are present.
Q	If this bit is set, the other fields (C, L, A, and P) included by the client are required.
A	If this bit is set, the client requests that the server perform dynamic DNS updates using the AAAA record.
P	If this bit is set, the client requests that the server perform dynamic DNS updates using the PTR record.
Reserved	This field must be zero.
Prefix-Size	If the C bit is set (i.e., a client address is included), this field specifies the number of leftmost bits in the client address that is used to determine the routing prefix.
Client Address	This field specifies the IP address to be allocated by the DHCP server for the client.
Preferred Lifetime	This field specifies the preferred lifetime of the IP address (in seconds). This is the lifetime that the DHCP client would like to have.
Valid Lifetime	This field specifies the valid lifetime of the IP address (in seconds). This is the lifetime determined by the DHCP server.
DNS Name	This field specifies the DNS name (ASCII text).

Time Offset Extension

The Time Offset Extension specifies the amount of time (in seconds) that the client's clock should be offset from Universal Time Coordinated (UTC). See Figure 12-13 for the format of the Time Offset Extension field.

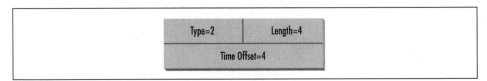

Figure 12-13. The Time Offset Extension

Domain Name Server Extension

The Domain Name Server Extension specifies the list of DNS servers that the client should use. See Figure 12-14 for the format of the Domain Name Server Extension field.

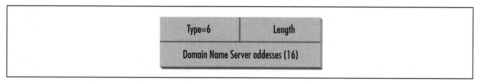

Figure 12-14. The Domain Name Server Extension

Domain Name Extension

The Domain Name Extension specifies the DNS domain name the client should use when resolving host names. The domain name is an ASCII string. See Figure 12-15 for the format of the Domain Name field.

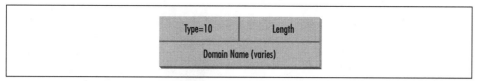

Figure 12-15. The Domain Name Extension

Summary

IPv6 and DHCPv6 are the future of the Internet. IPv6 overcomes many of the shortfalls of IPv4, producing an elegant and versatile release of the Internet Protocol. IPv6 provides a vast address space and a hierarchical address structure.

Although IPv6 supports stateless autoconfiguration of clients, DHCPv6 complements IPv6 by providing a stateful autoconfigure option to facilitate the automatic configuration of DHCP clients. DHCP clients can get configuration options such as DNS server addresses.

Although Windows 2000 does not support IPv6 yet, support needs to be added as more devices and networks migrate to the new standard.

Appendix:
DHCP Options

Pad (0)

Specifies that the following data fields will be aligned on a word (16-bit) boundary.

Time (2)

Specifies the Universal Time Coordinated (UTC) Offset in seconds.

Time Server (4)

Specifies a list of timeservers for the client in order of preference.

Name Servers (5)

Specifies a list of name servers for the client in order of preference.

Log Servers (7)

Specifies a list, in order of preference, of MIT_LCS User Datagram Protocol (UDP) log servers for the client.

Cookie Servers (8)

Specifies a list, in order of preference, of cookie servers (as specified in RFC865) for the client.

LPR Servers (9)

Specifies a list, in order of preference, for Line Printer Remote (as specified in RFC1179) servers for the clients.

Impress Servers (10)

Specifies a list of Imagen Impress servers for the client in order of preference.

Resource Location Servers (11)

Specifies a list, in order of preference, of RFC887-compliant Resource Location Servers for the client.

Hostname (12)

Specifies the hostname (maximum of 63 characters) for the client. NOTE: The name must start with an alphabetic character, end with an alphanumeric character, and contain only letters, numbers, or hyphens. The name can be fully qualified with the local DNS domain name.

Boot File Size (13)

Specifies the default size of the boot image file in 512-octet blocks.

Merit Dump File (14)

Specifies the ASCII path of a file in which the client's core dump can be stored in case of an application or system crash.

Swap Server (16)

Specifies the IP address of the client's swap server.

Root Path (17)

Specifies a path (in ASCII) for the client's root disk.

Extensions Path (18)

Specifies a file that includes information that is interpreted the same as the vendor extension field in the BOOTP response, except that references to Tag 18 are ignored. Note that the file must be retrievable through TFTP.

IP Layer Forwarding (19)

Specifies that IP packets should be enabled (1) or disabled (0) for the client.

Nonlocal Source Routing (20)

Specifies that datagram packets with nonlocal source route forwarding should be enabled (1) or disabled (0) for the client.

Policy Filters Mask (21)

Specifies a list in order of preference of IP address and mask pairs that specify destination address and mask pairs respectively. Used for filtering nonlocal source routes. Any source routed datagram whose next hop address does not match an entry in the list is discarded by the client.

Max DG Reassembly Size (22)

Specifies the maximum size datagram that a client can assemble. NOTE: The minimum size is 576 bytes.

Default Time to Live (23)

Specifies the Time to Live (TTL) that the client will use on outgoing datagrams. Values must be between 1 and 255 hops.

Path MTU Aging Timeout (24)

Specifies the timeout in seconds for aging Path Maximum Transmission Unit values. NOTE: MTU values are found using the mechanism defined in RFC1191.

Path MTU Plateau Table (25)

Specifies a table of MTU sizes to use when performing Path MTU (as defined in RFC1191). NOTE: The table is sorted from the minimum value (68 octets) to maximum value (576 octets).

MTU Option (26)

Specifies the MTU discovery size. NOTE: The minimum value is 68.

All Subnets are Local (27)

Specifies whether the client assumes that all subnets in the network use the same MTU value as that defined for the local subnet. This option is enabled (1) or disabled (0), which specifies that some subnets may use smaller MTU values.

Broadcast Address (28)

Specifies the broadcast IP address to be used on the client's local subnet.

Perform Mask Discovery (29)

A value of 1 specifies that the client should use ICMP (Internet Control Message Protocol) for subnet mask discovery, whereas a value of 0 specifies that the client should not use ICMP for subnet mask discovery.

Mask Supplier (30)

A value of 1 specifies that the client should respond to ICMP subnet mask requests whereas a value of 0 specifies that a client should not respond to subnet mask requests using ICMP.

Perform Router Discovery (31)

A value of 1 specifies that a client should use the mechanism defined in RFC1256 for router discovery. A value of 0 indicates that the client should not use the router discovery mechanism.

Router Solicitation Address (32)

Specifies the IP address to which the client will send router solicitation requests.

Static Route (33)

Specifies a list in order of preference of IP address pairs the client should install in its routing cache. NOTE: Any multiple routes to the same destination are listed in descending order or in order of priority. The pairs are defined as destination IP address/router IP addresses. The default address of 0.0.0.0 is an illegal address for a static route and should be changed if your non-Microsoft DHCP clients use this setting.

Trailer Encapsulation (34)

A value of 1 specifies that the client should negotiate use of trailers (as defined in RFC983) when using the ARP protocol. A value of 0 indicates that the client should not use trailers.

ARP Cache Timeout (35)

Specifies the timeout in seconds for the ARP cache entries.

Ethernet Encapsulation (36)

Specifies that the client should use Ethernet version 2 (as defined in RFC894) or IEEE 802.3 (as defined in RFC1042) encapsulation if the network interface is

Ethernet. A value of 1 enables RFC1042 whereas a value of 0 enables RFC894 encapsulation.

Default Time to Live (37)

Specifies the default TTL the client should use when sending TCP segments. NOTE: The minimum octet value is 1.

Keepalive Interval (38)

Specifies the interval in seconds for the client to wait before sending a keep-alive message on a TCP connection. NOTE: A value of 0 indicates that the client should send keepalive messages only if requested by the application.

Keepalive Garbage (39)

Enables (1) or disables (0) sending keepalive messages with an octet of garbage data for legacy application compatibility.

NIS Domain Name (40)

An ASCII string specifying the name of the Network Information Service (NIS) domain.

NIS Servers (41)

Specifies a list, in order of preference, of IP addresses of NIS servers for the client.

NTP Servers (42)

Specifies a list, in order of preference, of IP addresses of Network Time Protocol (NTP) servers for the client.

Vendor Specific Info (43)

Binary information used by clients and servers to pass vendor-specific information. Servers that cannot interpret the information ignore it, and clients that do not receive the data attempt to operate without it.

NetBIOS Over TCP/IP NBDD (45)

Specifies a list, in order of preference, of IP addresses for NetBIOS datagram distribution (NBDD) servers for the client.

X Window System Font (48)

Specifies a list, in order of preference, of IP addresses of X Window font servers for the client.

X Window System Display (49)

Specifies a list, in order of preference, of IP addresses of X Window System Display Manager servers for the client.

NIS + Domain Name (64)

Specifies a list of NIS + domain names in order of preference.

NIS + Server (65)

Specifies a list of NIS + servers in order of preference.

End (255)

Specifies the end of the DHCP packet.

Index

About the Author

Neall Alcott has been designing, building, and managing networks for the past 8 years. He is also an MCT who has been training students in the Delaware Valley for the past 4 years. Currently, he is a Senior Systems Engineer for Visalign LLC, a professional services firm specializing in web solutions, web infrastructure, and managed services for enterprise-wide clients in the pharmaceutical, financial services, power/utility, entertainment/media, emerging technology/growth, and state and local government industries. Neall's current role at Visalign is as an eBusiness Infrastructure Architect, planning and designing server architectures using Microsoft's .NET platform. Previously, Neall was responsible for overseeing the Intel platform infrastructure at one client's North American headquarters, as well as 16 remote sites across the United States.

Colophon

Our look is the result of reader comments, our own experimentation, and feedback from distribution channels. Distinctive covers complement our distinctive approach to technical topics, breathing personality and life into potentially dry subjects.

The animal on the cover of *DHCP for Windows 2000* is a frilled coquette hummingbird (*Lophornis magnificus*). There are over 300 species of humming-birds. They are found in all parts of the Americas, but the majority of species live in tropical South America. The hummingbird family includes the smallest of all birds; many species are less than 8 centimeters (3 inches) long.

Leanne Soylemez was the production editor and copyeditor for *DHCP for Windows 2000*. Nicole Arigo, Mary Sheehan, and Susan Carlson Greene provided quality control. Nancy Crumpton wrote and Brenda Miller edited the index.

Ellie Volckhausen designed the cover of this book, based on a series design by Edie Freedman. The cover image is a 19th-century engraving from the Dover Pictorial Archive. Emma Colby produced the cover layout with QuarkXPress 4.1 using Adobe's ITC Garamond font.

Alicia Cech and David Futato designed the interior layout based on a series design by Nancy Priest. Mike Sierra implemented the design in FrameMaker 5.5.6. The text and heading fonts are ITC Garamond Light and Garamond Book; the code font is Constant Willison. The illustrations that appear in the book were produced by Robert Romano using Macromedia FreeHand 8 and Adobe Photoshop 5. This colophon was written by Leanne Soylemez.

Whenever possible, our books use a durable and flexible lay-flat binding. If the page count exceeds this binding's limit, perfect binding is used.